Journal of International  Business

Management International Review

Jan Hendrik Fisch (Guest Editor)
Innovation and Internationalization
Guest Editor's Introduction

Alan M. Rugman/Cecilia Brain
Regional Strategies in Pharmaceuticals

Anca Metiu/Bruce Kogut
Distributed Knowledge and Creativity in the International Software Industry

John Cantwell/Katherina Glac/Rebecca Harding
The Internationalization of R&D – the Swiss Case

Marian Beise/Hans Georg Gemünden
Lead Markets

Alexander Gerybadze
Knowledge Management and Cognitive Coherence in MNCs

Dirk Holtbrügge/Nicola Berg
Knowledge Transfer in Multinational Corporations

Jan Hendrik Fisch
International R&D with Fuzzy Logic

D 21247

ISBN 978-3-409-12719-6   ISBN 978-3-322-91001-1 (eBook)
DOI 10.1007/978-3-322-91001-1

EDITORIAL BOARD

Professor Raj Aggarwal, Kent State University, Kent – U.S.A.
Professor Jeffrey S. Arpan, University of South Carolina, Columbia – U.S.A.
Professor Daniel van Den Bulcke, Universiteit Antwerpen – Belgium
Professor John A. Cantwell, Rutgers University, Newark – U.S.A.
Professor S. Tamer Cavusgil, Michigan State University, East Lansing – U.S.A.
Professor Frederick D.S. Choi, New York University – U.S.A.
Professor Farok Contractor, Rutgers University, Newark – U.S.A.
Professor John D. Daniels, University of Miami, Coral Gables – U.S.A.
Professor Peter J. Dowling, University of Canberra – Australia
Professor Santiago García Echevarría, Universidad de Alcála de Henares, Madrid – Spain
Professor Lawrence A. Gordon, University of Maryland, College Park – U.S.A.
Professor Sidney J. Gray, University of Sydney – Australia
Professor Geir Gripsrud, Norwegian School of Management, Sandvika – Norway
Professor Jean-François Hennart, Tilburg University – The Netherlands
Professor Georges Hirsch, Centre Franco-Vietnamien de Formation à la gestion, Paris – France
Professor Andrew Inkpen, Thunderbird, The American Graduate School of International Management, Glendale – U.S.A.
Professor Eugene D. Jaffe, Bar-Ilan University, Ramat-Gan – Israel
Professor Erdener Kaynak, Pennsylvania State University, Middletown – U.S.A.
Professor Yui Kimura, University of Tsukuba, Tokyo – Japan
Professor Michael Kutschker, Katholische Universität Eichstätt, Ingolstadt – Germany
Professor Reijo Luostarinen, Helsinki School of Economics – Finland
Professor Klaus Macharzina, Universität Hohenheim, Stuttgart – Germany
Professor Roger Mansfield, Cardiff Business School – United Kingdom
Professor Mark Mendenhall, University of Tennessee, Chattanooga – U.S.A.
Professor Rolf Mirus, University of Alberta, Edmonton – Canada
Professor Michael H. Moffett, American Graduate School, Phoenix – U.S.A.
Professor Krzysztof Y. Obloj, University of Warsaw – Poland
Professor Lars Oxelheim, Göteborg and Lund University – Sweden
Professor Ki-An Park, Kyung Hee University, Seoul – Korea
Professor Robert D. Pearce, University of Reading – United Kingdom
Professor Lee Radebaugh, Brigham Young University, Provo – U.S.A.
Professor Edwin Rühli, Universität Zürich – Switzerland
Professor Alan M. Rugman, Indiana University, Bloomington, U.S.A.
Professor Rakesh B. Sambharya, Rutgers University, Camden, U.S.A.
Professor Reinhart Schmidt, Universität Halle-Wittenberg – Germany
Professor Hans Schöllhammer, University of California, Los Angeles – U.S.A.
Professor Oded Shenkar, The Ohio State University, Columbus – U.S.A.
Professor Vitor Corado Simoes, Universidade Técnica de Lisboa – Portugal
Professor John Stopford, 6 Chalcot Square, London NW1 8YB – United Kingdom
Professor Daniel P. Sullivan, University of Delaware, Newark – U.S.A.
Professor Norihiko Suzuki, International Christian University, Tokyo – Japan
Professor Stephen Bruce Tallmann, University of Utah, Salt Lake City – U.S.A.
Professor George Tesar, Umeå University, Umeå – Sweden
Professor José de la Torre, Florida International University, Miami – U.S.A.
Professor Rosalie L. Tung, Simon Fraser University, Burnaby, BC – Canada
Professor Jean-Claude Usunier, University of Lausanne, Lausanne – Dorigny – Switzerland
Professor Alain Charles Verbeke, Vrije Universiteit Brussel, Brussels – Belgium
Professor Lawrence S. Welch, Mt Eliza Business School, Melbourne, Australia
Professor Martin K. Welge, Universität Dortmund – Germany
Professor Bernard Yin Yeung, New York University – U.S.A.
Professor Masaru Yoshimori, Yokohama National University – Japan

BOOK REVIEW EDITOR

Professor Dr. Johann Engelhard, Universität Bamberg – Germany

EDITOR

MANAGEMENT INTERNATIONAL REVIEW, *Professor Dr. Profs. h.c. Dr. h.c. Klaus Macharzina, Universität Hohenheim (510 E), Schloss-Osthof-Ost, D-70599 Stuttgart, Germany, Tel. (0711) 4 59-29 08, Fax (0711) 459-3288, E-mail: klausmac@uni-hohenheim.de, Internet: http://www.uni-hohenheim.de/~mir Assistant Editors: Professor Dr. Michael-Jörg Oesterle, Universität Bremen, Germany, Professor Dr. Joachim Wolf, Universität Kiel, Germany, Editorial office: Mrs. Sylvia Ludwig*

VOLUME 44 · SPECIAL ISSUE · 2004/3

CONTENTS

Guest Editor's Introduction 3

Alan M. Rugman/Cecilia Brain
Regional Strategies of Multinational Pharmaceutical Firms 7

Anca Metiu/Bruce Kogut
Distributed Knowledge and Creativity
in the International Software Industry 27

John Cantwell/Katherina Glac/Rebecca Harding
The Internationalization of R&D – the Swiss Case 57

Marian Beise/Hans Georg Gemünden
Lead Markets:
A New Framework for the International Diffusion of Innovation 83

Alexander Gerybadze
Knowledge Management, Cognitive Coherence, and Equivocality in
Distributed Innovation Processes in MNCs 103

Dirk Holtbrügge/Nicola Berg
Knowledge Transfer in Multinational Corporations:
Evidence from German Firms 129

Jan Hendrik Fisch
Allocating Innovative Activities in International R&D with Fuzzy Logic ... 147

GUIDELINE FOR AUTHORS

mir welcomes articles on original theoretical contributions, empirical research, state-of-the-art surveys or reports on recent developments in the areas of

a) International Business b) Transnational Corporations c) Intercultural Management d) Strategic Management e) Business Policy.

Manuscripts are reviewed with the understanding that they are substantially new, have not been previously published in whole (including book chapters) or in part (including exhibits), have not been previously accepted for publication, are not under consideration by any other publisher, and will not be submitted elsewhere until a decision is reached regarding their publication in **mir**. The only exception is papers in conference proceedings, which we treat as work-in-progress.

Contributions should be submitted in English language in a Microsoft or compatible format by e-mail to the Editor at klausmac@uni-hohenheim.de. The complete text including the references, tables and figures should as a rule not exceed 25 pages in a usual setting (approximately 7000 words). Reply papers should normally not exceed 1500 words. The title page should include the following elements: Author(s) name, Heading of the article, Abstract (two sections of about 30 words each), Key Results (20 words), Author's line (author's name, academic title, position and affiliation) and on the bottom a proposal for an abbreviated heading on the front cover of the journal.

Submitted papers must be written according to mir's formal guidelines. Only those manuscripts can enter the reviewing process which adhere to our guidelines. Authors are requested to

- use *endnotes* for clarification sparingly. References to the literature are indicated in the text by author's name and year of publication in parentheses, e.g. (Reitsperger/Daniel 1990, p. 210, Eiteman 1989). The references should be listed in alphabetical order at the end of the text. They should include full bibliographical details and be cited in the following manner: e.g.
    Reitsperger, W. D./Daniel, S. J., Dynamic Manufacturing: A Comparison of Attitudes in the U.S. and Japan, *Management International Review*, 30, 1990, pp. 203–216.
    Eiteman, D. K., Financial Sourcing, in Macharzina, K./Welge, M. K. (eds.), *Handwörterbuch Export und Internationale Unternehmung*, Stuttgart: Poeschel 1989, pp. 602–621.
    Stopford, J. M./Wells, L. T. Jr., *Managing the Multinational Enterprise*, New York: Basic Books 1972.
- avoid *terms* that may be interpreted denigrating to ethnic or other groups.
- be especially careful in dealing with gender. Traditional customs such as "... the manager wishes that **his** interest ..." can favor the acceptance of inequality were none exist. The use of plural pronouns is preferred. If this is impossible, the term "he or she" or "he/she" can be used.

In the case of publication authors are supplied one complimentary copy of the issue and 30 off-prints free of charge. Additional copies may be ordered *prior to printing*. Overseas shipment is by boat; air-delivery will be charged extra.

The author agrees, that his/her article is published not only in this journal but that it can also be reproduced by the publisher and his licensees through license agreement in other journals (also in translated versions), through reprint in omnibus volumes (i.e. for anniversary editions of the journal or the publisher or in subject volumes), through longer extracts in books of the publisher also for advertising purposes, through multiplication and distribution on CD ROM or other data media, through storage on data bases, their transmission and retrieval, during the time span of the copyright laws on the article at home and abroad.

Guest Editor's Introduction

This special issue of **mir** is published at Professor Klaus Macharzina's 65th birthday. Playing with words, is that a coincidence happening at random, by accident or by chance? Those who know that a German university professor generally retires at the age of 65 will doubt that *random* is the case. Others know that a professor of his generation has the right to defer the time of his retirement. They could possibly suspect that this "Festschrift" was prepared rashly as a farewell present and might turn out as an *accident* for the Guest Editor, since Klaus has exercised the option to stay in his affiliation. Indeed we have known for quite a while that Klaus would stay here and wish to seize this special issue as a *chance* to thank him for continuing his work, which has been extraordinarily successful and acknowledged by scholars and practitioners from all over the world.

Puzzling about the proper moment to launch a "Festschrift" for Klaus Macharzina is related to searching for the zenith of his scholarly work. When the first publications of this kind appeared on the occasion of his 60th birthday, it seemed obvious to be the right time because he was just confirmed in the office as president of the Hohenheim University for the subsequent four years. Looking back at the time since his second tenure ceased, we realize that the supposed zenith was rather the beginning of a plateau. As his assistant I can testify that he is still frequently asked to represent the university and even more frequently invited to represent the discipline of International Management. During his sabbatical at the University of Hawaii at Honolulu, he launched a fireworks of new publications. After a nine-year recess from teaching, he now endeavors to pass the experience he gained on to his students.

The ambition and success of his career were predominantly driven by two principles, which I chose for the title of this special issue: Innovation and Internationalization. As a field of research, the joint of innovation and internationalization is eminently fruitful because these two aspects of management have a reinforcing influence on one another. Innovation enables internationalization, internationalization triggers innovation. A balanced set of authors, from near to far and from upcoming to established, submitted papers for this special issue of **mir** and reflect the latest research in this area.

Guest Editor's Introduction

Alan M. Rugman's and *Cecilia Brain's* paper examines the R&D and strategies of the world's largest firms in the pharmaceuticals sector and finds a high degree of intra-regional sales. R&D and sales are more concentrated within North America and Europe than in Asia. In addition, the relative size of the US market, compared to other parts of the triad, creates imbalances with respect to R&D, sales and international strategy.

The paper written by *Bruce Kogut* and *Anca Metiu* addresses the question of what limits the international distribution of work between rich and poor countries in the software industry. Their research reveals a convergence among co-located and distributed projects. The results indicate that the managerial experience to support global outsourcing of intellectual labor is already advanced, while creativity remains more likely to be located in rich countries.

John Cantwell, Katherina Glac, and *Rebecca Harding* analyze the extent and the patterns of specialization of the internationalization of R&D since 1969 by the largest Swiss firms abroad, and by the largest non-Swiss firms in Switzerland. They find out that Swiss-owned firms abroad access technologies in the primary fields of their own industry, while foreign-owned firms conducting research in Switzerland demonstrate more technological diversification away from their own primary fields and into sources of local Swiss traditional technological strengths.

The article by *Marian Beise* and *Hans Georg Gemünden* tries to explain why countries lead the international diffusion of specific innovations. It suggests that five advantages on the demand side play a decisive role for the international competitiveness of the companies of a country. A company that is eager to develop internationally standardized innovations can leverage the lead market role of their home country for each innovation project.

Alexander Gerybadze's work investigates the sharing of knowledge in international networks of R&D locations. The paper differentiates between the degree to which knowledge is explicit or implicit and the degree to which it is canonical or equivocal. Situations of strong interpretive coherence and a dominance of canonical knowledge are favorable for knowledge sharing across locations. Problems arise for equivocal knowledge and in situations of interpretive divergence, even if a significant part of the knowledge base is explicit.

Dirk Holtbrügge and *Nicola Berg* distinguish between two dimensions of knowledge management: source and content. They explore in an empirical study of 142 subsidiaries of German MNCs how knowledge is transferred across organizational and national boundaries and find that the sources and characteristics of knowledge flows are affected by different firm-specific and country-specific variables.

The paper by *Jan Hendrik Fisch* develops a model to predict the appearance of specific R&D units in international locations using fuzzy logic. Grounding on information processing theory, this approach evaluates the local supply of technological information and demand for R&D information processing using fuzzy logic in order to determine the appropriate type of R&D unit. The model is tested with data from six German and Swiss MNCs.

Dear Klaus, we sincerely congratulate you on your 65th birthday! We wish you the best of luck and health and hope to see you active in this position for many more years.

On behalf of all authors
JAN HENDRIK FISCH

mir *Edition*

GABLER

Carsten Röh

IuK-Technik und internationale Unternehmensführung

Kommunikation – Koordination – Konfiguration

2004, XVII, 326 pages, pb., € 59,90 (approx. US $ 59,90)
ISBN 3-409-12552-3

Information technology and particularly the internet is at the centre of the current technology debate. It offers a large potential for business applications, especially in an international context.

This work focuses on and analyses new aspects of IT looking at its impacts on communication, coordination and configuration aspects of international management.

Target groups are students and teachers of business administration, especially in the fields of organisation and international management, scientists of international management and managers.

Betriebswirtschaftlicher Verlag Dr. Th. Gabler GmbH, Abraham-Lincoln-Str. 46, 65189 Wiesbaden

**Management
International Review**
© Gabler Verlag 2004

Alan M. Rugman/Cecilia Brain

Regional Strategies of Multinational Pharmaceutical Firms

Abstract

- Recent research on the world's 500 largest companies has established that the majority of international business occurs within regional clusters in the three largest economic regions of North America, Europe, and Asia (the triad). This finding extends to the 18 companies in the chemicals and pharmaceuticals sector, which is the most innovative in the world.

Key Results

- This paper examines the R&D and strategies of the world's largest firms in the pharmaceuticals sector and finds a high degree of intra-regional sales. R&D and sales are more concentrated within North America and Europe than in Asia. In addition, the relative size of the US market, compared to other parts of the triad, creates imbalances with respect to R&D, sales and international strategy.

Authors

Alan M. Rugman, L. Leslie Waters Chair and Director of the Center for International Business Education & Research, Professor of Management, Professor of Business Economics and Public Policy, Kelley School of Business, Indiana University, Bloomington, IN, USA.
Cecilia Brain, Principal and CEO of Braintrust, a Toronto-based consulting organization, Toronto, Canada.

Alan M. Rugman/Cecilia Brain

Introduction

A new research stream has demonstrated that the vast majority of international business activity is conducted on a regional basis, rather than globally. By regional is meant the large "triad" markets of the European Union (EU), the United States (or, more broadly, NAFTA), and Japan (or, more broadly, all of Asia). This research is illustrated in Rugman (2000) (2003), Rugman and Brain (2003), Rugman and Verbeke (2004), and Rugman (2005).

Of the world's 500 largest multinational enterprises (MNEs), the sector which is consistently one of the most innovative is chemicals and pharmaceuticals. In this paper we examine the R&D of the 18 MNEs in this sector and relate this to the regional nature of their sales. Of the 500 largest companies in the world, it is possible to find data on their geographic sales in the "broad" triad regions of Europe, North America, and Asia. These data exist for 380 of the 500 firms. Of these 380, 200 are in services, leaving 180 in manufacturing, see Table 1. Of the 180 manufacturing MNEs, there are 18 in the chemicals and pharmaceuticals sector.

Of these 18 MNEs in the chemicals sector, data are available for all 18 (one company, Pharmacia, was acquired by Pfizer in 2002) and these can be classified

Table 1. The Top 500 MNEs, by Industry

Industry Category	No. of Firms in the Fortune 500	No. of Firms in the RNGMA	% of total
Manufacturing	206	180	87.4
1 Aerospace and Defense	11	11	100.0
2 Chemicals and Pharmaceuticals	19	18	94.7
3 Computer, Office & Electronics	39	36	92.3
4 Construction, Building Materials and Glass	12	11	91.7
5 Energy, Petroleum & Refining	43	31	72.1
6 Food, Drug & Tobacco	18	14	77.8
7 Motor Vehicle and Parts	31	29	93.5
8 Other Manufacturing	13	13	100.0
9 Natural Resource Manufacturing	20	17	85.0
Services	294	200	68.0
1 Banks	62	40	64.5
2 Entertainment, Printing & Publishing	9	9	100.0
3 Merchandisers	77	63	81.8
4 Other Financial Services	58	27	46.6
5 Other Services	25	21	84.0
6 Telecommunications & Utilities	43	27	62.8
7 Transportation Services	20	13	65.0
Total	500	380	76.0

Source: Data are for 2001

as shown in Table 2:

Global	0
Bi-regional	4
Host bi-regional	2
Home region	11
Insufficient Information	1

Table 2. The Regional Nature of the Chemical and Pharmaceutical MNEs

Company	Region	Revenues in bn US$	F/T Sales	% intra regional	North America (%)	Europe (%)	Asia Pacific (%)
Bi-Regional							
7 Bayer	Europe	27.5	na	41.3	30.6	41.3	16.6
9 Aventis*	Europe	21.6	91.2	36.4	44.8	36.4	6.4
10 Novartis	Europe	20.9	98.0	47.0	47.0	33.0	17.0 f
11 Roche Group	Europe	19.2	98.2	37.1	38.0 z	37.1	13.6
Host-region oriented							
2 GlaxoSmithKline	Europe	42.6	95.7	28.6	50.9 z	28.6	na
13 AstraZeneca	Europe	17.8	na	31.9	55.6	31.9	5.5 j
Home-region oriented							
1 Merck	North America	51.8	16.0	84.0	84.0 z	na	na
3 Johnson & Johnson	North America	36.3	38.1	61.9	61.9 z	21.0	11.5 f
4 Pfizer	North America	32.4	35.9	64.1	64.1 z	na	29.8 j
5 BASF	Europe	30.6	78.4	58.9	24.2	58.9	15.7 f
8 DuPont de Nemours (E.I.)	North America	24.0	52.4	53.4	53.4	26.3 m	7.3
12 Bristol-Myers Squibb	North America	18.2	37.6	62.4	62.4	22.2 m	na
14 Abbott Laboratories	North America	17.7	37.8	65.1	65.1 a	na	na
15 Wyeth	North America	14.6	36.7	63.3	63.3	5.1 u	na
16 Mitsubishi Chemical	Asia-Pacific	13.4	16.0	85.5	na	na	85.5
17 Akzo Nobel	Europe	13.3	94.0	52.0	27.0 a	52.0	11.0
18 Eli Lilly	North America	11.1	41.0	59.0	59.0 z	19.5 w	na
Insufficient Information							
6 Dow Chemical	North America	27.6	59.2	40.8	40.8 z	33.4	na
Other							
19 Pharmacia	(Acquired by Pfizer in July 2002).						
Weighted Average**		24.47		54.5			
Total		440.5					

Source: Data are for 2002
Note: * Regional data on Aventis are calculated using data for its core business, which represents 85% of revenues.
To calculate revenues in US dollars, where the company did not provide a figure, the following exchange rates were used: euro (0.9495); Swiss Franc (0.64505) and Pound (1.50377)
** % intra regional average is weighted according to revenues.
z. United States; a. Canada and the United States; m. Europe, Middle East and Africa; u. United Kingdom; w. Western Europe; f. Africa; j. Japan.

The regional sales of these 18 MNEs, across the triad, are also reported in Table 2. Their average home-region sales are 54.5%, while for all 180 MNEs in manufacturing it is 62%.

Table 3 examines the R&D of these MNEs. The average R&D to sales percent for these chemical and pharmaceutical MNEs is 9.9%. Eli Lilly had the highest R&D to sales expenditures at 19.4%, followed by other pharmaceutical companies such as: – AstraZeneca at 17.2%; Aventis at 16.6%, and Pfizer at 16%. In contrast, there were relatively low R&D expenditures by chemical firms: – BASF at 3.5%; Dow Chemicals at 3.9%; and DuPont at 5.3%. These data suggest that pharmaceutical companies conduct greater R&D than chemical MNEs.

In this paper we analyze such innovation differences in the chemicals sector, especially in pharmaceuticals which records consistently higher R&D expenditures than pure chemical MNEs. Once a drug has been developed and patented, few substitutes if any, can compete with it over a prescribed period of time. Patients suffering from disease, especially those that are terminal or which produce discomfort, have a significantly inelastic demand for drugs as do the doctors working with health insurance schemes. Since the cost of manufacturing a drug is often marginal, pharmaceutical firms depend on national patent protection for their discovery to

Table 3. Research and Development in the Chemical and Pharmaceutical Industries

Company	Industry	Region	Revenues in bn US$	R&D in bn US$	R&D % of Sales
1 Merck	Pharmaceutical	North America	51.8	2.7	5.2
2 GlaxoSmithKline	Pharmaceutical	Europe	42.6	4.4	10.2
3 Johnson & Johnson	Pharmaceutical	North America	36.3	4.0	10.9
4 Pfizer	Pharmaceutical	North America	32.4	5.2	16.0
5 BASF	Chemical	Europe	30.6	1.1	3.5
6 Dow Chemical	Chemical	North America	27.6	1.1	3.9
7 Bayer	Chemical	Europe	27.5	2.4	8.7
8 DuPont de Nemours (E.I.)	Chemical	North America	24.0	1.3	5.3
9 Aventis	Pharmaceutical	Europe	21.6	3.6	16.6
10 Novartis	Pharmaceutical	Europe	20.9	2.8	13.4
11 Roche Group	Pharmaceutical	Europe	19.2	2.7	14.3
12 Bristol-Myers Squibb	Pharmaceutical	North America	18.2	2.2	12.2
13 AstraZeneca	Pharmaceutical	Europe	17.8	3.1	17.2
14 Abbott Laboratories	Pharmaceutical	North America	17.7	1.6	8.8
15 Wyeth	Pharmaceutical	North America	14.6	2.1	14.3
16 Mitsubishi Chemical	Chemical	Asia-Pacific	13.4	0.6	4.8
17 Akzo Nobel	Chemical	Europe	13.3	0.9	6.5
18 Eli Lilly	Pharmaceutical	North America	11.1	2.1	19.4
19 Pharmacia	(Acquired by Pfizer July 2002)				
Average*			24.5	2.4	9.9
Total			440.5	43.7	

Data are for 2002
* Average R&D % of Sales is weighted according to revenues.

generate profits. Over the last decade, the development of drugs has become more and more expensive and produced lower profits than in previous decades. Yet, as a pharmaceutical's survival is dependent on new drug development, R&D expenditures are the only way of assuring the long-term survival of the company.

The products of chemical companies, on the other hand, are often not necessities and have many substitutes. Marketing a differentiated product to the consumer is often the only way to obtain a premium price. R&D investment might produce a better paint, textile, pesticide, or plastic but many chemical products are now commodities, with low returns to R&D.

It is often difficult to disentangle chemical companies and pharmaceutical companies as they tend to engage in similar businesses. For instance, companies

Table 4. The Chemical and Pharmaceutical Industries, a Comparison

Company	Region	Revenues in bn US$	F/T Sales	% intra regional	R&D % of Sales
Chemical Industry					
1 BASF	Europe	30.6	78.4	58.9	3.5
2 Dow Chemical	North America	27.6	59.2	40.8 z	3.9
3 Bayer	Europe	27.5	na	41.3	8.7
4 DuPont de Nemours (E.I.)	North America	24.0	52.4	53.4	5.3
5 Mitsubishi Chemical	Asia-Pacific	13.4	16.0	85.5 f	4.8
6 Akzo Nobel	Europe	13.3	94.0	52.0	6.5
Average*		**22.7**	**62.4**	**52.7**	**5.4**
Total		**136.4**			
Pharmaceutical Industry					
1 Merck	North America	51.8	16.0	84.0 z	5.2
2 GlaxoSmithKline	Europe	42.6	95.7	28.6	10.2
3 Johnson & Johnson	North America	36.3	38.1	61.9 z	10.9
4 Pfizer	North America	32.4	35.9	64.1 z	16.0
5 Aventis*	Europe	21.6	91.2	36.4	16.6
6 Novartis	Europe	20.9	98.0	47.0	13.4
7 Roche Group	Europe	19.2	98.2	37.1	14.3
8 Bristol-Myers Squibb	North America	18.2	37.6	62.4	12.2
9 AstraZeneca	Europe	17.8	na	31.9	17.2
10 Abbott Laboratories	North America	17.7	37.8	65.1 a	8.8
11 Wyeth	North America	14.6	36.7	63.3	14.3
12 Eli Lilly	North America	11.1	41.0	59.0 z	19.4
Average		**25.3**	**54.8**	**55.3**	**12.0**
Total		**304.17**			

Data are for 2002

Note: Averages for F/T Sales exclude companies for which data is not available. If the same companies were excluded from the % intra-regional column, the averages would be 55.5% for chemicals and 56.7% for pharmaceuticals. If the same companies are excluded from R&D as % of sales, the averages are 4.5% for chemicals and 11.6% for pharmaceuticals.

z. United State; a. Canada and the United States; f. Africa.

* F/T average, % intra regional average and R&D as a % of Sales average are weighted according to revenues.

in both sectors engage in biotechnology, and some chemical companies have pharmaceutical operations. It is no surprise that Bayer, which has a large pharmaceutical arm, is the chemical company with the highest R&D to sales ratio. In Table 4, the R&D to sales ratios of the six chemical and twelve pharmaceutical MNEs are reported. On average, pharmaceutical companies spend 12% of revenues on R&D, more than twice that spent by chemical companies.

Pharmaceutical companies also tend to be slightly more intra-regionally oriented with regards to revenue. This might reflect a relatively tougher set of regulations for pharmaceutical companies. At nearly twice the size of the European market, the United States is the largest world market for pharmaceuticals. It is also the fastest growing, and not surprisingly, where most large pharmaceutical companies prefer to operate.

The Boston Consulting Group estimates that 40% of all research facilities of large pharmaceutical companies in the world are located in the United States. While a major reason for this is the large size of the US market, most importantly, on average US residents pay more than twice as much as Europeans for pharmaceutical products. Price controls in European countries can influence upwards the extra-regional percentage of sales for European pharmaceutical MNEs while decreasing the extra-regional percentage sales of US pharmaceutical MNEs.

Most firms tend to have a larger portion of their R&D facilities in their home region of the triad. Indeed, looking at Table 5, which shows the distribution of R&D facilities across the triad for a selected number of pharmaceuticals, all of the firms show over 50% of their R&D facilities to be in their home region. This, however, understates the significance of home-region based R&D. The number of facilities tells us little about the particular importance, or of the resources devoted to research, in a given geographic region. A more telling statistic would be the amount of R&D expenditure in each region. This information is generally not available. R&D is highly centralized in the home region of the firm, even when sales are spread more across regions. For instance, host-region oriented European-based firms, like AstraZeneca and GSK, continue to have

Table 5. Chemical Multinationals' Distribution of R&D Facilities Across the Triad

Company	Country	Region	North America % of total	Europe % of total	Asia Pacific % of total
1 AstraZeneca	Sweden	Europe	33.3	55.6	11.1
2 Merck	United States	North America	50.0	41.7	8.3
3 Pfizer	United States	North America	54.5	27.3	18.2
4 DuPont	United States	North America	53.3 z	na	na
5 Aventis	France	Europe	25.0	50.0	25.0
6 GlaxoSmithKline	United Kingdom	Europe	25.0	70.0	5.0
7 Roche Group	Switzerland	Europe	36.8	52.6	10.5

Source: Individual Annual Reports, 2002
Notes: z. United States only

over 50% of their R&D facilities in Europe. Bayer, the bi-regional chemical company, allocates over 70% of its R&D budget to Europe even though this region accounts for only 41.3% of total revenues.

Barriers to Global Strategy in the Pharmaceutical Industry

A set of stringent local and regional regulations prevent pharmaceutical companies from adopting a global strategy. R&D and sales are more concentrated within North America and Europe than in Asia. In addition, the relative size of the US market for pharmaceuticals creates a significant imbalance that shapes the industry and defines international strategy. In chemicals, a lower dependency on patents, the existence of multiple substitutes, and the commodity nature of products results in lower R&D spending and more geographically spread sales.

The pharmaceutical industry is heavily regulated by national and regional governments. The first set of regulations that pharmaceutical firms must overcome is the drug approval process. Presently, this approval is attained at a national level, so pharmaceuticals must test their products and follow the procedures in each jurisdiction. The EU, however, is moving towards a regional approval process to take effect in 2004 or later (FDA News 2003). The liability for damage caused by drugs also varies across nations and must be taken into account when introducing a new drug.

Another set of regulations is price controls. Some countries have price controls for pharmaceuticals in the form of fixed pricing, reference price lists, or volunteer agreements with the pharmaceutical sector. The United States, the largest pharmaceutical market in the world accounting for nearly half of the world's market for pharmaceuticals, takes a more *laissez faire* approach to pharmaceutical pricing; thus there is more R&D in the United States than in Europe.

In Germany, the government has adopted regulations to decrease the overall expenditure on pharmaceuticals. A reference price system forces patients to pay the difference between the reference price and the market price. Since most patients are not willing to pay this difference for many drugs, pharmaceutical companies are forced to bring their prices down to the reference price or face a huge decrease in sales of prescription drugs. The French government encourages the use of generics and directly regulates prices of prescription drugs. In 2003, the Italian government implemented a pharmaceutical-reimbursement policy that would only offer refund to a level set by the Health Ministry. The Department of Health of the UK has the power to regulate prices for pharmaceutical products and control the profits of pharmaceutical companies. As a result, a voluntary agreement was reached in which manufacturers can set initial prices for their drugs, but price increases are regulated.

Marketing is done at a national level. This is because governments not only approve a drug and might set prices, but they also regulate distribution and advertising. The type of packaging and labeling that is permitted and whether a drug is sold only with a prescription is the decision of each government. Governments may even force pharmaceuticals to license the rights to produce their patented drugs. Some governments allow pharmaceuticals to market directly to consumers; others restrict this practice while others ban it altogether.

Many pharmaceutical (and chemical) companies are also in the crop-science business and must plan their strategies to conform to individual government regulations and customer perceptions about genetically modified crops.

Despite such barriers to trade, pharmaceutical products have some of the lowest percentage of intra-regional sales among manufacturing industries. A number of factors explain this. (1) Most pharmaceutical products need not be heavily adapted (in some cases only the packaging and labeling is different) for each geographic market. (2) Large pharmaceutical companies own the rights to brand-name drugs that are essential for healthcare across the world. (3) Once research and development costs are sunk, pharmaceutical companies will continue to sell the drug despite government price control as long as a profit on production costs is made. What governments are doing is basically regulating monopolies on patented drugs which may have very inelastic demand curves.

Case Studies

We now examine the strategies of six pharmaceutical MNEs in a set of case studies. In these case studies we analyze the strategy and structure of the MNE, especially in relation to its R&D. We use frameworks from international business strategy, such as Rugman and Verbeke (1990) with their focus on firm-specific advantages (FSAs) and country-specific advantages (CSAs). The MNEs to be examined are:

  Bi-Regionals: Aventis
                  GlaxoSmithKline
                  AstraZeneca
  Home Region: Merck
                  Pfizer-Pharmacia
                  Eli Lilly

Aventis

In 1999, Hoechst of Germany and Rhône-Poulenc of France combined their businesses to create Aventis a bi-regional pharmaceutical company that researches, develops, manufactures, and markets branded prescription drugs. In 2002, Aventis employed 71,000 people in 100 countries around the world. Although 91.2% of its revenues are derived from sales in foreign markets, the European region accounts for 36.4% of revenues. The most important market for Aventis is North America, where it derives 44.8% of its revenues. Asia-Pacific accounts for approximately 6.4% of sales.

Aventis is organized across business lines. Its core businesses include: prescription drugs, human vaccines, and animal health. The company markets its products through its commercial subsidiaries. The most important of these are located in the United States, Japan, France and Germany, which together account for 64% of Aventis' core business sales. Presently, Aventis is aggressively seeking expansion in the US market. The company currently derives just below 40% of its sales from this country, significantly less than other large European pharmaceuticals. Aventis' structure is centralized in terms of drug development and is decentralized in terms of marketing. The company is divided into three core businesses, and its commercial operations are nationally responsive units in major markets. Its North American marketing operations are just as important as the European ones.

Aventis' strategy is one of low levels of economic integration in terms of marketing and high levels of national responsiveness. Once a drug has been developed, it must be approved by each national government in which it operates. Marketing must also be done in accordance with local legislation, the structure of the healthcare system which influences the distribution of drugs, price controls, and individual cultures and preferences of clients. The locally-based structure of the pharmaceutical industry makes high levels of economic integration in distribution and marketing impossible and forces firms to be nationally responsive. Even in terms of manufacturing, whether a drug will be produced locally or imported across national borders is highly dependent on the regulations of the nation and regional trade treaties.

R&D centers for Aventis are located across the triad. Two research centers are based in Europe; there is one in North America and one in Asia-Pacific. Thus R&D shows high levels of economic integration. Indeed, Aventis' development of a drug can take place in any of its R&D labs across the world and lead to a drug product that can be sold in all jurisdictions. Like all other pharmaceuticals, Aventis is faced with the increasing cost of production and marketing new drugs. The development of new and expensive R&D technology and the increasing layers of regulation in each national market increase the cost of bringing new drugs to market. On the revenue side, governments at all levels and other bulk clients are seeking to reduce healthcare expenditure. At the same time, a growing population with higher life expectancy is increasing the demand for pharmaceuticals. In industrialized countries the aging population seeks to live healthier lives by ensuring access to medication.

One major FSA that Aventis possesses is its drug portfolio and the R&D for its continued development. This is potentially a global advantage if a drug could be sold across the world. Unfortunately, individual national regulations prevent such global production and sales. Its pipeline of drugs in development and its researchers constitute FSAs that are potentially global but not in practice. The expertise of each individual marketing subsidiary is also an FSA. The CSAs are regional. The intellectual hubs that foster the ability of researchers have allowed Aventis to expand its R&D capabilities across the triad. There is one R&D facility in North America, one in Asia-Pacific, and two in Europe. For the firm, each region has a set of regulations that it must adhere to. In the case of North America, its most important market, those regulations are dominated by those of the United States. The United States takes a more favorable stance on genetically modified foods than the EU, and this is echoed by the population. Thus, Aventis would have a much easier time marketing GM products in the United States than in Europe.

GlaxoSmithKline

With £ 28.3 billion in revenues, and 100,000 employees, GlaxoSmithKline (GSK) is one of the largest pharmaceutical companies in the world. The company markets over 70 prescription drugs and a variety of consumer healthcare products. Although incorporated in the UK, over half of its sales originate in the United States. It is a host-region, bi-regional company.

Approximately 30 years ago, British Glaxo was a small company in the dry milk, antibiotics, respiratory drugs, and nutritional businesses. The discovery of Zantac, a drug to treat stomach ulcers, catapulted the company into the mainstream pharmaceuticals market and financed its expansion into the US market. As the patent for Zantac was about to expire, Glaxo found itself in a sticky situation. Up to that point, the company had relied on internal R&D, but this had failed to develop the R&D capabilities for sustainable long-term growth. In 1995, the company merged with Wellcome, a company known for its strength in R&D and its lack of marketing capabilities. The merger was successful in that the new company produced a stream of new drugs that could be marketed using Glaxo's expertise. In 2000, Glaxo Wellcome merged with SmithKline Beecham. According to Sir Richard Sykes, then chairman of Glaxo Wellcome, the deciphering of the human genome would transform the industry and only large companies who can afford to invest to work with this new information would succeed. Together, these two companies are immune to the problem of losing a major blockbuster drug; no one drug accounts for more than 12% of the company's revenues.

Based on location of consumers, the United States is GSK's largest market, accounting for 50.9% of revenues. If we consider only pharmaceuticals, the US market becomes even more significant accounting for 54.4% of revenues. With

Canada, this number increases to 56.8%. GSK derives 28.6% of its sales from its home-market region of Europe. In the heavily-regulated pharmaceutical market alone, GSK derives an even lower portion of its sales from the region, at 26.1%. The European market accounts for 25% of the world market for pharmaceuticals.

GSK's strategy is one of low economic integration in terms of marketing and high levels of national responsiveness. Government regulations, the structure of the local healthcare system, and cultural differences do not allow pharmaceutical firms to adopt strategies of high economic integration in distribution and marketing. GSK must be significantly more responsive to its host region of North America as it is its primary market. Nonetheless, R&D shows high levels of economic integration. Indeed, GSK's development of a drug can take place in any of its R&D labs across the world and lead to a drug product that can be sold across all regions. It has developed a network where "best practice" in its R&D labs can be used anywhere in the network.

The first step in the development of a drug is research and development. GSK spends over £2.6 billion in R&D and has over 15,000 researchers in 28 major R&D sites around the world. Of these, 14 are located in Europe, 10 in the UK, and one in each of Belgium, France, Italy, and Spain. In North America, the United States houses five R&D facilities and Canada one. In Japan, the company has R&D operations in the Tsukuba Science City in Takasaki.

GSK spreads R&D around the world to take advantage of CSAs in terms of human resources and institutional infrastructure that might help it develop a new drug. For instance, it links to an academic department in a major research university with a teaching medical center that is exploring a new drug treatment. Another reason is to monitor more closely the research progress of its competitors, most of which also have R&D facilities in all areas of the world. Finally, R&D facilities might be better able to respond to the particular needs of regional communities.

Once GSK has developed a new drug, it must obtain government approval. This must be done for each individual nation in which the company markets the product, and the process can be significantly different in each jurisdiction.

Production and marketing are the next steps for a new drug. GSK's supply chain is divided into a primary supply chain and a secondary supply chain. The primary supply chain manufactures active ingredients for its products and ships them to the secondary supply chain, which manufactures the end product. There are six primary supply chain sites: Australia, India, Ireland, Singapore, the United States, and the UK. In Europe, there are 17 secondary supply chain sites. North America houses an additional six secondary supply chains. The rest of the world houses 32 secondary sites in 19 countries (the Middle East and Africa houses five sites, 22 sites are located in Asia-Pacific, and Latin America accounts for the remaining five sites).

Proximity and regional regulations prevent multinationals from segmenting national markets. As a result, GSK was not able to continue selling drugs to

Spain under a two-price system, one for local consumption and one for exports into the EU. Similarly, the integration of the North American market under NAFTA makes preventing the importation of Canadian pharmaceuticals into the United States difficult despite the health section having been exempted from the national treatment provisions of NAFTA. Indeed, pharmaceutical companies are struggling with supplying drugs to the Canadian market that erode their profits in the US market. Beneficiaries from this intra-regional trade of drugs are considering whether to challenge the US government and GSK under NAFTA to continue to trade in pharmaceuticals.

Although the United States and Europe account for nearly 80% of GSK's sales, developing countries took center stage over AIDS medications. In 2000, Cipla of India offered to produce generic versions of AIDS drugs to underdeveloped countries at a 90% markdown. GSK and other pharmaceuticals sued the South African government to stop the drug from being imported, but this sparked a public relations nightmare. Oxfam, a development NGO, accused the pharmaceuticals of waging war on the world's poor. The companies had a difficult time explaining to their developed-country consumers how they could potentially let millions die of AIDS when a cure was readily available. Under a storm of criticism, the drug companies withdrew the suit and paid the South African government's legal costs.

AstraZeneca

In 1999, British Zeneca merged with Swedish Astra to create what at the time was the third largest pharmaceutical company in the world. The merger was considered a union of equals. Astra was a leader in the ulcer market, with Prilosec, at the time the world's best selling drug. Yet the dependency on this one drug made the company highly vulnerable as its patent was projected to expire in 2001. Today, 55.6% of European AstraZeneca's $17.8 billion in revenues is derived from North America. Its home region of Europe accounts for only 31.9% of revenues. Japan accounts for a mere 5.5%, and the remaining 7% is derived from other markets. It is a host-region oriented firm.

In 1999, Imperial Chemical Industries (ICI) divested its pharmaceutical business under the name Zeneca. ICI, the world's largest producer of paint, remained a chemical manufacturer. While Zeneca continued to prosper independently, the separation proved devastating for ICI. In the four years that followed, ICI's shares were significantly undervalued, and the company sought acquisitions, including companies it had divested to strengthen its position.

AstraZeneca is a good example of the marketing difficulties pharmaceuticals face even after they have cleared drug regulatory bodies. Each national jurisdiction has its own rules for marketing drugs, forcing companies to structure their marketing strategies to fit the local environment, and preventing the development of a global strategy.

Astra Zeneca's strategy is one of low levels of economic integration in terms of marketing and high levels of national responsiveness. In R&D, however, it has high levels of economic integration. Indeed, Aventis' development of a drug can take place in any of its R&D labs across the world and lead to a drug product that can be sold in all jurisdictions.

The weight of the safety and marketing regulations in each national jurisdiction is too large relative to overall operations for AstraZeneca to develop a global strategy. The emergence of regional blocks means another set of regulations and barriers that AstraZeneca must take into account. Therefore, the company cannot have a uniform global strategy. Governments are nationally responsive to the demands of their citizens. Drugs are perceived differently across national borders. In addition, local communities may react differently to drugs. There is also an entire industry built around the approval process that governments have an interest in maintaining.

A significant risk for pharmaceutical companies is the discovery of new or more dramatic side effects that were not discovered during clinical testing. In late 2002, the Japanese government restricted the use of Iressa, a drug aimed at patients with lung cancer, after over 100 deaths were reported linked to taking the drug. Clinical trials showed that lung-cancer patients showed significant improvement after taking the drug. The Japanese Ministry of Health did not ban the drug as it considered the benefits to late-stage cancer patients outweighed the risks. However, the discovery prompted AstraZeneca to change its labeling to reflect the risks and the Japanese Ministry of Health to require that patients taking the drug be hospitalized for four weeks to monitor side effects. In clinical trials, Japanese patients taking Iressa benefited significantly more from the drug than other patients. However, it turned out that they were also far more likely to suffer from interstitial lung disease (ILD), a side effect of the drug. ILD, the cause of all Iressa-related Japanese deaths, occurs in all cancer treatments. Yet, a media panic in Japan made international news and threatened to jeopardize Iressa's approval in the United States and Europe.

In the case of Iressa, AstraZeneca made the decision to launch the drug in the Japanese market first. The panic that ensued compromised drug approval in its two largest markets of Europe and North America. Although a regional strategy is required for drug marketing, the strategic launching of pharmaceuticals must be thought of on a global basis. Panics in the media do not remain regional. AstraZeneca's mistake was to launch Iressa without examining or taking into consideration that the Japanese were more likely to suffer interstitial lung disease. Even though they were also more likely to benefit from the drug, the risks associated with it were far higher than for other regions.

In conclusion, while AstraZeneca has to be careful in its European domestic market, it also faces regulations in its large North American market and in the Asian market. These prevent the company from adopting a worldwide strategy. At the same time, it can be argued that regional effects might have worldwide repercussions. It needs to think regionally rather than globally, but continue to consider the intra-regional effects of its regional actions.

Merck

Merck is a US based firm deriving 84.0% of its revenues from its home national market. That Merck derives most of its profits from the United States is no surprise. This is the case for most large pharmaceutical companies. After all, the United States is the largest market, and it has the least price regulation among all industrialized countries. Most of Merck's research is conducted in North America, where the company has six research facilities (five in the United States and one in Canada). Yet, despite the dominance of the North American region, the company also has five R&D facilities in Europe and one in Japan.

Merck's strategy is one of high economic integration and low national responsiveness. Although the company is facing different market conditions in Europe which would require developing a nationally responsive strategy, this only accounts for a small fraction of its operations.

The company is organized on the basis of products and services. Merck's revenues are derived from prescription, therapeutic, and preventive products. Medco Health revenues are derived from the sale of prescription drugs in the United States through managed prescription drug programs. Merck has "global" product lines (i.e. run in a uniform manner from head office). The firm is basically divided across business lines. There is no significant geographic segmentation in terms of business units. A product/service based structure that includes nationally-based Medco Health gives Merck a competitive advantage against other competitors in the US market, but it does nothing to help it compete in other regions of the world. Merck's strategy is based on centralized product/service lines, not regional ones. That is, there is no European SBU to integrate all European operations. In addition, the European market is fractured in terms of language, culture, and healthcare structure, making a regional strategy more difficult to achieve.

Ray Gilmartin, Chairman of Merck, stands by the motto, "Medicine is for the people. It is not for the profits. The profits follow." This is why the company stood aside while the pharmaceutical industry restructured through a wave of mergers in the late 1990s. At the time, Merck faced the same problems plaguing the entire industry: (1) the patent expiry of some of its most important drugs; (2) competition from generic companies; (3) increased price regulation by national and sub-national governments; (4) increase costs of developing a drug; and most importantly (5) a slowdown in the number of successful new products that it develops. Yet, while competitors rushed to buy rivals to increase overall R&D expending, Merck chose to go at it alone relying on the strength of its research force. This strength is undisputed. Between 1996 and 2000, the company patented 1,933 new compounds, the highest in the industry. That this is done with a lower R&D budget than that of other large pharmaceuticals only increases the reputation of Merck as a research-oriented company. The benefit of such a vision is that the company can lure some of the best scientists, or, at the very least, some of the more dedicated to their research.

One of Merck's FSAs is the caliber of its researchers. Other FSAs include its patented compounds, its pipeline of drugs in progress, and its portfolio of current drugs in the market. Merck's reputation is also an FSA. Not only is the quality of its research well regarded by the public, but it is also well regarded in terms of corporate responsibility.

As a US based firm, Merck is located in the largest pharmaceutical market in the world, where most R&D is performed, so it is a hub of innovation that Merck can use to improve its competitive position. R&D facilities are often built to take advantage of specific human resources in an area or region to take account of government incentives or institutional infrastructure, as well as to monitor competitors.

Merck has also had to take a different stance in poorer countries where the cost of medication is prohibitive for many patients. In 2001, Merck, in collaboration with other large pharmaceuticals, launched a lawsuit against the South African government. At the time, the country was switching to generic drugs to combat AIDS, which was affecting 10% of its population. Drug costs were often higher than salaries, and, like Brazil, the country had to decide to either honor the patents of large MNEs to produce its own or to import it from countries that already legalized generics and produced them at a fraction of the cost. Throughout the world, protestors rose up against the lawsuit, forcing pharmaceutical companies to justify letting 250,000 people die every year. Merck was the quickest to realize the public relations hole which it had dug, and it acted to broker an agreement between the industry and developing countries. Merck no longer makes a profit from selling HIV drugs in the poorest of countries. Others in the industry complain that this inhibits future research, but Merck was quick to point out that as long as pharmaceuticals can continue to make significant profits in the developed world, research will continue at the same pace.

Pfizer Pharmacia

In 2000, Pfizer offered $90 billion to Warner-Lambert shareholders to win a hostile takeover and snatch the company from American Home Products, which was already negotiating a friendly merger with Warner-Lambert. Only two years later the company offered $60 billion for Pharmacia. These acquisitions turned Pfizer into the largest pharmaceutical company in the world with an estimated $37.5 billion in revenues and a $7 billion R&D budget.

Pfizer is a home-region oriented company with 64.1% of its sales in the United States. Its R&D is headquartered in its home region of the United States. Excluding Pharmacia, six of the pre-merger company's R&D facilities are in the North American region (one in Canada and five in the United States). Europe hosts three Pfizer R&D facilities and Japan two labs.

The company operates in two business segments: pharmaceuticals and consumer products. The pharmaceutical segment is the largest, accounting for 92% of Pfizer's business and includes human and health pharmaceuticals and capsugel, a capsule-making sub-segment. Pfizer's Consumer Healthcare business manufactures over the counter healthcare products, including Listerine, Rolaids, Vizine, and BenGay. International operations include both the pharmaceutical and consumer product segments. Marketing is conducted through subsidiaries and through distributors.

In an industry where constant innovation is the most valuable long-term predictor of wealth creation, Pfizer is better known for the capabilities of its sales force. To date, its competitive advantage has been marketing. Pfizer's 11% world market can be attributed to the company's sales force of 35,000 representatives.

Even if Pfizer cannot compete as an innovator, it is well positioned to profit from the innovations of others. This might be the company's saving grace since a large R&D budget has produced very little relative to the industry. It costs Pfizer more than three times as much to discover a compound that can be patented than it costs its largest US competitor, Merck. Between 1996 and 2001, Pfizer patented 1,217 compounds at a cost of $17.5 million each. For the same period, Merck patented 1,933 compounds at a cost of $6 million each. One of the most compelling reasons given for mergers and acquisitions, a large R&D budget, has not yet proven fruitful. For a discussion of the international expansion of Pfizer, see Fina and Rugman (1996).

Small pharmaceuticals that can produce a prize drug are willing to partner up with Pfizer to have the product pitched through their marketing machine. Lipitor was produced by Warner-Lambert and marketed through a joint venture with Pfizer. This drug alone justified Pfizer's hostile takeover. Celebrex and Aricept, two other best selling drugs in Pfizer's portfolio, were also discovered by smaller players, Searly and Eisai of Japan.

Eli Lilly

Eli Lilly, the Indiana-based pharmaceutical company, is a home-region oriented company with 59% of its sales derived from within the United States. Western Europe accounts for an additional 19.5% of sales. The remaining 21.5% of sales originate in non-specified foreign countries. In terms of assets Eli Lilly is even more intra-regional. Nearly 74% of all long-lived assets are located in the United States. Western Europe accounts for an additional 15.6%. One main explanation for the relative importance of the US market is that prices in the United States are significantly higher than in the rest of the industrialized countries. As a result, revenues in Eli Lilly's home region tend to be higher regardless of similar unit sales in other regions.

Eli Lilly only operates in one industry segment, pharmaceuticals. Its business units are divided according to product lines which are defined by the type of ailment they target. In the United States, Lilly markets its products through 35 wholesale distributors, three of which account for nearly 50% of domestic sales. Although the government and managed care institutions account for a large portion of sales, direct sales by Lilly are not material; it is the wholesalers who process these orders. Lilly takes a more direct role in marketing its drugs. This is done through sales representatives who contact physicians, wholesalers, hospitals, managed-care organizations, and governments. These representatives are divided in terms of product lines, neurosciences, endocrinology, cardiovascular, etc. A special group is dedicated to marketing to managed care organizations and to the government. The efforts of sales representatives are complemented with advertising in medical journals, distribution of pamphlets, and samples to physicians; and, in the United States and Canada, advertising targeted directly to customers.

Eli Lilly's products are sold internationally despite different regulatory environments because it is to the benefit of each country to approve a new medicine. Internationally, promotion, distribution and marketing are highly dependent on national regulation. Most products are marketed through sales representatives. In the majority of foreign countries, Lilly has its own sales force, but in others, it uses independent distributors. In 2002, Lilly's R&D budget was $2.1 billion, or 19.4% of total revenue. In the United States, R&D facilities are located in Indiana and Greenfield. There are also four European based R&D facilities and three Asia-Pacific based R&D facilities.

Lilly's strategy is one of high economic integration and low national responsiveness. Although the company faces different market conditions in Western Europe that require developing a nationally responsive marketing strategy, this only accounts for about 20% of its operations. In its home region, Lilly requires a high degree of economic integration. Eli Lilly's FSAs include its portfolio of patented drugs, its pipeline of new drugs, its biotechnology competencies, and its R&D centers. In terms of marketing, FSAs are its distribution routes and its sales representatives, both in the US market and internationally. Changes in patent legislation that allow generic firms and large pharmaceuticals to produce a competing drug reduce Lilly's FSAs. Its biotechnology competencies and its R&D centers all contribute to developing drugs that can one day be patented drugs that can be sold across borders. FSAs relating to marketing, however, are not transferable to other countries or regions. This is because of differences in regulations not only in each country, but also because of cultural differences, including language.

Conclusion

Innovation in the chemicals and pharmaceuticals industry occurs largely within the home region bases of the large MNEs. There are two distinctive markets in North America and Europe for pharmaceuticals; these markets are segmented by strong regulations and different institutional frameworks for distribution and marketing. Even within the EU, there are strong national differences in regulatory regimes. These segmented national and regional markets deny MNEs the potential R&D and marketing global scale economies in production that they might otherwise wish to achieve. Pharmaceutical MNEs, in particular, are not global. Chemical MNEs can be more global, but such MNEs are much less innovative than pharmaceutical ones. Both sets of MNEs have regional, rather than global, strategies.

Sources for Cases

Aventis: Adapted from Aventis, *Annual Report*, 2002; "Rhine or shine", *The Economist*, March 7, 2002 and Brian O'Reilly, "Reaping a Biotech Blunder", *Fortune*, February 8, 2001.

Website: www.aventis.com

GlaxoSmithKline: Adapted from GlaxoSmithKline, *Annual Report*, 2002; "Searching for a new formula", *The Economist*, May 21, 2002; "Glaxo's expanding galaxy", *The Economist*, November 23, 2000 and Viviene Walt. "AIDS Drug War Heats Up", *Fortune*, June 20, 2001.

Website: www.gsk.com

AstraZeneca: Adapted from AstraZeneca, *Annual Report*, 2002; "Misleading drug ads slip under regulators' radar", *USAToday*, January 5, 2003; "FTC investigates AstraZeneca marketing", *Philadelphia Business Journal*, March 10, 2003 and "Drug linked to 124 deaths in Japan", *CBSNews.com*, January 10, 2003.

Website: www.astrazeneca.com

Merck: Adapted from Merck, *Annual Report*, 2002; "The acceptable face of capitalism"? *The Economist*, December 12, 2002 and Melanie Warner, "Can Merck Stand Alone", *Fortune*, July 9, 2001.

Website: www.merck.com

Pfizer: Adapted from Pfizer, *Annual Report*, 2002; John Simons, "King of the Pill", *Fortune*, March 30, 2003; Lee Clifford, "Pharmacia: Tyrannosaurus Rx", *Fortune*, February 18, 2001 and Pfizer, "Pfizer and Pharmacia Combine Operations, Creating World's Largest Research-Based Pharmaceutical Company", *News Release*, April 16, 2003.

Website: www.pfizer.com

Eli Lilly: Adapted from Eli Lilly, *Annual Report*, 2002; "Bloom and blight", *The Economist*, October 24, 2002; "Marketing madness", *The Economist*, July 19, 2001 and "A Bitter Pill", *Fortune*, July 24, 2001.

Website: www.lilly.com

References

Anonymous, Europe Standardizing Drug Approval Process, *FDA News*, May 30, 2003.
Finn, E./Rugman, A. M., A Test of Internalization Theory and Internationalization Theory: The Upjohn Company, *Management International Review*, 36, 3, 1996, pp. 199–213.
Rugman, A. M., *The End of Globalization*, London: Random House and New York: Amacom-McGraw Hill 2000.
Rugman, A.M., Regional Strategy and the Demise of Globalization, *Journal of International Management*, 9, 4, 2003, pp. 409–417.
Rugman, A. M./Brain, C., Multinationals are Regional, not Global, *Multinational Business Review*, 11, 1, Spring 2003, pp. 3–12.
Rugman, A. M./Verbeke, A., *Global Corporate Strategy and Trade Policy*, London: Routledge 1990.
Rugman, A. M./Verbeke, A., The Regional and Global Strategies of Multinational Enterprises, *Journal of International Business Studies*, 35, 1, 2004, pp. 3–18.
Rugman, A. M., *The Regional Multinational*, Cambridge: Cambridge University Press 2003.

Management International Review

Neuerscheinungen

Joachim Scholz
Wert und Bewertung internationaler Akquisitionen
2001
XXII, 365 S. mit 40 Abb.,
(mir-Edition),
Br. € 79,–
ISBN 3-409-11602-8

Joachim Wolf
Strategie und Struktur 1955–1995: Ein Kapitel der Geschichte deutscher nationaler und internationaler Unternehmen
2000
XXXII, 673 S. mit 156 Abb.,
7 farb. Abb. (mir-Edition),
Br. € 94,50
ISBN 3-409-11637-0

Dodo zu Knyphausen-Aufseß (Hrsg.)
Globalisierung als Herausforderung der Betriebswirtschaftslehre
2000
XVIII, 285 S. (mir-Edition),
Br. € 64,–
ISBN 3-409-11719-9

Laila Maija Hofmann
Führungskräfte in Europa. Empirische Analyse zukünftiger Anforderungen
2000
XXVIII, 414 S. mit 89 Abb.,
129 Tab., Diss. Augsburg 2000
(mir-Edition),
Br. € 64,–
ISBN 3-409-11704-0

Frank Niederländer
Dynamik in der internationalen Produktpolitik von Automobilherstellern
2000
XXVIII, 296 S. mit 111 Abb.,
36 Tab., Dissertation Eichstätt 2000
(mir-Edition),
Br. € 59,–
ISBN 3-409-11722-9

Jan Hendrik Fisch
Structure Follows Knowledge. Internationale Verteilung der Forschung und Entwicklung in multinationalen Unternehmen
2001
XXII, 247 S. mit 84 Abb., 10 Tab.
(mir-Edition),
Br. € 49,–
ISBN 3-409-11802-0

Betriebswirtschaftlicher Verlag Dr. Th. Gabler, Abraham-Lincoln-Str. 46, 65189 Wiesbaden

Management
International Review
© Gabler Verlag 2004

Anca Metiu/Bruce Kogut

Distributed Knowledge and Creativity in the International Software Industry[1]

Abstract

- The growth of outsourcing of intellectual work has provoked a major debate in wealthy countries concerning the loss of jobs to developing countries. However, what is the limit to this distribution of work?
- We interviewed several software and client companies as well as conducted extended field research. The qualitative work was matched by a questionnaire.

Key Results

- These triangulated methods indicated a surprising convergence among co-located and distributed projects, indicating that firms have acquired a body of skills to manage intellectual work across distance and national boundaries. The efficacy of these practices is contingent on the importance of a heavyweight manager to oversee the project. However, the more creativity was required, the more likely work would be co-located than dispersed.
- These results indicate that the managerial experience to support global outsourcing of intellectual labor is already advanced, while creativity remains more likely to be located in rich countries.

Authors

Anca M. Metiu, Assistant Professor of Organizational Behavior, INSEAD, Fontainebleau, Cedex, France.
Bruce Kogut, Professor of Strategy and Management, INSEAD, Fontainebleau, Cedex, France.

Introduction

In the first part of the 19th century, Great Britain entertained an active debate regarding the dangers of the transmission of knowledge across borders. This debate led first to the enactment of laws that forbade the migration of skilled workers and that became a cause of grievance between England and the backward United States. In the later debates that eventually led to the repeal of these acts, other voices such as Andrew Ure noted that the success of the UK did not lie in its preservation, but its creation of knowledge (Ure 1835). England, and Birmingham more exactly, was to be the innovative leader of the world economy.

It is not coincidental that Charles Babbage, famed today as the inventor of the mechanical computer, should have proposed a division of mental labor (Babbage 1835). Since brains were scarce and expensive, it made sense to assign less skilled (including women and children) to low paying and less skilled jobs. The vertical division of mental labor concluded with the more intellectually capable directing work and the innovative process.

These two elements of the geography of innovation and the vertical division of mental labour have become the background knowledge of the modern world. Innovation is done in the Silicon Valley, Toulouse, Baden-Württemberg, Tokyo, and Seoul. This list suggests that the world has changed since Ure and Babbage, but it is still an unequal world, with a handful of largely western and a few Asian countries dominating the indices of innovation.

The explanation of this persistence is both simple and complicated. The simplicity is that innovation addresses the needs of advanced consumers located in richer countries. Since it is intensive in human capital, its location favors countries rich in educational resources. A smart person in less advantaged parts of the world either had not the luxury to be educated, or if schooled, could not easily participate in innovation. These observations are easily confirmed by migration flows of educated people from poor countries to rich countries, but until recent times, rarely in the reverse. Human capital migrated to be in proximity with physical capital.

The complicating aspect of this story is to ask why this situation should endure? One possibility is to posit a path dependence in which past investments have resulted in localized knowledge, much of it held tacitly as the background knowledge of how intellectual work is done. The design of semiconductors, or the combinatorial chemistry of biotechnology, consists of knowledge encoded in books and articles which are not nevertheless easily accessible. Participation in the networks of knowledge is vital in order to acquire the technological skills for innovation and valued intellectual work. For this reason, the little evidence regarding innovative regions that we have appears suggests that the job movement of skilled workers loyal to a region is critical to innovative success (Almeida/Kogut 1999). Perhaps in this regard, the British concern over the migration of skills was not entirely nonsensical.

These two explanations are not competitors, but complements. They raise the interesting question what would happen if the economics of space should be eliminated. Imagine that the transport of ideas, and products, should be of zero cost. Would regions still exist?

This hypothetical question has become a practical reality in the past decade, primarily in the software and information technology industries. The expansion of information technologies amplifies the division of mental labor among countries and regions. A long tradition in the economics of location explains the distribution of firm activities across space based on the economics of weight and transportation. However, when ideas can be encoded in electronic bytes, considerations of weight and transportation vanish. Due to similar quality training available in many – though not all – countries, (e.g. US, India, Ireland, Israel, Germany, France), human capital for mental work exists in many locations throughout the world. Consequently, costs and productivity should, by economic logic, drive location decisions.

Software is an exemplar case of study for the study of the meaning of geography in the absence of the standard spatial costs. Because intellectual work uses ideas as inputs and outputs to the production process, and since the transport of these ideas is not bounded by weight, any two points in the world appear as co-located from the point of view of economic transportation. This economic implication lies at the heart of the current debate in many rich countries regarding the outsourcing of skilled jobs to India and other Asian countries.

Our aim in this study is to analyze the international division of mental labor by identifying the limits and potentials of the spatial distribution and coordination of software design and programming. We begin with a simple hypothesis that software projects requiring a greater creative content are more likely to be located in the United States for the period under study. From this perspective, we examine how the digitalization of task content, the increased sophistication of communication technology, and spatial coordination are rapidly changing parameters to the decisions of companies in the software industry. Our study provides an analytical window into a rapidly moving frontier that has implications far broader than those currently impacting the software industry. Similar dramatic changes affect all activities that can be encoded in bytes and transmitted over distances.

Software design and production are activities common to many industries. As the content of work continues to shift from material processing to knowledge creation, the demand for software increases, no matter if the company is in the computer industry, in insurance, or in the creative arts. The digitalization of content, the ability to provide services remotely, and the replacement of mechanical by electronic design are all driven by the writing and maintenance of software code. To the extent that such activities as film making and editing, back office processing of data and text, education, or service support (to name a few examples) can be digitally-encoded and transmitted, the software industry is representative of a far-reaching revolution in the nature of work.

To avoid confusion, it is useful to define at the outset the central terms used throughout this paper. Onshore activities refers to development activities carried by US firms in the US. Offshore activities refers to the software development work done by US firms in their own Indian offshore development centers. Outsourcing refers to the software development done in India, by Indian for US companies. Hybrid projects are those partly done in the US and partly done in India. Co-location designates the physical proximity of two or more activities.

We rely upon two types of data: interviews and administered questionnaires. The interviews were conducted in Bangalore, Singapore, and in the United States with American, Indian, and Singaporean managers involved in software development. These interviews revealed somewhat distinct perceptions of managers who operate in different environments. Managers who operate mainly in the US perceived the impact of the digital revolution as a force to be recognized but one that would not dramatically affect the location and organization of work. However, the executives who are closely involved in offshore operations emphasized the implications posed by the new technologies for the compression of time and space.

There is good reason to believe that the demand for software will only be met by a rapid globalization of work. In India, this young industry (the first software companies were established in the mid-1980's) has been growing at annual rates of 50–55% over the past ten years. According to Nasscom[2], the Indian software and services exports grew from $ 6.5 Billion in 1998 to $ 9.8 Billion in 2003. Out of this volume 67.7% of software exports are to the US. It is also significant that over time, the offshore activities grew much faster than the services provided by Indian companies at their clients' site.

The very fluidity of the environment makes the findings of our study even more valuable. By capturing the factors that impact this dynamism, we can understand the motivations and the limits of this growing phenomenon. Clearly, a complex dynamic is here at work. The technology makes possible increasingly richer interactions across distances, a process that reinforces firms' propensity to locate abroad in their search for economic rents and for talents. In their turn, the demands of coordination among distant locations require even more sophisticated communication links, and this need pushes the technologies even further. We recognize that the phenomenon of offshore location is largely driven by this dynamic.

At the same time, this dynamic is also influenced by the need to collocate activities requiring creativity. As Analee Saxenian (1996) has shown in her study of the Silicon Valley, the region's success is supported by a culture of free communication among engineers. The information technology revolution poses, therefore, a fundamental question that lies at the center of our inquiry: does the observed division of labor reflect the limits to the virtual coordination of creative work?

We address this question by investigating the spatial distribution of software work among various locations worldwide and the influences of three factors on the location decision: shared context of the strategic mission, task and product design, and communication. These dimensions are empirically grounded in an ethnographic study of dispersed software development teams (Metiu 2001).

In summary, the increasing digitalization of work makes intellectual tasks such as software writing virtually co-located. However, we hypothesize that the decision to locate intellectual activities also hinges on factors representing the limits imposed by human and machine languages, as well as on the shared context of human interaction. Because the knowledge needed for some tasks is not easily communicated among distant parties, we find that particular projects are retained at locations even where factor costs are higher.

The International Software Industry

To understand our research design, it is instructive to consider first the traditional models of software design and the importance of the software industry for the study of the growing distribution of mental labour. The software industry's digital, and at the same time modular and systemic character, makes it a perfect setting for the study of the international division of intellectual labor. During the last several decades the US have largely dominated this industry; however, in the last ten years, we have witnessed the rise of software writing centers in several regions of the globe. The most prominent centers are located in India, Ireland and Israel. While many US firms outsource parts of software development and maintenance to Irish or Indian firms, other multinationals have set up development centers that operate on the basis of long-term agreements on prices for time and materials.

The issue of internal development versus outsourcing in software development has been the focus of modeling in recent research (Whang 1992, Richmond/Seidmann/Whinston 1992). Wang, Barron, and Seidmann (1997) argue that such models are limited by their neglect of the informational disparities inherent in software contracting. They show that the developers' skill and business knowledge are not invariant with different sources or providers because outsourcers tend to specialize in a particular industry, where they develop industry specific know-how. Consequently, Wang et al. (1997) take into account explicitly the necessity of communication between parties. Their model and numerical experiments show that an internal developer has a substantial advantage over an outsourcer. Two recent empirical studies support this claim. Nelson et al. (1996) examine 186 projects from five firms and find that 75% were done internally. Also, the case studies of Lacity et al. (1996) lead to the recommendation that organizations develop internally projects that require familiarity with existing business processes.

The tension between creative and well-understood tasks is present in studies of the software industry in general. Cusumano (1991) documented the emergence, first in the United States, of the concept of a software "factory" designed to rationalize the process of software production, as well as the adoption and implementation of this concept in the Japanese companies Hitachi, Toshiba, NEC, and Fujitsu. In the attempt to make the development of software more cost-effective, firms proceeded to standardize software tools and environments and to re-use code in different projects. This approach culminated in an attempt to rationalize the entire cycle of software production, installation, and maintenance through the establishment of factory-like procedures and processes. At issue, however, is whether the factory concept increases quality and productivity only at the cost of flexibility, creativity, and the adequate meeting of specific customer needs. Cusumano's view is that software factories were not the answer to new and complex systems because the processes involved in this type of projects are only imperfectly understood.

Ultimately, these studies aimed at improving project performance. However, very few of them attempted to assess this outcome via large scale surveys. An earlier quantitative study by Cusumano and Kemerer (1990) compares the performance of 24 US and 16 Japanese software development projects. The analyses indicate that Japanese software projects perform at least as well as US counterparts in basic measures of productivity, quality, and reuse of software code. Similarly, in one of the few surveys of software development projects, Kraut and Streeter (1995) found that their coordination will be difficult when specifications are incomplete, when the knowledge needed is not documented and therefore not easily available. They also found that coordination was impeded as project size and complexity increase, and that the maintenance of informal communication networks was an important determinant of project success.

The most modest of the strategies involved in distributed activities is to exploit simply the cost advantage by assigning routine tasks to offshore sites. These tasks might be the maintenance of legacy systems, developing highly specialized but routine modules, or completing entirely the detailed design work of a software project. Modularity is easy to achieve, communication requirements are low, and there is little concern over shared context. As shown in Figure 1 for the traditional waterfall model, module tasks are separable and, thus, easy to locate in different places.

Figure 1. The Waterfall Model Minimizes the Need for Coordination and Communication because it Sees the Process of Software Development as a Cascade of Phases, the Output of One Being the Input to the Next

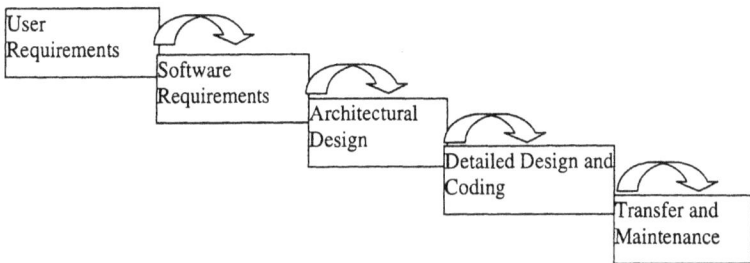

The waterfall model is a stylized view of programming that is often rejected by software engineers. In a research workshop held with software designers from many firms and countries, a manager of a highly innovative project characterized the waterfall model as possible for only routine work. Creative work, he insisted, demanded a chaotic model in which the design of the downstream steps simultaneously caused alterations in the upstream architecture. This model of development was highly interactive and dynamic.

The waterfall model has served as a principal point of reference for the design of international software projects. Interviews with software engineers, as discussed below, indicate that the waterfall model had been the operating guide for the assignment of software programming to contractors located in India. These contractors provided so-called "Offshore Development Centers" or ODCs. The larger contractors maintained several ODCs as separate "silos", that is, under strict confidentiality not to share information with the other centers. In some cases, these ODCs functioned as virtual units to the contracting American firm. These centers have also been called "bodyshop" centers to denote that their value-added has been traditionally the writing of code to meet the requirements and architecture determined already by the onshore contracting customer. It is not surprising that a waterfall model appears to fit well the "bodyshop" services provided traditionally by offshore contractors.

In trying to understand the decision to locate programming offshore, it is critical to consider two boundaries: the national boundary (i.e. the decision to locate "offshore") and the firm boundary (i.e. the decision to contract or not). Both of these boundaries posed difficulties for coordination which are often addressed through innovative efforts to integrate the "offshore" and "outsourced" contractor within the firm. An indication of the efforts to integrate was the investment by a large American financial services firm in communication systems, including the assignment of internal phone numbers to the Indian programmers. As a result, an American employee composed only the last numbers of an internal exchange (such as, x4329) to call the Indian contractors located in India.

There is, in effect, an important element of caution regarding the potential for selection bias in the research design. We witness only the projects that have already been made, that is, the projects deemed feasible to outsourcing and/or contracting. Once the decision is made, many of the critical dimensions that determined location may appear similar among onshore and offshore work. However, some dimensions may represent features that cannot be easily resolved by investments in communication or organization. As we will argue and show below, the most important dimension that differentiates onshore from offshore work is the saliency of creativity. It is this dimension that has been argued, as we noted above, to be the less amenable to the implementation of a waterfall type of production process.

The Spatial Distribution of Work

Software is the writing of symbolic code to achieve particular functions to be executed by computers and electronic devices. Since the capital investment consists largely of computers, software, and communication infrastructure, its production is heavily biased towards mental labour relative to traditional capital-intensive industries. As wage rates and the availability of brains vary by geography, there are strong economic incentives to source software from distributed locations.

We wish to understand the motives for, and the limits of, the spatial distribution of work tasks in a distributed intelligence environment in reference to the co-location decision. The variables of interest are a) location of software development activities (on shore or offshore) and b) project dimensions. In addition to the dimensions of coordination and communication, property rights issues may impact location decisions for certain software tasks (e.g. source code), as well as labor cost differentials between various locations. For example, at the time of the first data collection, an entry level software programmer recruited by one of India's top domestic software companies expected to earn about $ 500 a month; his American counterpart earned approximately $ 3,000 (*Financial Times* December 2, 1998).

Any model of the geography of production points to a few central determinants of location: the factor costs of production, transportation costs, location of demand. The expansive literature on economic development stresses the importance of "backward and forward linkages" to other industries. Though these linkages have been difficult to conceptualize and analyze, work by Becker and Murphy (1992) provides the interesting insight that the division of labor is influenced by the general degree of knowledge available in a system. In their work, production is characterized by the constraint that all elements to a task must be accomplished such that the minimally efficient task determines global efficiency. Much of software writing has, in fact, this characteristic, whereby the product cannot be shipped until all modules are completed and integrated.

This analytical frame captures the explanation offered by Babbage that we discussed earlier, namely, that differences in productivity and wages among classes of workers give rise to a "mental" division of labor (Babbage 1835). This division of labor is, consequently, a vertical hierarchy, in which less complex work is assigned to less productive and less expensive labor. The more skilled workers are reserved for more complex work, where their higher wages are justified by their higher productivity at mental labor. It is important to underline here that Becker and Murphy imply that productivity differences among workers can be explained by differences in the degree of general knowledge available to them. This point is especially significant in light that highly educated workers in an offshore site may be less productive due to inefficiencies in the local economic environment.

Leaving aside coordination costs, the economics of software would suggest a tremendous advantage for offshore production. Factor costs are remarkably less expensive in, say, India. Though energy provision is highly problematic, small firms internalize such costs by purchasing an assemblage of batteries for outages, while larger firms install small generator facilities. Costs are still estimated to be substantially below sites in developed countries. Transportation costs are negligible, since the product is transmitted by satellites. Satellite communication also avoids the costs and uncertainties of depending upon local networks and roads. Human capital is rapidly deepening, since countries like India and Ireland (where the wage costs are substantially higher) have developed efficient institutions of technical education.

If factor and transportation costs indicate the absolute advantage of offshore location, what then are the forces that determine the decision to locate software in a given site? A critical determinant in the decision to locate a project must be the costs of coordination. We focus upon three elements that influence the costs of coordination over distance: the dimensions of the task, the limits to communication by various media, and the importance of shared context.

Dimensions of Task: Tacitness and Hidden Knowledge of Modules

Work tasks display a great diversity in terms of the underlying knowledge bases, as well as the type of effort required for their successful completion. Our paper gives due attention to the finding that knowledge transfers are not abstract transactions between information-transmitters and information-receivers, but exchanges in which the identity of the two parties is crucial for success. As Brown and Duguid (2001) have argued, significant amount of innovation takes place in the informal communities of practice existing in each firm. These informal groups linking individuals within and across formal organizational boundaries are the loci for innovation, because individuals and groups create knowledge as they interact with the things and activities of the social and physical world (Brown/Duguid 2001). This line of thinking clarifies the reason why knowledge cannot be simply transferred among various firms.

This conception of firms has been explored by organizational scholars interested in the tacit aspects of work processes that will make technology difficult to imitate and transfer within and across organizations. Expanding upon Rogers (1980) and Winter (1987), Kogut and Zander (1992) propose that the firm is a repository not only of information, but also of social knowledge or know-how, which is largely tacit hence difficult to communicate and imitate. That firms act as social communities for the creation and communication of knowledge is apparent in their statistical results that found that the transfer of innovations among Swedish firms was significantly affected by the extent to which the knowledge can be articulated in documents and software, as well as by the extent to which workers can be trained in schools or on the job (Kogut/Zander 1993; Zander/Kogut 1995).

The challenge of knowledge articulation is also apparent in the work of Szulanski (1996). Like von Hippel (1994), he refers to the 'stickiness' of knowledge as the factor impeding the transfer of best practices within the same firm. Sticky knowledge is causally ambiguous and unproven. Causal ambiguity captures the extent to which the precise reasons for success or failure in replicating a capability in a new setting cannot be determined even *ex post*. In another study of knowledge transfer within a large multinational enterprise, Hansen (1999) shows that the transmission of knowledge that is noncodified and dependent is difficult to communicate across divisions, and its transfer necessitates frequent and close ties between a firm's divisions.

Clearly, the limitations imposed by the complex, dependent, and tacit character of knowledge can be offset, in part, by modularity. Modules permit the use of "hidden knowledge". Software engineers responsible for one module only need to know the interface with other modules, not their internal code. Some competencies can be joined with modular design as long as each task results in a module that can be assembled independent of knowing the competence of each team. Also, in the process of designing a modular product, some of the tacit knowledge about components and their interfaces becomes explicit. However, some tasks cannot be modularized; or, if a certain degree of modularization can be achieved, the task still requires large overlaps between various knowledge bases. In such cases, rich and intense communication is needed for the sharing of both tacit and explicit competencies. In the words of Frederick Brooks, "since software construction is inherently a systems effort – an exercise in complex interrelationships – communication effort is great, and it quickly dominates the decrease in individual task time brought about by partitioning" (1975, p. 19).

However, the emphasis on the sharing and transfer of knowledge obscures an important aspect of work design: transfer occurs subsequent to, or concomitant with, innovation and creativity. A main dimension that emerged in our study is creativity. Radical creativity can be defined as revolutionary changes that depart from existing practices and solutions (Dewar/Dutton 1986). Traditionally however, creativity was conceptualized as more adaptive adjustments to established practices. For example, Perrow (1967, 1970) introduced the concept of routineness – defined as a function of the extent to which the task contains variety and is analyzable – in order to arrive at a definition of creativity. In this view, creative tasks involve either tasks that cannot be broken down into small and well-defined components, or those that require variation in the needed knowledge bases.

This concept of creative tasks is also supported by psychologists, who argue that "novelty can arise from either or both of two sources: novelty of the component mental operations, and novelty of the content of the problems" (Gardner/Sternberg 1994, p. 40).

We would like to stress this alternative conception of innovation that emphasizes the importance of interactivity in the generation of new knowledge. As we discussed above, the emergence of knowledge in communities of practice is one of the reasons for the tacitness of the produced knowledge. Similarly, the work of von Hippel (1988) stresses the role of interactivity between firms and their users. His work shows how, contrary to common-sense views, many new innovative ideas come from the end users.

Communication Media

The difficulty of transmitting some kinds of knowledge required for software production over digital media is an important element to our understanding of why there are lasting differences between the tasks performed in different regions. There is a vast literature, not entirely consistent, regarding the relationship of media and communication across distance. Table 1 reviews the vast literature on the sophistication of new communication media such as the computer and the video, and their effects on perceived complexity, dependence, and even tacitness. As a result of this range of work, it is not practical to review all of these many studies. We consequently highlight a few that are particularly relevant to our findings.

A frequent claim is the argument that ambiguity and non-routineness (or innovativeness) bias communication toward face-to-face or voice media. Daft and Lengel, among others, argue that particularly in the case of ambiguous tasks,

Table 1. A Review of Empirical Research on the Effects of Communication Media

Issue	Studies	Face-to-Face Communication (FTF)	Computer-Mediated-Communication (CMC)
WORK TASKS			
Decision making			
Time to reach decision	Dubrovsky et al. (1991), Siegel et al. (1986)		four to ten times longer to reach a decision than FTF groups
	Arunachalam and Dilla (1992), Daly (1993), George et al. (1990)		longer time than FTF
	Reid et al. (1997)		much longer than FTF
Types of decisions	McGuire et al. (1986), Siegel et al. (1986), Weisband (1992)		riskier decisions, and more choice shift
Quality of decisions	Hiltz et al. (1986), Hollingshead (1996 a)	no difference	no difference
	Hedlund et al. (1998)	much better decision accuracy	
Satisfaction with decision	Reid et al. (1997)	better	
	Gallupe et al. (1988)	more satisfaction with the decision process	
	Gallupe et al. (1988)	more confidence in their decisions	
	Gallupe and McKeen (1990)		significantly less satisfied with decision process than FTF groups
Idea-generation			
number of unique ideas	Straus and McGrath (1994)	higher number of unique ideas than CMC	worse
	Daly (1993)	same number of correct solutions	same
	Gallupe et al. (1992)		more nonredundant ideas than FTF groups in 4- and 6-member groups, but not in the 2-member groups
	Gallupe et al. 1988 (task was crisis management)		more alternatives were generated than in FTF
	George et al. (1990) (task is idea generation/ intellective)	same number of unique alternatives	

Table 1. A Review of Empirical Research on the Effects of Communication Media (continued)

Issue	Studies	Face-to-Face Communication (FTF)	Computer-Mediated- Communication (CMC)
Quality of ideas	Straus and McGrath (1994)	same	same
	Gallupe et al. (1992)		better ideas than FTF groups in 4- and 6-member groups, but not in the 2-member groups
	Gallupe et al. (1988)		better quality decisions were generated than in FTF
	George et al. (1990)	same quality of decisions	
Judgement task: achieve goal consensus	Straus and McGrath (1994), Reid et al. (1997)	better	worse
	McLeod and Liker (1992)	better on the decision-making task, which required a response to in-basket correspondence	
Intellective task (pick correct solution)	Straus and McGrath (1994)	same	same
	Hollingshead (1996b)	better on intellective task (when given instructions to rank-order decision alternatives)	
	McLeod and Liker (1992)		better than FTF groups; the task also required consensus in terms of the proper sequence of activities
Number of errors	Daly, B. (1993), task is intellective	lower number of errors	higher
Creativity	Cummings et al. (1995), task was essay generation	At the beginning, FTF-generated essays were more complex	Over time, essays generated via CMC were more complex
Negotiation			
	Hollingshead et al. (1993)	better on negotiation and intellective tasks than CMC groups	
Transfer-pricing negotiation	Arunachalam and Dilla (1992)	higher performance	lower outcomes, and distributed resources more unequally, and deviated from the integrative agreement, and maintained more inaccurate perceptions of the interaction

Table 1. A Review of Empirical Research on the Effects of Communication Media (continued)

Issue	Studies	Face-to-Face Communication (FTF)	Computer-Mediated-Communication (CMC)
INTERACTION PROCESS			
Volume and frequency of communication	Hiltz et al. (1986)	more	less
	McGuire et al. (1987) (task is investment decision)	more	less
	Siegel et al. (1986)	more	less
Content of communication	Hiltz et al. (1986)		larger % of task-oriented messages
	McLeod and Liker (1992)	longer responses; greater awareness of underlying problems	more task-oriented behavior
	Weisband (1992)		more task-irrelevant remarks
	Dubrovsky et al. (1991), Weisband (1992)		more diverse opinions or decision recommendations
	Smith and Vanecek (1990) (complex intellective task; participants were volunteers from professional organizations and several corporations)	FTF groups shared more of the important info needed for finding the correct solution, derived more correct reasons for eliminating wrong alternatives, and perceived more progress than CMC groups	
	Hollingshead (1996a)		information more readily accessible
	Weisband (1992)		more implicit preferences and explicit proposals; more social pressure remarks
Discussion Style	Reid et al. (1997)	more factual	more normative
	Dubrovsky et al. (1991) Siegel et al. (1986) Weisband (1992)		less inhibition, more personal expression (including profanity and insults)
	Sproull and Kiesler (1986)		more uninhibited and nonconforming behavior through electronic mail

Table 1. A Review of Empirical Research on the Effects of Communication Media (continued)

Issue	Studies	Face-to-Face Communication (FTF)	Computer-Mediated-Communication (CMC)
	Straus (1991)		same degree of negative interpersonal communication as FTF; higher proportion of positive interpersonal communication than FTF
	Arunachalam and Dilla (1992)		more competitive flaming behavior; more tendency to reach coalitional agreements
	Kiesler et al. (1985) (task is dyads getting to know each other)		subjects evaluated each other less positively and were more uninhibited in their comments
Social effects			
Equalization of participation	McGuire et al. (1987), Siegel et al. (1986), Weisband (1992), Daly (1993), George et al. (1990)		equalization of team members' participation (because of anonymity)
	Hollingshead (1996a)		information suppression effect, which really accounts for the equalization of participation
	McLeod and Liker (1992) (tasks are intellective ranking and decision-making)	no difference	no difference
Status differences	Dubrovsky et al. (1991)		high status members less likely to dominate the discussion
	Hiltz et al. (1986)	dominant member more likely to emerge	
	Weisband et al. (1995)	high status members participated more and had greater influence than low status members	high status members participated more and had greater influence than low status members
	Spears and Lea (1994)		the technology may be used by high status individuals to exert greater power and influence over low status individuals

Table 1. A Review of Empirical Research on the Effects of Communication Media (continued)

Issue	Studies	Face-to-Face Communication (FTF)	Computer-Mediated-Communication (CMC)
Group development			
degree of cohesiveness	Chidambaram et al. (1991) (task is decision making w/o 'correct' answers)	manual (i.e., paper-and-pencil) groups did better initially (first 2 weeks)	CMC groups became more cohesive in the 3rd and 4th sessions
conflict management within the group	Chidambaram et al. (1991)	manual (= paper-and-pencil) groups did better initially (first 2 weeks)	CMC groups managed conflict better in the 3rd and 4th weeks
	Gallupe et al. (1988)	less conflict in group discussions than CMC groups	
Affect			
Anxiety level	Daly (1993)		higher (reported) level of anxiety and nervousness during experiment
	Gallupe et al. (1992)		less evaluation apprehension than FTF groups

communication requirements are much higher than for routine tasks (Daft/Lengel 1986). Also, Galbraith (1977) shows that task routineness influences the groups' communication structure because it determines the information processing requirements of the group.

The social psychology literature has addressed some of the issues related to the types of tasks for which co-location and face-to-face interactions are important. This literature holds that face-to-face communication is needed for substantial consensus decisions, and when the equivocality of the task is high. McKenney, Zack, and Doherty's (1992) study of the communication patterns in a programming team concludes that electronic mail and face-to-face are complementary media: while email provides efficiency in well-defined contexts, face-to-face has the ability to build a shared understanding and definition of the task. Coordination at a distance is costly if not impossible because the medium of communication (mainly the computer) misses a whole host of non-verbal cues that influence message reception and understanding. In the same vein, Nohria and Eccles (1992) argue that face-to-face communication has three main advantages over electronic communication: the existence of a shared context among participants, its richness which encompasses the full bandwidth of physical senses and psychoemotional reactions, and its capacity for interruption, repair, feedback and learning.

More detailed studies of the limitations of computer-mediated communication have been discussed by authors such as McGrath and Hollingshead (1994). They observe that this medium often alters communication times, as well as the sequence and synchrony of messages. At the same time, it increases ambiguity because the sender cannot be confident that failure of any given member to reply to a given message in a timely fashion reflects that member's deliberate choice (1994, p. 21). Groups using computer-mediated communication try to supplement the lack of nonverbal cues by using "emoticons" as well as a) longer and more complex syntax; b) jargon, argot, and other shared nonstandard language that relies on culturally shared connotative meanings; c) punctuation and format conventions; and d) redundancy (McGrath and Hollingshead 1994, p. 19). However, all these supplements can only provide a low-quality substitute for what humans routinely do with nonverbal cues.

Our project paid attention to several mechanisms used to coordinate effort in distributed teams. Our interviews sought out managers who specifically fulfill the role of liaison between teams situated at large distances and who provide such coordination. We also attended the planned and unplanned meetings that bring together people in routine or exceptional circumstances (Metiu 2001). We believe that tracing the reasons for face-to-face meetings over the course of the projects will further shed light on the relationship between certain types of tasks and the need for physical proximity.

Shared Context

The rise of new technologies such as the video and especially computer-mediated communication has led to a vast literature that has examined the virtues of various communication media on work performance. As seen from Table 1, this literature is rife with interesting yet contradictory findings. For example, some studies find that face-to-face communication generates a higher number of unique ideas; however, other studies find that computer-mediated communication generates more nonredundant ideas; yet other studies find no difference between the two types of communication media in terms of the number and quality of ideas generated. We believe that the lack of robustness of these results is due to the spuriousness caused by the lack of attention to contextual factors. As most of this research has been primarily experimental, it has neglected the degree of impact that a shared context has on people's interactions.

Some tasks require close interactions with customers, and this is a common explanation given by many of the Indian firms to explain why they are less innovative. Our study recognizes the importance of close interaction with the customer when the requirements are unclear, or are changing during the course of the project. However, it is also important that the information to be gleaned from customers cannot be easily parametized. When the software developers are unfamiliar with the functionality of the end product of their work, the communication of the product's features may be difficult.

The impact of a shared context is particularly important in the case of creative and highly tacit tasks. Work in the area of creativity has always been confronted by the difficulty that creativity is difficult to organize as a task and thus cannot be easily parametized along the dimensions of complexity and non-modularity.

Creativity, therefore, is linked to a host of "unobservables" such as creativity climate or labor supply characteristics. Saxenian's (1996) study of the Silicon Valley is a good example of an attempt to identify the factors that have led to the region's continued inventiveness. Apart from the role played by venture capital firms and major universities in the Bay Area, the region's rich creativity is largely tied to a certain culture of free communication among engineers, to a sustained desire and effort to invent something new. Saxenian's work, as well as Almeida and Kogut's (1999) study of the networks of relationships linking engineers in the semiconductor industry, highlight the role of spatial proximity in sustaining an intense atmosphere of creativity.

Also, tasks with a high tacit component may require physical co-location. As competences are often non-articulable, they can only be transmitted through common participation in an activity. Lave and Wenger (1991) show that learning some crafts requires not simply a transmission of abstract concepts, but also effective co-participation in an activity. Such concrete actions, performed together, give access to and refine a wealth of nonverbal communication cues that can enhance understanding and speed execution. More importantly, the knowledge being created in face to face interactions entails often the assessment of others' degree of involvement in the common activity. It is this part of the knowledge produced during face to face interactions that is largely non-articulable.

We hypothesize that tasks that are non-modular, complex, creative, tacit, and require a shared context with the customer, as well as a high degree of coordination and customer interaction, will be co-located, and will not be located overseas in spite of the cost advantages of such locations.

Methodology

We explored the issues delineated above via a questionnaire. The research design and survey instrument were created after we conducted extensive interviews with executives and engineers in US, Indian and Irish firms.

The main analyses in this study employ the project as their unit of analysis. For example, creative and non-modular tasks are hypothesized to be co-located. In contradistinction, creative and modular projects could be dispersed. However, we allow for the possibility that various stages in the development process may differ according to dimensions such as creativity or tacitness, and that such differences may account for the division of labor among countries in terms of software development. Consequently, our design will permit us to check whether the fault lines between onshore and offshore work lie along the project development stages (requirements, design, coding). This approach is warranted on the basis of our interviews, some of which indicated that stages of project development are best done in a co-located mode.

We will compare projects done in a collocated fashion (in onshore locations) with dispersed projects. Because our study is exploratory and affected by selection bias as discussed above, the statistical results need to be interpreted with caution. Generalizing the results to the location decisions of small, or new firms should be done with care, because we have chosen projects done by large, established US firms. When the subjects are highly heterogeneous, the results for any subgroup are likely to be imprecise because of unobserved variation. This imprecision may lead to a lack of confidence in the validity of the results; in turn, such imprecision precludes generalization. In other words, we factored out potential contamination of the statistical results by selective design.

Apart from location, the other dependent variable of interest is project performance. Our sampling technique reflects that many projects are for internal use rather than for external customers. We assess the performance of software projects by using several measures such as quality, time to completion, cost, and creativity. Hence we are able to avoid the selection bias problem generated by the use of commercial success as the sole performance measure. The managers and engineers to whom we talked explained the variety of motives for which firms decide to do offshore development. One of the main reasons is to achieve 24-hour development, especially critical for products in very competitive markets.

The questionnaire also provided part of the raw data for the study of coordination mechanisms between distantly located teams. Our interviews have revealed that many unplanned meetings occur at critical junctures in the projects, and often it is deemed that only a face-to-face encounter (often lasting several days) can solve the problem satisfactorily.

Data

We have obtained a sample of 40 projects from several firms. Ten of these projects were collocated (i.e., they were accomplished in only one location) and 30 were accomplished across at least two different sites or locations. Out of the collocated projects, 7 were done in India and 3 in Singapore. The 30 dispersed

Table 2. Project Characteristics

	Collocated	Dispersed	Total
Total projects:	10	30	40
– out of which ongoing	5	21	26
Average project length (in months)	10	22	19
Internal projects	4	5	9
External client projects	10	21	31

projects were done over locations in the US, India, Singapore, China, Japan, Finland, Switzerland, and the UK. Out of the 30 dispersed projects, only 2 were done in more than 2 locations. Table 2 provides a description of our sample along several dimensions of interest.

The length of the projects ranged widely, from 1 month to 60 months. However, the respondents were competent to evaluate the projects given that the average project, at the time of the survey administration, had been operating for 10 months in the case of collocaded, and 22 months in the case of dispersed projects. Both collocated and dispersed projects involve system software, middleware, and application customisations.

The respondents were project managers, out of which 80% had a background in engineering, 5% in management, and 11% some other background. When asked to choose their current professional identity, 23% said engineering, and 77% responded they identified with management. This pattern of response reflects the typical career path in software engineering where after several years in technical positions, people take on management responsibilities.

Results

Several results merit attention. First, the striking result of our study is that once a firm decides to use a remote location, the properties of the projects, whether collocated or dispersed, are about the same. A comparison of the collocated and dispersed projects reveals that they do not differ significantly along the dimensions of coordination, modularity, and tacitness.

Creative Work

Given our findings about the many dimensions on which collocated and dispersed projects are done, the question becomes: what does differentiate the two types of projects? The interesting dimension of differentiation turns out to be creativity. In the software industry, creativity remains hard to source from far away. Projects that are supposed to find innovative solutions tend to be accomplished in a dispersed rather than in a collocated fashion (t-test significant at the 0.05 level)[3].

Further analyses advance an explanation for the findings, an explanation related to the need for proximity to customers. Our survey asked respondents to list which activities (collecting user requirements, architecture, coding etc.) were done at each location. An examination of the activities performed in various locations for the dispersed projects reveals a telling picture.

Of the 30 dispersed projects, all but one did the user requirements phase in locations other than India or Singapore. Also, only on 15 projects was the software requirements phase done in India or Singapore (or China). On 22 projects the architecture phase was done in India or Singapore or China. On 25 projects the coding was done in India or Singapore or China. The transfer and maintenance phase of 17 involved India or Singapore or China; naturally, this phase also involved the developed world locations in the case of 21 projects. Figure 2 portrays the trend above by displaying the proportion of the dispersed projects' activities done in offshore locations (India, Singapore, China).

Figure 2 illustrates quite powerfully the main findings of our study. The first is that creativity is an important challenge in distributed work. The need to create products for sophisticated customers located in developed countries does not pose technical problems to remote developers; clearly, they can often (50% of the time in our sample) translate the user requirements into software requirements, and even do the architectural design of products in over 70% of cases in our setting. However, what is hard to outsource at a distance is the knowledge of customer needs, particularly when those needs are not familiar to workers in the developing world. Of course, one of the implications of our findings is that if it weren't for this constraint, much more work will get sent to offshore locations.

Figure 2. Proportion of the Share of Work Done Offshore for Each Stage of a Software Development Project

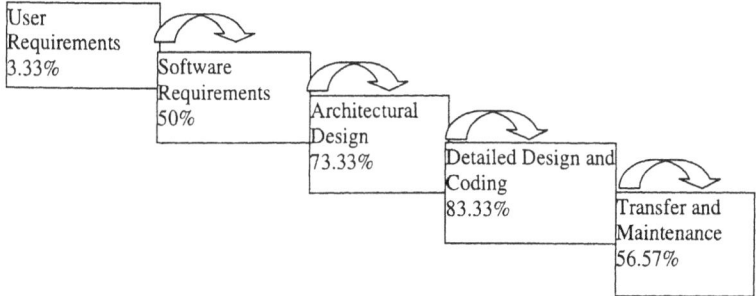

The lack of familiarity of workers in offshore sites with the requirements of most sophisticated clients is a challenge to offshore sites and managers. To the question 'this product was a common item in the project members' lives', the answers from dispered projects were much lower then those from collocated projects (t-test significant at the 0.05 level).

Even more surprisingly, and related to the above, our respondents rated dispersed projects higher on the dimension of importance of the product to the firm's future stream of products (t-test significant at the 0.05 level). The progress made by offshore sites in securing work on strategically important projects has been quick and explains the rapid growth of offshore activities in several countries. The finding that dispersed projects involved software that was considered to be important to the firm's future stream of products documents the increasing competency of offshore sites in providing high-quality services to their clients. It also therefore explains the sustained growth of offshore centers such as Bangalore.

Process Management

To the practicing manager, the challenges posed by tacit knowledge are addressed by process tools. We asked first did problems occur. Secondly, we asked how such problems were resolved.

In examining the way collocated and dispersed projects are managed, we found no significant differences in the two types of projects in terms of the frequency or the type of problems encountered. 80% of the collocated and 87% of the dispersed projects report having encountered technical problems. Also, 20% of the collocated and 40% of the dispersed projects report having encountered people-related problems. While the dispersed projects seem to experience higher proportions of people-related problems, these differences are not significant.

For the resolution of these problems, the dispersed projects relied more on the activities of a heavyweight manager (t-test significant at the 0.05 level). The results illustrate the importance of a manager who, in dispersed projects, conveys information across sites and solves problems as they come along. Heavyweight managers have been found to be crucial to innovative capabilities, such as in automobiles (Clark/Fujimoto 1991) and pharmaceuticals (Cockburn/Henderson 1998). This finding shows that dispersed projects may be similar in most regards to onshore projects because of the organizational capability of the contracting firm to manage such projects through heavyweight managers.

Communication

Our data does not reveal a difference in the amount of face-to-face interactions in the two types of teams. In fact, the two types of teams seem to use face-to-face and email communications in similar proportions. The difference comes with teleconferencing and videoconferencing, of which distributed teams make more use (but the differences only approach significance). Our findings enable us to suggest that the emphasis on face-to-face interactivity may have been over-rated.

The bias towards a priori over-rating the importance of face-to-face communication arises out of the tendency to take collocated settings, and the face-to-face type of interactivity that is specific to these settings, as the norm. Indeed, managers of collocated projects rate the importance of face-to-face interactions for project success more highly than managers of dispersed projects (means of 5.67 vs. 5.27). Clearly, both categories of managers rate quite highly the importance of face-to-face interactions. However, managers with experience in dispersed environments have learned efficient ways of getting around the constraint of face-to-face communication.

Factor Analyses

In an exploratory study, it is of interest to look for patterns in the data that are not expected *a priori*. A common technique for such exploration is factor analysis. Since our sample is not large, we report simply the loadings with the caution that these results are suggestive.

Table 3. Factor Analyses

	Formalization	Iterativeness	Novelty
Ease of monitoring	**0.49914***	−0.43210	−0.30398
Requirements were clear	**0.40612**	−0.45481	0.39184
Cultural differences not a problem	**0.54121**	0.31483	−0.65689
Location not affected by culture	**0.58168**	0.45715	0.45343
Easy to monitor progress	**0.75379**	0.38343	−0.20316
Modularity	**0.50548**	0.36003	0.07591
Easy to work independently	**0.73823**	−0.09056	0.24679
Degree of documentation	**0.72506**	0.17305	0.07861
Newcomers learn quickly	**0.52130**	−0.11115	0.40160
GAP analysis easy	0.33658	−0.14831	0.17162
Technical solutions were innovative	0.29939	0.13343	−0.13016
Iterativeness	0.04322	**0.41304**	0.09652
User interfaces	0.24591	**0.40468**	−0.23592
Product was familiar to workers	0.11211	**0.64284**	−0.13104
Work was codified	0.04016	**0.35713**	0.15818
Change affects other projects	0.21749	0.47699	**0.58908**
Product solved a novel problem	−0.20469	0.39287	**0.51133**
Reused components	0.06565	0.05815	**0.68880**
Contact of personnel was important	−0.11079	0.34148	**0.39583**
Documentation was an important output	−0.16230	0.12759	0.34972
Process synchronization was important	0.04361	−0.25668	0.28870

* factors >0.35 are highlighted.

The questionnaire was designed to look at project characteristics along the dimensions of tacitness and modularity, communication, and shared context,. These items were analyzed using principal components and varimax rotation. A three-factor structure was revealed, as seen in Table 3.

The first group of variables loads on project characteristics related to modularity, work independence, clarity of requirements, ease of monitoring progress and of bringing newcomers up to speed, amount of documentation. We call this underlying factor 'project formalization' as a measure of the routinization of knowledge. A second group of factors pertains to need for process synchronization, the amount of contact among personnel, the need to solve a new problem, the amount of changes in requirements, the familiarity of personnel with the product. A third group has to do with the familiarity with the product, with the need to design user interfaces, with the fact that the work was not coded in manuals, and with the iterativeness of the project (as opposed to waterfall). This group of factors has to do basically with the creativity that needs proximity to the customer.

Discussion

This exploratory study shows that creativity is the main obstacle to the dispersion of mental work across space. While outsourcing of software activities grows at a fast pace, the closeness to customers who provide ideas and inputs for innovativeness remains important. This result is consistent with a body of literature that has emphasized the interactive nature of innovation.

It is also consistent with the results of our interviews, in which offshore managers repeatedly mentioned the acquisition of domain knowledge as their most significant challenge. Software development managers distinguish between two types of knowledge needed for project accomplishment. Technical knowledge involves expertise with hardware and software, mastery of programming languages, and understanding the documentation. The managers interviewed did not see technical knowledge as posing problems for the accomplishment of work in offshore sites. Domain knowledge however, is a challenge. It involves understanding the product, the requirements, and learning the application domain (for ex., healthcare systems, or telecommunications). These types of knowledge were seen as major hurdles for offshore sites. As the manager of an Indian subsidiary of a US firm said "My main challenge is understanding how the product impacts the customer. Knowing the big picture, how my work is impacting the product is key.":

In other words, the obstacle to distributed work was not the tacitness of technical knowledge. Engineers felt this type of information was amenable to communication over distance. Rather, the primary obstacle was the communication of the larger picture, how a piece of programming is important to the project and, ultimately, to the client.

Interestingly, we found similarities in terms of the process of coordination in the two types of projects. Both encountered comparable levels of technical and people-related problems. Respondents reported non-significant differences for the importance of face-to-face interactions. This result is surprising, as the general consensus among managers and management scholars has been that collocated groups are efficient at coordination because they can talk out problems together, keep all the details of the task in focus, and organize work (Nohria/Eccles 1992, Kameda et al. 1992).

We advance two alternative explanations for this result. The first points to the expertise at managing across distance that managers and developers involved in dispersed projects have developed. Furthermore, the companies that provide outsourcing services have developed process management capabilities that carefully store project-related knowledge and, when appropriate, transferred it to new projects. Of course, part of the attention to process is due to the need to reassure customers who may not trust from the beginning the outsourcing team's competence and motivation. The second explanation is that our sample contains only projects that had been deemed appropriate for outsourcing. Since our sample did not contain projects that were done completely in the developed world, we cannot discriminate between these two explanations. Further work that will include a variety of projects (completely outsourced, hybrid, and completely done in the developed world) will be able to address this issue more directly.

While surprising, the finding that managers of dispersed projects have identified and are successfully practicing efficient ways to coordinate activities in the absence of face-to-face communication helps to explain our result of the similarity in project dimensions and coordination. The major challenge for dispersed projects, therefore, is one of closeness to customers who are the source of requirements and of product ideas.

The larger implication of our finding is that the division of labor among various regions is changing. This observation has obvious implications for new software centers outside of India. Initially, the developed world did not only the user requirements stage, but also the software requirements and particularly the architecture stage. As long as that kind of division of labor persisted, engineers in the developed countries did not feel threatened by their counterparts in outsourcing centers. However, as our research has uncovered, that division of labor has been changing rapidly over the past few years. The recent heating of the debates over outsourcing and over H1B visas[4] in the US are an echo of this phenomenon.

Conclusions

The current debate over out-sourcing in the United States and Europe reflects a concern over the loss of skilled jobs to developing countries. It is easy to respond to these criticisms by an implicit appeal to general equilibrium in which increased earnings of workers in poor countries lead to an increase in goods produced by rich countries. Indeed, the striking element of a visit to a Bangalore firm is the presence of state-of-the-art computers and software bought from western countries.

Whatever the general equilibrium argument, the rapid rise of new regions in poor countries producing the infrastructural software supporting information technologies speaks to certain arbitrage gains. As we have noted in the context of open source software (Kogut/Metiu 2001), one of the most wasteful features of the global economy is the failure to incorporate fully 2/3 of the world's brains in the production of new ideas. The expansion of communication infrastructures, and the digitalization of work and product, permits an arbitrage of this potential that has not ever been possible.

Because this arbitrage potential is so large, it is to be expected that growth rates of software production can be remarkably high during this period in the few regions in poor countries able to educate a skilled workforce. This explosion obscures the continued presence of severe obstacles to the distribution of intellectual labour globally. Our study has especially noted the obstacles for software products that require innovative work.

The experience of managing distributed work is still immature, but managerial processes are already surprisingly efficient. However, a key element in the global management of intellectual work is the so-called "heavy-weight manager". It is a page from a science fiction script that even in the most technologically advanced industrial frontiers, human intervention and management remains salient.

Endnotes

1 We would like to thank INSEAD for the funding of this research and Professor Uwe Fischer for the opportunity to contribute to this collection in honor of Professor Klaus Macharzina.
2 India's National Association of Software and Service Companies.
3 All t-tests are one-tailed.
4 H-1B visas are nonimmigrant visa issued by the US government to individuals who seek temporary entry in a specialty occupation as a professional. Many of the visa holders are software developers from countries such as India. For the fiscal year 2004, beginning October 2003, there is a maximum of 65,000 H-1B visas issued.

References

Almeida, P./Kogut, B., Localization of Knowledge and the Mobility of Engineers in Regional Networks, *Management Science*, 45, 7, 1999, pp. 905–917.
Arunachalam, V./Dilla, W., Computer-mediated Communication and Structured Interaction in Transfer Pricing Negotiation, *Journal of Information Systems*, 6, 2, 1992, pp. 149–170.
Babbage, C., *On the Economy of Machinery and Manufactures*, fourth edition, London: C. Knight 1835.
Becker, G. S./Murphy, K. M., The Division of Labor, Coordination Costs, and Knowledge, *Quarterly Journal of Economics*, CVII, 1992, pp. 1137–1160.
Brooks, F. P. Jr., *The Mythical Man-Month*, Reading, MA: Addison-Wesley 1975.
Brown, J. S./Duguid, P., Organizational Learning and Communities-Of-Practice: Toward a Unified View of Working, Learning, and Innovating, *Organization Science* 2, 1, 1991, pp. 40–57.
Chidambaram, L./Bostrom, R. P./Wynne, B. E., The Impact of GDSS on Group Development, *Journal of Management Information Systems*, 7, 3, 1991, pp. 3–25.
Clark, K. B./Fujimoto, T., *Product Development Performance: Strategy, Organization, and Management in the World Auto Industry*, Boston, MA: Harvard Business School Press 1991.
Cockburn, I. M/Henderson, R. M., Absorptive Capacity, Coauthoring Behavior, and the Organization of Research in Drug Discovery, *Journal of Industrial Economics*, 46, 2, 1998, pp. 157–182.
Cummings, A./Schlosser, A./Arrow, H., Developing Complex Group Products: Idea Combination in Computer-Mediated and Face-to-Face Groups, *Computer Supported Cooperative Work*, 4, 1995, pp. 229–251.
Cusumano, M. A., *Japan's Software Factories*, New York: Oxford University Press 1991.
Cusumano, M. A./Kemerer, C. F. A., Quantitative Analysis of US and Japanese Practice and Performance in Software Development, *Management Science* 36, 11, 1990, pp. 1384–1406.
Daft, R./Lengel, R., Organizational Information Requirements, Media Richness and Structural Design, *Management Science*, 32, 1986, pp. 554–571.
Daly, B., The influence of Face-to-Face Versus Computer-mediated Communication Channels on Collective Induction, *Accounting, Management & Information Technology*, 3, 1, 1993, pp. 1–22.
Dewar, R. D./Dutton, J. E., The Adoption of Radical and Incremental Innovations: An Empirical Analysis, *Management Science*, 32, 1986, pp. 1422–1433.
Dubrovsky, V./Kiesler, S./Sethna, B., The Equalization Phenomenon: Status Effects in Computer- and Face-to-Face Decision-making Groups, *Human-Computer Interaction*, 6, 1991, pp. 119–146.
Galbraith, J., *Organizational Design*, Menlo Park, CA: Addison-Wesley 1977.
Gallupe, R. B./DeSanctis, G./Dickson, G., Computer-based Support for Group Problem Solving: An Experimental Investigation, *MIS Quarterly*, 12, 1988, pp. 277–296.
Gallupe, R. B./McKeen, J., Enhancing Computer-mediated Communication: An Experimental Study into the Use of a Decision Support System for Face-to-Face versus Remote Meetings, *Information and Management*, 18, 1990, pp. 1–13.
Gallupe, R. B./Denis, A. R./Cooper, W. H./Valacich, J. S./Bastianutti, L. M./Nunamaker, J. F., Electronic Brainstorming and Group Size, *Academy of Management Journal*, 35, 1992, pp. 350–369.
Gardner, M. K./Sternberg, R. J., Novelty and Intelligence, in Sternberg, R. J./Wagner, R. K. (eds.), *Mind in Context: Interactionist Perspectives on Human Intelligence*, New York: Cambridge University Press 1994, pp. 38–73.
George, J./Easton, G./Nunamaker, J./Northcraft, G., A Study of Collaborative Group Work with and without Computer-based Support, *Information Systems Research*, 1, 4, 1990, pp. 394–415.
Hansen, M., The Search-Transfer Problem: The Role of Weak Ties in Sharing Knowledge Across Organization Subunits, *Administrative Science Quarterly*, 44, 1999, pp. 82–111.
Hedlund, J./Ilgen, D. R./Hollenbeck, J. R., The Effect of Computer-mediated versus Face-to-Face Communication on Decision Making in Hierarchical Teams, *Organizational Behavior and Human Decision Processes*, 76, 1998, pp. 30–47.
Hiltz, S. R./Johnson, K./Turoff, M., Experiments in Group Decision Making: Communication Process and Outcome in Face-to-Face versus Computerized Conferences, *Human Communication Research*, 13, 1986, pp. 225–252.

Hollingshead, A. B., Information Suppression and Status Persistence in Group Decision Making: The Effects of Communication Media, *Human Communication Research*, 23, 1996a, pp. 193–219.
Hollingshead, A. B., The Rank-order Effect in Group Decision Making, *Organizational Behavior and Human Decision Processes*, 68, 1996b, pp. 181–193.
Hollingshead, A./McGrath, J. E./O'Connor, K. M., Group Performance and Communication Technology: A Longitudinal Study of Computer-Mediated versus Face-to-Face Work Groups, *Small Group Research*, 24, 3, 1993, pp. 307–333.
Kameda, T. M./Stasson, F./Davis, J. H./Parks, C. D./Zimmerman, S. K., Social Dilemmas, Subgroups, and Motivation Loss in Task-oriented Groups: In Search of an "Optimal" Team Size in Division of Work, *Social Psychology Quarterly*, 55, 1992, pp. 47–56.
Kiesler, S./Zubrow, D./Moses, A. M./Geller, V., Affect in Computer-mediated Communication: An Experiment in Synchronous Terminal-to-Terminal Discussion, *Human Computer Interaction*, 1, 1985, pp. 77–104.
Kogut, B./Metiu, A., Open Source Software Development and Distributed Innovation, *Oxford Review of Economic Policy*, 17, 2, 2001, pp. 248–264.
Kogut, B./Zander, U., 1992, Knowledge of the Firm, Combinative Capabilities, and the Replication of Technology, *Organization Science*, 3, 1992, pp. 383–397.
Kogut, B./Zander, U., Knowledge of the Firm and the Evolutionary Theory of the Multinational Enterprise, *Journal of International Business Studies*, 24, 1993, pp. 625–645; reprinted in Egelhoff, W. G. (ed.) *Transforming International Organizations*, Northampton, MA: Edward Elgar Publishing, 1997.
Kraut, R. E./Streeter, L. A., Coordination in Software Development, *Communications of the ACM*, 38, 1995, pp. 69–81.
Lacity, M.C./Willcocks, L. P./Feeny, D. F., The Value of Selective IT Sourcing, *Sloan Management Review*, Spring 1996, pp. 13–25.
Lave, J./Wenger, E., *Situated Learning*, Cambridge: Cambridge University Press 1991.
McGrath, J. E./Hollingshead, A. B., *Groups Interacting with Technology*, Thousand Oaks: Sage Publications, 1994.
McGuire, T. W./Kiesler, S./Siegel, J., Group and Computer-mediated Discussion Effects in Risk Decision Making, *Journal of Personality & Social Psychology*, 52, 1987, pp. 917–930.
McKenney, J. L./Zack, M. H./Doherty, V. S., Complementary Communication Media: A Comparison of Electronic Mail and Face-To-Face Communication in a Programming Team, in Nohria N./Eccles, R. G. (eds.), *Networks and Organizations*, Boston, MA: Harvard Business School Press 1992, pp. 262–287.
McLeod, P. L./Liker, J. K., Electronic Meeting Systems: Evidence from a Low Structure Environment, *Information Systems Research*, 3, 1992, pp. 195–223.
Metiu, A., Faraway, So Close: Code Ownership over Innovative Work in the Global Software Industry, Unpublished dissertation, The Wharton School 2001.
Nelson, P./Richmond, W./Seidmann, A., Two Dimensions of Software Acquisition, *Communications of the ACM*, 39, 1996, pp. 29–35.
Nohria, N./Eccles, R. G., Face-to-Face: Making Network Organizations Work, in Nohria N./Eccles, R. G. (eds.), *Networks and Organizations*, Boston, MA: Harvard Business School Press 1992.
Perrow, C., A Framework for the Comparative Analysis of Organizations, *American Sociology Review*, 32, 1967, pp. 194–208.
Perrow, C., *Organizational Analysis: A Sociological View*, Belmont, CA: Wadsworth, 1970.
Reid F. J. M./Ball, L. J./Morley, A. M./Evans, J. S. T., Styles of Group Discussion in Computer-mediated Decision Making, *British Journal of Social Psychology*, 36, 1997, pp. 241–262.
Richmond, W. B./Seidmann, A./Whinston, A. B., Incomplete Contracting Issues in Information Systems Development Outsourcing, *Decision Support System*, 8, 4, 1992, pp. 459–477.
Rogers, E., *Diffusion of Innovations*, New York: Free Press 1980.
Saxenian, A., *Regional Advantage: Culture and Competition in Silicon Valley and Route 128*, Cambridge: Harvard University Press, 1996.
Siegel, J./Dubrovsky, V./Kiesler, S./McGuire, T., Group process in computer-mediated communication, *Organizational Behavior & Human Decision Processes*, 37, 1986, pp. 157–187.
Smith, J./Vanecek, M., Dispersed Group Decision Making Using Nonsimultaneous Computer Conferencing: A Report of Research, *Journal of Management Science*, 7, 2, 1990, pp. 71–92.

Spears, R./Lea, M., Panacea or Panopticon: The Hidden Power in Computer-Mediated Communication, *Communication Research*, 21, 1994, pp. 427–459.
Sproull, L./Kiesler, S., Reducing Social Context Cues: Electronic Mail in Organizational Communication, *Management Science*, 32, 1986, pp. 1492–1512.
Straus, S. G./McGrath, J. E., Does the Medium Matter? The Interaction of Task Type and Technology on Group Performance and Member Reactions, *Journal of Applied Psychology*, 79, 1994, pp. 87–97.
Straus, S., *Does the Medium Matter: An Investigation of Process, Performance and Affect in Computer-mediated and Face-to-Face Groups*, Unpublished doctoral dissertation, University of Illinois, Urbana-Champaign 1991.
Szulanski, G., Exploring Internal Stickiness: Impediments to the Transfer of Best Practice within the Firm, *Strategic Management Journal*, 17, 1996, pp. 27–43.
Ure, A., *The Philosophy of Manufactures*, London: C. Knight 1835.
Von Hippel, E., *The Sources of Innovation*, NY, NY: Oxford University Press 1988.
Von Hippel, E., 'Sticky Information' and the Locus of Problem Solving: Implications for Innovation, *Management Science*, 40, 1994, pp. 429–439.
Wang, E./Barron, T./Seidmann, A., Contracting Structures for Custom Software Development: The Impacts of Informational Rents and Uncertainty on Internal Development and Outsourcing, *Management Science*, 43, 1997, pp. 1726–1744.
Weisband, S. P., Group Discussion and First Advocacy Effects in Computer-mediated and Face-to-Face Decision Making Groups, *Organizational Behavior & Human Decision Processes*, 53, 1992, pp. 157–188.
Weisband, S. P./Schneider, S. K./Connolly, T., Computer-mediated Communication and Social Information: Status Salience and Status Differences, *Academy of Management Journal*, 38, 1995, pp. 1124–1151.
Whang, S., Contracting for Software Development, *Management Science*. 38, 3, 1992, pp. 307–324.
Winter, S., Knowledge and Competence as Strategic Assets, in Teece, D. (ed.), *The Competitive Challenge-Strategies for Industrial Innovation and Renewal*, Cambridge, MA: Ballinger 1987, pp. 159–184.
Zander, U./Kogut, B., Knowledge and the Speed of the Transfer and Imitation of Organizational Capabilities: An Empirical Test, *Organization Science*, 6, 1995, pp. 76–92.

mir *Edition*

GABLER

Andreas Wald

Network Structures and Network Effects in Organizations

A Network Analysis in Multinational Corporations

2003, XVIII, 238 pages, pb., € 49,90 (approx. US $ 49,90)
ISBN 3-409-12395-4

Network structures have been praised as the organizational form of today's multinational corporation. Building on conceptual work on network organizations, a quantitative network analysis of formal and informal organizational structures is performed in this study. It is tested whether network structures can be identified empirically. Moreover, the effects of organizational structures on strategic decision making in two multinational corporations are analyzed. A theoretical framework is provided by an exchange model and by social capital theory.

The book is addressed to scholars of international management and organizational studies.

Betriebswirtschaftlicher Verlag Dr. Th. Gabler GmbH, Abraham-Lincoln-Str. 46, 65189 Wiesbaden

Management
International Review
© Gabler Verlag 2004

John Cantwell/Katherina Glac/Rebecca Harding

The Internationalization of R&D – the Swiss Case

Abstract

- Technological activity is becoming increasingly internationally dispersed and international linkages of technological activity through cross-border knowledge flows are playing an ever more important role in the competitiveness of MNCs and domestic companies.

- This paper analyses the extent and the pattern of specialization of the internationalization of R&D since 1969 by the largest Swiss firms abroad, and by the largest non-Swiss firms in Switzerland, focusing both on changes in indigenous technological capabilities as well as the role of inward and outward foreign direct investment in the process.

- The evidence used is the geographical and sectoral profiles of invention revealed by patents granted in the US to the world's largest firms.

Key Results

- Swiss-owned firms abroad access technologies in the primary fields of their own industry, since they are world class companies but have at home only the science and technology base of a small country.

- However, foreign-owned firms conducting research in Switzerland demonstrate more technological diversification away from their own primary fields and into sources of local Swiss traditional technological strengths.

Authors

John Cantwell, Professor of International Business, Rutgers Business School, Newark, NJ, USA, and Professor of International Economics, University of Reading, UK.
Katherina Glac, Ph.D. Candidate, Rutgers Business School, Newark, NJ, USA.
Dr. Rebecca Harding, Senior Research Fellow in Entrepreneurship, London Business School, London, UK.

John Cantwell/Katherina Glac/Rebecca Harding

Introduction

The thinking on research and development (R&D) activity by large firms, particularly multinational corporations (MNCs) has undergone a significant change since the 1970s. The focus of theorizing and scholarly work in the late 1970s and the 1980s revolved around conceptual integration in the aspiration of moving towards a generalizable theory of international business (IB) itself, as was reflected in the theme of an MIR special issue in 1991 on frontiers in IB research (Macharzina/Englehard 1991). R&D in MNCs did not receive much attention as a distinct and prominent area of inquiry, given that its internationalization was thought of as a special case of technology transfer processes that were on the whole better analyzed by other means, with reference to a broader context. In contrast, since that time, knowledge has been increasingly recognized as the key wealth creating asset, and the attention of the IB field has turned towards the globalization of technology, innovation and know how (Macharzina 2003).

So in the early years of scholarly work on internationalization of R&D, still with the traditional product cycle theory at its center, MNCs were supposed to undertake technological activity mainly in the home country's headquarters and essentially just to adapt home-based technology in host countries as local markets and production conditions required. Many studies have since then contributed to a change in perspective. The focus shifted from internationalization as the creation of networks of international trade and production to globalization as the closer integration of those networks, which includes the closer coordination by MNCs of geographically dispersed R&D and other innovative activities (Cantwell 1995, Cantwell/Janne 1999b, Pearce 1989, Pearce/Singh 1992). It is now widely acknowledged that technological activity is more internationally dispersed and that these international linkages of technological activity through cross-border knowledge flows are playing an ever more important role in the competitiveness of the MNC and domestic companies (Bartlet/Ghoshal 1989, Cantwell/Piscitello 2000).

Two reasons have been emphasized as to why MNCs should take an internationally integrated approach to technological development (Cantwell 1992, 1995, Dunning 1993, Howells/Michie 1997). First, technological activity in any industry is locationally differentiated in accordance with the varied participation of MNCs in different national systems of innovation, whose patterns of technological competence are fairly stable, even over long periods of time, with changes only occurring gradually (Cantwell 2001, Freeman 1995, Lundvall 1988, Mariotti/Piscitello 2001, Patel/Pavitt 1991, Vertova 1999). Furthermore research on clustering indicates that significant economies of agglomeration exist in the geographical location of innovation (Audretsch/Feldman 1996, Baptista/Swann 1998, Cantwell 1991, Dosi 1988, Feldman 1993). Since knowledge diffusion remains geographically bounded, involving distinct characteristics of innovation in each country, MNCs can acquire an important source of competitive advantage by geographically dispersing research facilities to gain access to differentiated but complementary streams of new knowledge creation, and integrating them at a corporate level (Cantwell 1989, Kogut/Chang 1991).

Secondly, and closely connected with the first reason, the geographical dispersion of research to gain access to new lines of innovation may be related to a new impetus towards corporate technological diversification (Cantwell/Piscitello 2000). With the emergence of a new techno-economic paradigm, in which knowledge is becoming the key wealth-creating asset, the range of technologies that firms need to combine in their innovation and production processes has become wider, resulting in what have now been termed multi-technology products and companies (Torrisi/Granstrand 2004). This increased technological complexity and interrelatedness (Cantwell/Barrera 1998) compels firms to broaden their technological activity in part through an international strategy as a means of supporting technological development even in their own immediate primary field of interest.

Both rationales are particularly important when examining the internationalization of Swiss R&D. Switzerland is a small country and small countries tend to be more internationalized and specialized in their technological activities than are large ones (Archibugi/Pianta 1992). In 1980 the largest 15 Swiss-owned MNCs had no less than 75% of their global employment abroad, and for the largest six Swiss companies it was as much as 83% (Borner 1986). Small and open economies are to some extent forced to specialize in selected niches due to a relative lack of resources and technological expertise to carry out comparatively expensive experimental R&D that entails many risks and uncertainties in order to remain competitive in the global marketplace (Duysters/Hagedoorn 2001). As a result they usually rely disproportionally on international flows and research cooperation and the dependence on foreign sources of technology is at the core of their R&D strategy (Katzenstein 1985). In this setting, a small open economy can be a leader only in a limited range of technologies. Another important issue to bear in mind is the interaction between national systems of innovation and the activities of large firms, particularly if an economy is dominated by a few large firms, as in the Swiss case, and these firms are the main focus of R&D policies (Katzenstein 1985) and R&D spending (BBW 2004). The innovative activity of large firms both reflects their home national strengths but also has a major impact on the rate and direction of their home countries' technological activities (Patel/Pavitt 1991).

This paper aims to explore in detail the internationalization of Swiss R&D over the period 1969–1995, focusing both on changes in indigenous technological capabilities as well as the role of inward and outward foreign direct investment in the process. In the next section we describe the data and methods.

Subsequently we examine in greater detail the specific position of Swiss-owned firms abroad, and foreign-owned firms in Switzerland. Then the discussion turns to the internationalization of activity in some selected Swiss industries, and the technological specialization of selected leading Swiss-owned companies abroad. The last section summarizes and concludes.

A Note on Data and Methodology

This paper follows a similar methodology to some earlier studies (Cantwell/Hodson 1991, Cantwell/Kotecha 1997, Cantwell/Harding 1998, Cantwell/Janne 1999a). The data on technological activity presented here relate to patents granted in the USA between 1969 and 1995. These data are extremely valuable because of the variety of information provided on each patent granted. It is possible to separately identify the firm to which the patent has been granted, the location of the research facility originally responsible for the innovation, and a sectoral classification of the technological activity with which each patent is associated. It has also proved possible to establish the ultimate ownership of patents where they are granted to the affiliates of MNCs.

The technological activity of international corporate groups has been consolidated for the world's largest 792 industrial firms as of 1982, derived from the listings in the Fortune 500 (Dunning/Pearce 1985). Of these 792 companies, patenting activity was recorded for 730 firms during the period 1969–1995. In addition, a further 40 of the world's largest firms that are not in the Fortune 500 listing were included, because they are among the most technologically important either historically or recently as represented in the US patent statistics (for example, AT&T and RCA). The consolidated firms were also allocated to their primary industry of output according to the product distribution of their sales (Dunning/Pearce 1985) so that corporate patenting was then divided into 16 broad industrial groups. Each patent was also classified by the type of technological activity with which it is primarily associated, using a classification scheme derived from the US patent class systems. It should be emphasized that this technological classification of each patent is quite distinct from the industry (output) classification of the firm to which the patent is granted. Finally, the country of origin of the parent company was recorded.

The relative merits and de-merits of patent data as a measure of innovativeness are well documented in the literature and it is not our intention to enter significantly into this debate here (see for example Cantwell 1993, Cantwell 1995, Griliches 1990, Patel/Pavitt 1991, Pavitt 1988). However, some points are worth highlighting, as they relate directly to the use made of these data in this paper.

Firstly, patents represent a measure of inventions and advances in knowledge, which are generated by firms as inputs into the development of new products and processes, and are thus a proxy for downstream technological activity. They can thus be used as a proxy measure for technological activity as a whole and, as such, are a powerful tool in making cross-country comparisons of the extent of foreign location of and foreign participation in local development efforts (Cantwell 1995, Patel/Pavitt 1991). Secondly, at a corporate level, patents are useful, again as a proxy, in measuring the inventive output of formal in-house R&D, especially for large firms that are likelier to have a formal corporate research division and to patent the results of research. Lastly, patents are the best, indeed perhaps the only, detailed source of information on the sectoral and geographical composition of innovative capacity within firms, and are therefore particularly useful in making empirically-based comparisons across industries and across countries (Cantwell/ Andersen 1996, Cantwell/Harding 1998, Patel/Pavitt 1991).

Used judiciously, then, patents represent a powerful means of assessing the geographical or sectoral distribution of innovation of the largest companies in an industry or nation. Care has been taken to construct ratios or indices from the data such that absolute values are not used, since different industries have different propensities to patent. All the data reported here are in the form of ratios and shares to avoid the problems associated with use of absolute values. Similarly, US patenting is used as a proxy measure to avoid the problems of non-uniform legal and classification systems.

The large number of patents usually available for analysis is one of the key advantages of using patent statistics. Unfortunately in the case of Switzerland the technological activity is, compared to larger countries, fairly limited and narrow, posing a problem of small numbers. In order to ensure statistically useful results the breadth of industries and technological fields across which we consider the patenting of the largest firms needs to be reduced to a selected few, in which a sufficient number of patents is available. Therefore, the analysis is limited in that it might overstate the focus of technological activity domestically and abroad and understate the breadth of companies that are involved in internationalization of their R&D because some industries and technological fields have been eliminated from our consideration. Therefore, the findings and interpretation need to be considered with this limitation in mind.

The Case of Switzerland

Table 1 shows the share of US patents of the largest Swiss firms attributable to research outside Switzerland and organized by the industrial group of the parent

Table 1. The Share of US Patents of the Largest Swiss Firms Attributable to Research Outside Switzerland Organised by the Industrial Group of Parent Firms (1969–1995) (%)

	1969–1972	1973–1977	1978–1982	1983–1986	1987–1990	1991–1995
Food Products	56.00	45.16	49.04	64.84	98.39	97.37
Chemicals	38.54	36.49	38.97	40.43	43.92	52.22
Pharmaceuticals	65.25	61.35	60.22	49.92	53.29	58.40
Metals	56.78	44.81	46.85	34.48	36.75	29.38
Mechanical Engineering	13.28	25.40	31.75	33.24	30.17	39.20
Electrical Equipment	37.73	33.25	29.38	39.40	45.38	51.44
Total	44.38	43.63	43.79	41.59	44.50	52.52

Source: US patent database developed by Professor John Cantwell, with the assistance of the USPTO.

company. Overall, the table shows a trend towards greater internationalization with the total share of US patents of Swiss-owned firms attributable to research conducted outside Switzerland rising by 8.14% over the period as a whole, from 44.38% in 1969–1972 to 52.52% in 1991–1995. There was a slight decrease in internationalization during the 1970s and 1980s but the level of the late 1960s was surpassed in the late 1980s, and the beginning of the 1990s was marked by a strong increase in internationalization. Despite the volatility, this share has been consistently among the highest when compared to other countries. Only firms from Belgium and the Netherlands, both small countries as well, have uniformly higher shares of internationalization of R&D throughout the period 1969–1995, and since the mid-1980s the highly internationalized firms of the UK (Cantwell/Kosmopoulou 2002). In contrast, firms from the largest countries with a strong domestic technological base – Japan, the United States, and until quite recently Germany – have had a much weaker propensity to undertake their technological activity abroad, with shares of foreign-located R&D in the most recent period of only 1.08%, 8.62% and 20.72% respectively (Cantwell/Janne 1999a).

Taking a look at the industrial breakdown of the overall trend, one can observe that Swiss-owned technological activity abroad is concentrated in only a few industries and firms. Out of the 6 industrial groups 4 show a net increase in internationalization. There was a substantial net rise in internationalization in food products, from an already high level of 56% to 97.37%, which is a 41.37% increase. While in general the food industry is the most internationalized due to demand-led pressures for adaptation, and shows an overall level of internationalization of 26.87% in the period 1991–1995 for the world's largest firms, the extraordinarily high level of internationalization of the Swiss-owned food companies is remarkable. It is even higher than the highest share of foreign R&D in Dutch firms in the same industry, which was 85.38% (Cantwell/Hodson 1991, Cantwell/Janne 1999a). The chemicals (13.68%), mechanical engineering (25.92%) and electrical equipment industry (13.71%) exhibited an increase in internationalization as well. However, only in mechanical engineering has the rise in internationalization been continuous over the period. Food products and chemicals exhibit a net centralization, i.e. a decrease in internationalization, between the first and second periods, and electrical equipment exhibits net centralization from the first through to the third period. Net centralization took place over the period as a whole in pharmaceuticals and metals (of −6.85% and −17.58% respectively). For pharmaceuticals there is a marked recovery of internationalization by 5.11% between 1987–1990 and 1991–1995, but for metals the net centralization is a consistent trend over the entirety of the period in question.

These same data, i.e. the share of US patents of the largest Swiss-owned firms attributable to research conducted outside Switzerland, are classified in Table 2 by the sectoral composition of the technological activity (instead of the industrial group) for comparative purposes. There is an increase in internationalization over the period as a whole in all fields except one. Specialized industrial equipment saw a net centralization of 18.90% with the centralizing trend evident in all time periods except from 1973–1977 to 1978–1982 and in the most recent period, which showed a slight increase in internationalization compared to the period of 1987–1990.

Table 2. The Share of US Patents of the Largest Swiss Firms Attributable to Research Outside Switzerland, Classified by Technological Activity, 1969–1995 (%)

	1969–1972	1973–1977	1978–1982	1983–1986	1987–1990	1991–1995
Chemicals	45.98	41.88	46.35	38.15	38.88	47.64
Chemical processes	42.05	40.07	50.14	42.80	46.67	50.79
Organic chemicals	47.29	43.28	48.43	42.74	40.53	48.18
Pharmaceuticals	53.82	55.02	45.76	51.99	57.34	59.72
Metals	34.00	45.40	41.76	33.62	41.52	62.31
Non-electrical machinery	39.52	41.22	41.39	39.32	37.91	42.82
Chemical and allied equipment	43.66	54.74	47.77	51.49	46.72	50.70
Specialised industrial equipment	56.52	39.73	41.13	37.67	36.94	37.62
Electrical equipment	32.31	36.73	35.90	42.01	43.21	49.01
Electrical systems	36.00	30.83	30.00	40.50	48.09	55.28
General electrical equipment	23.94	48.24	44.00	47.27	48.68	39.24
Professional and scientific instruments	42.54	48.79	40.59	53.85	55.95	73.83
Non-photographic instruments	41.60	49.19	39.69	50.00	54.72	73.71
Total	44.38	43.63	43.79	41.59	44.50	52.52

Source: As for Table 1.
Note: Sectoral headings in bold represent collective categories, while those not in bold represent sub-headings under the heading in bold immediately above them.

The most substantial increase in internationalization occurred in three fields of technological activity. Non-photographic instruments saw a net rise in internationalization by 32.11%, professional and scientific instruments by 31.29% and metals by 28.31%. Further strong trends towards greater internationalization were also witnessed in general electrical systems (19.28%), general electrical equipment (15.3%) and electrical equipment (16.70%). In no field of technological activity was the rise in internationalization continuous throughout the whole period, and some fields such as chemical processes exhibited considerable volatility until 1983–1986. Otherwise the trend is generally towards greater internationalization, which is consistent with the notion that firms require a broader range of technological capability to support even a narrower range of products (Pavitt et al. 1989). What emerges when comparing Tables 1 and 2 is that the trend towards an increased internationalization of research by firms involved in a particular industry is not necessarily related to the trend in the equivalent primary technological field in which they are most immediately involved, but in other (presumably related) fields. For example, the strong growth of internationalization of research by chemical companies is not matched by a corresponding increase in the internationalization of the creation of chemical technological development itself. This phenomenon is even more marked when comparing the trend in the metals industry and that in metals as the equivalent primary field of technological activity. While the industry shows a centralization of its foreign R&D, the equivalent technological field shows a substantial internationalization, the combination of which implies that it must be the firms of other industries that have increased their development of complementary metals technologies abroad. This pattern of technological diversification abroad is consistent with that of other countries or for the world's largest firms when considered collectively (Cantwell/Janne 1999a, Cantwell/Kosmopoulou 2002).

It is also worth noting that three of the fields in which the foreign research share is now highest are related to the technological fields in which Switzerland has held traditional strengths, namely instruments, metals and pharmaceuticals. This might lead to the expectation that, in relation to others of the world's largest companies, Swiss-owned companies have relatively increased their research abroad in these key fields. Comparing the Swiss case with world trends should show whether the cross-sectoral pattern of the increase in internationalization of Swiss-owned companies was concentrated in their fields of traditional strength, or whether it was simply a reflection of the industries and technologies in which international dispersion has been greatest in general. The relative internationalization of research by Swiss firms compared to the largest firms of all other nationalities can be seen in Table 3, which shows the ratio of the share of patenting of Swiss-owned firms due to research abroad relative to the aggregate foreign research share in total patenting for all firms in the world as a whole, broken down by the industrial grouping of parent companies. The amount by which this ratio exceeds unity shows the extent to which Swiss-owned firms are especially internationalized in their research compared to the average of firms of other nationalities.

Table 3 shows that by the standards of others, Swiss firms have always been more reliant upon research located outside of Switzerland in all the industries represented, undertaking around 4 times as much technological activity abroad as did all the other firms during 1969–1995. Although it had been declining until the mid-1980s, the ratio of Swiss-owned foreign-origin patenting to world foreign-origin patenting has even increased very slightly by 0.27 over the period as a whole. There were increases in mechanical engineering of 1.42, in electrical equipment of 1.81 and in food products of 0.51. There was a substantial reduction in the ratio in metals of 3.24, which reflects the strong centralization of Swiss-owned research in this industry already reported in Table 1. In other words, the net centralization of the foreign research activity of Swiss-owned metal firms was not just a reflection of general trends in this industry worldwide, but a de-facto decrease in the extent of international research activity of the Swiss-owned metal firms in particular. Reductions in the ratio for chemicals and pharmaceuticals were relatively small, at 0.04 and 0.59 respectively.

To complement our understanding, Table 4 shows the share of US patents of the largest Swiss firms attributable to research abroad relative to the world share of foreign-origin patenting classified by technological activity instead of the industrial grouping of parent companies. There are increases in the relative foreign research ratio in professional and scientific instruments (4.03), non-photographic instruments (3.14), general electrical equipment (2.30), and metals (2.04). A slight increase is also exhibited in electrical systems (0.53). In other fields of technological activity the trend is downwards, albeit by relatively small amounts. For example, in organic chemicals the ratio declined by 1.03 while in chemical processes it declined by 0.29 and in pharmaceuticals it declined by 0.52. Reduc-

Table 3. The Share of US Patents of the Largest Swiss Firms Attributable to Research Abroad Relative to the Equivalent Share of the World's Largest Firms Considered Together, for Each Industrial Group of Parent Firms, 1969–1995

	1969–1972	1973–1977	1978–1982	1983–1986	1987–1990	1991–1995
Food Products	3.32	2.18	2.09	2.62	4.15	3.83
Chemicals	3.12	2.71	2.89	2.93	3.05	3.08
Pharmaceuticals	3.87	3.21	3.50	3.05	2.92	3.28
Metals	5.21	4.88	4.30	3.52	3.14	2.97
Mechanical Engineering	1.29	2.51	2.78	2.32	1.99	2.71
Electrical Equipment	3.66	3.36	3.34	4.05	4.43	5.47
Total	4.38	4.08	4.13	3.76	3.91	4.65

Source: As for Table 1.

Table 4 The Share of US Patents of the Largest Swiss Firms Attributable to Research Abroad Relative to the Equivalent Share of the World's Largest Firms Considered Together Classified by Technological Activity, 1969-1995

	1969-1972	1973-1977	1978-1982	1983-1986	1987-1990	1991-1995
Chemicals	3.97	3.51	3.93	3.36	2.87	3.06
Chemical processes	4.09	3.80	4.65	3.88	3.75	3.80
Organic chemicals	3.76	3.36	3.82	3.69	2.75	2.73
Pharmaceuticals	3.37	3.02	2.40	2.57	2.64	2.85
Metals	3.81	4.57	4.10	2.88	3.71	5.85
Non-electrical machinery	3.61	3.53	3.46	3.03	2.82	3.53
Chemical and allied equipment	3.92	4.64	4.48	4.33	3.31	3.66
Specialised industrial equipment	4.04	2.65	2.51	2.32	2.41	2.65
Electrical equipment	3.49	4.05	4.39	4.37	4.38	5.07
Electrical systems	4.39	3.61	4.04	4.04	4.53	4.92
General electrical equipment	3.08	6.12	5.54	5.88	5.88	5.38
Professional and scientific instruments	4.92	5.26	4.52	5.63	6.42	8.95
Non-photographic instruments	4.64	5.02	3.94	4.79	5.57	7.78
Total	4.38	4.08	4.13	3.76	3.91	4.65

Source: As for Table 1.
Note: Sectoral headings in bold represent collective categories, while those not in bold represent sub-headings under the heading in bold immediately above them.

tions in the ratio are also seen in specialized industrial equipment (1.39), chemicals (0.91) and non-electrical machinery (0.08).

The evidence presented thus far suggests that Swiss technological activity abroad is strongly internationalized, with growing overall internationalization since the mid-1980s after years of volatility. We can also see that international technological activity is relatively focused in a few industries and technological fields. This focus is becoming even narrower, since in 3 out of 6 industries the internationalization is decreasing, compared to firms of other nationalities.

The Pattern of Inward R&D Activity: Patents Emerging from the Research Activities of the World's Largest Firms in Switzerland

We move on to examine foreign-owned research in Switzerland. If technology develops along a national trajectory of specialization that is both supportive of and underpinned by the technological activities of a country's largest companies, then we might expect to see inward R&D activity seeking to exploit the technological advantages of a particular nation in key industries of the economy. As we have already seen, Switzerland tends to be specialized in a relatively small number of industries and fields of technological activity and the level of patenting outside these is very low. We would expect, therefore, to see inward R&D reflecting the traditional strengths of the Swiss economy and flowing into those technological fields that show the most increase and absolute level in internationalization as we have seen above, i.e. instruments, metals, pharmaceuticals and electrical systems and equipment. It is to this that the discussion now turns.

Table 5 shows the share of all of the world's largest companies' patenting attributable to research in Switzerland relative to patenting attributable to research in all locations outside their respective home countries, broken down by industrial grouping (expressed as a percentage). Overall the share of foreign R&D in Switzerland fell by 1.51%, from 2.92% in 1968–1972 to 1.41% in 1991–1995. By 1991–1995, the industry in which Switzerland was relatively most attractive to R&D by foreign-owned firms was the food industry with 4.09%, followed by mechanical engineering and electrical equipment, with 1.55% and 1.44% respectively. Overall, the table illustrates that Switzerland has declined in attractiveness as a location for foreign research activity, which reduction was particularly marked in chemicals (3.28%), mechanical engineering (3.07%), metals (2.26%), and electrical equipment (1.34%). There was a slight decline in the ratio for pharmaceuticals over the same period (0.14%). Only in food products was the increase relatively large at 3.67%, although a smaller increase of 0.14% was also seen in pharmaceuticals. All industries exhibit a volatile trend, and all except food products exhibit reductions between the last two periods (1987–1990 and 1991–1995). The decline in Swiss attractiveness for foreign research is particularly interesting in the chemicals and mechanical engineering industries, since in these industries the world's largest firms have exhibited overall a growing internationalization of their technological activity, but this trend has not been to the benefit of Switzerland (Cantwell/Janne 1999a).

Table 5. The Share of US Patents of the Largest Non-Swiss Firms Attribuatble to Research in Switzerland as a Proportion of Non-Swiss Firm Patenting from Research in all Foreign Locations, Organised by Industrial Group of Parent Firm, 1969–1995 (%)

	1969–1972	1973–1977	1978–1982	1983–1986	1987–1990	1991–1995
Food Products	0.42	1.68	1.06	2.75	1.08	4.09
Chemicals	4.15	1.50	0.76	0.85	0.98	0.87
Pharmaceuticals	1.15	0.67	1.86	1.51	2.15	1.29
Metals	2.91	4.22	3.70	2.79	1.03	0.65
Mechanical Engineering	4.62	6.59	5.50	3.79	2.84	1.55
Electrical Equipment	2.78	3.74	5.54	4.41	2.64	1.44
Total	2.92	2.55	2.69	2.52	1.85	1.41

Source: As for Table 1.

Table 6 examines the equivalent data broken down by field of technological activity. While the traditionally strong fields of Swiss expertise as described earlier are also the ones attracting the most foreign-owned firm research activity (non-photographic instruments [2.43%], electrical equipment [2.37%], electrical systems [2.36%], and professional and scientific instruments [2.24%]), the data show a marked decline in the attractiveness of Switzerland as a location for foreign-owned R&D over the whole period in question. All fields of technological activity show a net reduction. Higher reductions were seen in organic chemicals (2.68%), non-photographic instruments (2.37%), chemicals (2.17%), specialized industrial equipment (2.09%), chemical and allied equipment (2.08%), and professional and scientific instruments (2.08%). In all fields of technological activity except metals, the trend was variable over the period.

Comparing Tables 5 and 6 one result seems noteworthy. The food industry is the only industry that shows an increase in local participation in foreign-owned firm R&D activity. However, foreign firms in the food industry did not focus on the equivalent food technological fields, but neither do local firms. What this indicates is that the research activity of foreign-owned firms in the food industry that come to Switzerland focuses rather on engineering-related technological fields, such as machinery, electrical equipment and systems and instruments, in

Table 6. The Share of US Patents of the Largest Non-Swiss Firms Attributable to Research in Switzerland as a Proportion of Non-Swiss Firm Patenting due to Research in all Foreign Locations, Classified by Technological Activity, 1969–1995

	1969–1972	1973–1977	1978–1982	1983–1986	1987–1990	1991–1995
Chemicals	2.98	1.60	1.52	1.67	1.23	0.81
Chemical processes	1.96	2.05	2.85	3.16	1.71	0.80
Organic chemicals	3.51	1.40	0.64	0.77	0.90	0.83
Pharmaceuticals	1.10	0.27	0.96	0.54	0.45	0.91
Metals	2.24	2.21	2.00	1.55	0.85	0.98
Non-electrical machinery	2.88	2.84	2.58	2.31	1.64	1.00
Chemical and allied equipment	3.11	3.06	2.12	4.46	2.07	1.03
Specialised industrial equipment	2.82	1.38	2.33	1.61	1.55	0.73
Electrical equipment	3.44	4.06	5.76	4.37	2.97	2.37
Electrical systems	3.79	4.75	5.11	3.09	4.22	2.36
General electrical equipment	3.31	2.62	3.17	4.35	0.93	2.23
Professional and scientific instruments	4.32	3.87	5.08	4.05	3.26	2.24
Non-photographic instruments	4.80	4.23	4.44	3.66	3.16	2.43
Total	2.92	2.55	2.69	2.52	1.85	1.41

Source: As for Table 1.
Note: Sectoral headings in bold represent collective categories, while those not in bold represent sub-headings under the heading in bold immediately above them.

which Switzerland has been traditionally strong. This finding is consistent with the general trends identified in our opening remarks, in which we suggested that the internationalization of R&D activity is driven by technological diversification and the need of foreign-owned MNCs to access fields of local technological specialization.

For a better understanding of the contribution of foreign-owned firms to research in Switzerland, Table 7 shows the foreign-owned share of research in Switzerland organized by industry. Where the ratio increases between two periods, it indicates that the role of foreign-owned firms in Swiss-based research is increasing. Conversely, where a figure declines over time it indicates that Swiss-owned company research at home is increasing faster (or falling more slowly) than the research of foreign-owned firms in Switzerland.

Once again the table shows a net decline over the period as a whole, suggesting a reduction in the attractiveness of Switzerland as a location for non-Swiss R&D. The total reduction in the proportion of non-Swiss firms conducting research in Switzerland was 1.41% between 1969 and 1995. There were particularly large reductions in non-Swiss firm patenting attributable to research in Switzerland in metals (26.29%) and mechanical engineering (10.18%). The quite dramatic loss of attractiveness of Switzerland for foreign-owned firms in the metals industry coincides with the reduction of the international research activity of the domestic firms in this industry, as discussed above in connection with Tables 1, 3 and 5. This combined pattern may be an indication that the increased concentration of research activity by Swiss-owned metal firms at home has begun to deter foreign-owned firms in the same industry from locating their R&D in the same vicinity (Cantwell/Piscitello 2004). Other net reductions can be seen in chemicals (4.47%), and electrical equipment (7.30%). In all fields except metals the trend was varied over the period. There were increases in the share of foreign participation in Switzerland in food and pharmaceuticals. Indeed, in food, the increase was particularly marked at 73.08% over the whole period.

Table 7. The Share of US Patents of the Largest Non-Swiss Firms Attributable to Research in Switzerland as a Proportion of Those due to Research in Switzerland by all Firms, Organised by the Industrial Group of Parent Companies, 1969–1995 (%)

	1969–1972	1973–1977	1978–1982	1983–1986	1987–1990	1991–1995
Food Products	15.38	19.05	10.17	31.91	85.71	88.46
Chemicals	8.65	2.90	1.76	2.43	3.13	4.18
Pharmaceuticals	2.28	1.38	4.77	4.46	8.78	6.31
Metals	30.14	20.83	17.68	13.64	7.08	3.85
Mechanical Engineering	18.68	21.88	18.75	16.32	11.66	8.50
Electrical Equipment	32.00	30.96	28.96	33.92	26.16	24.70
Total	15.76	11.15	12.56	15.65	13.48	14.35

Source: As for Table 1.

There were large increases in this industrial grouping between 1978–1982 and 1983–1986 (21.74%) and from 1983–1986 to 1987–1990 (53.90%). In pharmaceuticals the trend was generally upward (4.03%), although with some fluctuations.

Table 8 examines the equivalent share of foreign-owned firms in Swiss research, but this time broken down by field of technological activity (expressed as a percentage). The greatest reductions over the period as a whole were in chemical and allied equipment (21.93%), specialized industrial equipment (23.61%), metals (15.75%) and non-electrical machinery (15.32%). However, only in non-electrical machinery was the downward trend consistent across the whole period. Alongside these reductions there were increases in foreign participation in Switzerland in six fields of technological activity. These were pharmaceuticals (2.28%), electrical equipment (7.53%), electrical systems (6.20%), general electrical equipment (2.14%), professional and scientific instruments (10.36%), and non-photographic instruments (9.73%). Particularly marked increases in the latest period were seen in four of these: electrical equipment (8.48%), general electrical equipment (13.64%), professional and scientific instruments (10.34%), and non-photographic instruments (11.22%). However, there was no consistently upward trend over the period as a whole in any field.

Table 8. The Share of US Patents of the Largest Non-Swiss Firms Attributable to Research in Switzerland, as a Percentage of the Number due to Research in Switzerland by all Firms Classified by Technological Activity, 1969–1995 (%)

	1969–1972	1973–1977	1978–1982	1983–1986	1987–1990	1991–1995
Chemicals	7.70	3.31	4.15	5.22	4.79	4.87
Chemical processes	16.30	13.59	16.67	20.54	14.12	8.78
Organic chemicals	6.51	2.14	1.47	2.13	3.09	4.33
Pharmaceuticals	2.21	0.67	2.84	2.14	2.15	4.49
Metals	29.79	17.59	12.39	13.48	6.54	14.04
Non-electrical machinery	26.47	25.24	20.05	19.82	15.24	11.15
Chemical and allied equipment	34.43	30.34	15.46	36.36	19.75	12.50
Specialised industrial equipment	29.58	12.87	19.78	9.90	10.26	5.97
Electrical equipment	38.60	40.84	40.27	40.68	37.55	46.03
Electrical systems	34.02	36.64	36.36	27.27	40.87	40.22
General electrical equipment	22.86	22.81	17.65	26.58	11.36	25.00
Professional and scientific instruments	34.19	26.59	32.96	37.78	34.21	44.55
Non-photographic instruments	34.82	26.04	28.66	33.60	33.33	44.55
Total	15.76	11.15	12.56	15.65	13.48	14.35

Source: As for Table 1.
Note: Sectoral headings in bold represent collective categories, while those not in bold represent sub-headings under the heading in bold immediately above them.

The data set out thus far present a picture of greater outward internationalization of research by Swiss-owned companies alongside an overall decline in attractiveness of Switzerland for foreign-owned R&D. Only in food and pharmaceuticals, arguably core industries, has there been a substantial increase in foreign participation in research in Switzerland. The foreign-owned firms in these industries then take advantage of a select number of technological fields in which Switzerland has been traditionally strong (electrical equipment and instruments). This pattern of a decline in attractiveness in most industries and technological fields, coupled with an increased attention to a few, traditionally strong industries and technologies seems to indicate that the overall tendency in the internationalization of R&D on both the outward and inward sides has been towards a greater specialization of the expertise of Swiss innovatory activity, thus reinforcing its niche character. The remainder of the paper now turns to see whether this contention is consistent with evidence on changes in the geographical profile of international technological specialization of individual companies.

The Profiles of Technological Specialization of Foreign-owned Firms in Switzerland and Swiss-owned Firms Abroad

The revealed technological advantage (RTA) index is a measure of technological specialization across different fields of activity. The RTA of a firm (or a group of firms) in a particular sector of technological activity is given by its share of US patents in that field granted to companies in the same industry, relative to the firm's overall share of all US patents assigned to firms in the industry in question. Denoting as P_{ij} the number of US patents granted in the field of activity i to firm (or selected group of firms) j in a particular industry, then the RTA index is defined as follows:

$$RTA_{ij} = (P_{ij}/\sum_j P_{ij})/(\sum_i P_{ij}/\sum_{ij} P_{ij})$$

The index varies around unity, such that values greater than one suggest that a firm (or group of firms) is comparatively specialized in the activity in question relative to the other firms in the same industry. Similarly, values less than one are indicative of a lack of specialization by the standards of the industry. Just as difficulties can be created when constructing ratios that rely on small numbers of patents, as discussed above, so there are particular problems associated with the use of small numbers when using an RTA index (Cantwell 1989, 1993). Due to these problems the analysis is restricted to sectors in which over 1,200 US patents were granted to large firms in the industry in question between 1969 and

1995. Sectors that do not meet this criterion are omitted from the RTA values reported from Table 9 onwards. The tables are constructed for three industries: chemicals, pharmaceuticals and electrical equipment. These are the industries in which the bulk of Swiss research is based.

Table 9 illustrates the RTA of non-Swiss firms in Switzerland relative to firms in the world as a whole in each of the three industries. Non-Swiss-owned chemical companies specialized in Switzerland in 7 out of the selected 13 technological fields: organic chemicals, non-electric machinery, chemical and allied equipment, specialized industrial equipment, electrical systems, professional and scientific instruments and non-photographic instruments. The level of specialization was especially high in specialized industrial equipment (2.02) and non-photographic instruments (1.81). Of the chemical fields, non-Swiss chemical companies were specialized only in organic chemicals (1.10).

Non-Swiss pharmaceutical companies in Switzerland had high levels of specialization in Switzerland in 5 of the 9 technological fields considered: most markedly in chemical processes (2.78), metals (3.28) and non-electrical machinery (1.88). Other specializations were in chemicals (1.10) and chemical and allied equipment (1.10). This again reflects a relatively diverse range of specialization across a range of technological activities but with a slight focus on chemical and machinery related technologies.

In electrical equipment specialization by non-Swiss firms in Switzerland is less diverse. Specialization is in four fields only (out of 12 selected fields): electrical equipment (1.24), electrical systems (1.27), professional and scientific in-

Table 9. The Revealed Technological Advantage of Non-Swiss Firms in Switzerland Relative to all Firms in that Industry Across Fields of Technological Activity, 1969–1995

	Chemicals	Pharmaceuticals	Electrical Equipment
Chemicals	0.94	1.10	0.51
Chemical processes	0.73	2.78	0.68
Organic chemicals	1.10	0.49	0.06
Pharmaceuticals	0.76	0.50	n/a
Metals	0.52	3.28	0.35
Non-electrical machinery	1.67	1.88	0.77
Chemical and allied equipment	1.14	1.10	0.77
Specialised industrial equipment	2.02	n/a	0.46
Electrical equipment	0.76	n/a	1.24
Electrical systems	1.50	n/a	1.27
General electrical equipment	0.51	n/a	0.56
Professional and scientific instruments	1.47	0.66	1.44
Non-photographic instruments	1.81	0.66	1.48

Source: As for Table 1.
Notes: n/a = not applicable.
Sectoral headings in bold represent collective categories, while those not in bold represent sub-headings under the heading in bold immediately above them.

struments (1.44), and non-photographic instruments (1.48). Here there is evidence of specialization in equipment and instrument related fields. It is interesting to note that the electrical equipment industry is one of the three industries that were most attractive to foreign-owned R&D in Switzerland and it also exhibits specialization in exactly those fields that seem to reflect traditional Swiss technological strengths, and which also happen to be the ones in which Swiss-owned companies show a high level of internationalization.

Table 10 looks at the technological specialization of Swiss-owned companies in their domestic base across a range of technological activities. It shows specialization in relatively few fields by Swiss-owned companies in Switzerland across the three industries, and perhaps a greater focus in R&D than is true of non-Swiss companies conducting research in Switzerland. In the chemical industry, Swiss-owned companies are specialized in pharmaceuticals (1.97) and organic chemicals (1.34). An additional specialization occurs in the primary field of chemicals (1.20) as a whole, and in the field of non-photographic instruments (1.12).

Swiss pharmaceutical companies are specialized in just two of the selected fields of technological activity – organic chemicals (1.60) and chemicals (1.44). In all other fields covered by Table 10, Swiss-owned companies in Switzerland are relatively unspecialized or there are insufficient patents to allow the RTA to be calculated. Again, however, this suggests a high degree of focus in their indigenous research by Swiss-owned companies within Switzerland.

Table 10. The Revealed Technological Advantage of Swiss-owned Firms in Switzerland in Selected Industries Across Fields of Technological Activity, 1969–1995

	Chemicals	Pharmaceuticals	Electrical Equipment
Chemicals	1.20	1.44	0.59
Chemical processes	0.67	0.57	0.70
Organic chemicals	1.34	1.60	0.20
Pharmaceuticals	1.97	0.77	n/a
Metals	0.20	0.08	2.09
Non-electrical machinery	0.34	0.39	1.61
Chemical and allied equipment	0.37	0.57	0.78
Specialised industrial equipment	0.41	n/a	0.63
Electrical equipment	0.09	n/a	0.96
Electrical systems	0.10	n/a	1.37
General electrical equipment	0.07	n/a	1.48
Professional and scientific instruments	0.90	0.42	0.86
Non-photographic instruments	1.12	0.42	1.00

Source: As for Table 1.
Notes: n/a = not applicable.
Sectoral headings in bold represent collective categories, while those not in bold represent sub-headings under the heading in bold immediately above them.

Finally, in electrical equipment, Swiss companies have an RTA of greater than 1 in four equipment and machinery related fields. Interestingly, in metals the level of specialization is relatively high at 2.09. In the three other fields of technological activity the level of specialization yields an RTA of 1.61 for chemical and allied equipment, 1.48 for general electrical equipment, and 1.37 for electrical systems. These data suggest a degree of focus in some key primary electrical equipment and in allied machinery technological fields by Swiss-owned companies in the electrical equipment industry.

Table 11 provides us with some insights into understanding the process by which Swiss companies have internationalized their technological activities. It shows the RTA of Swiss companies outside Switzerland across fields of technological activity in the same three industries, namely chemicals, pharmaceuticals and electrical equipment. Once again, it shows that Swiss-owned companies tend to be relatively focused in their R&D, particularly in the pharmaceuticals and electrical equipment industries and are also focused on the same technological fields as in their domestic research.

Swiss-owned chemical companies' research outside Switzerland is specialized in the primary fields of chemicals (1.08), including organic chemicals (1.18), and pharmaceuticals (2.25). They are further specialized in professional and scientific instruments (1.45), and especially in non-photographic instruments (1.77). Swiss-owned pharmaceutical companies' research outside Switzerland is specialized in just two of the selected fields: chemicals (1.40) and organic chemicals (1.63). Since the latter is a special case of the former, there is clearly a high degree of focus.

Table 11. The Revealed Technological Advantage of Swiss-owned Firms Outside Switzerland in Selected Industries Across Fields of Technological Activity, 1969–1995

	Chemicals	Pharmaceuticals	Electrical Equipment
Chemicals	1.08	1.40	0.57
Chemical processes	0.81	0.41	0.67
Organic chemicals	1.18	1.63	0.27
Pharmaceuticals	2.25	0.81	n/a
Metals	0.36	0.11	1.94
Non-electrical machinery	0.46	0.42	1.09
Chemical and allied equipment	0.37	0.60	0.55
Specialised industrial equipment	0.83	n/a	0.32
Electrical equipment	0.08	n/a	0.97
Electrical systems	0.02	n/a	1.42
General electrical equipment	0.11	n/a	1.66
Professional and scientific instruments	1.45	0.46	0.83
Non-photographic instruments	1.77	0.46	0.96

Source: As for Table 1.
Note: Sectoral headings in bold represent collective categories, while those not in bold represent sub-headings under the heading in bold immediately above them.

There is also evidence of a clear focus in their research outside Switzerland on the part of Swiss-owned electrical equipment companies. Relative specialization is shown in metals (1.94), non-electrical machinery (1.09), electrical systems (1.42), and general electrical equipment (1.66). This suggests a concentration upon the primary fields of the industry, and on some related machinery and equipment technologies in development efforts conducted abroad.

What is remarkable from Tables 10 and 11 is the sharp degree of focus of Swiss-owned companies in both their domestic research and research conducted outside Switzerland. Although the focus of research by chemicals companies abroad is slightly wider than in their research conducted at home, there is still evidence of a clear focus upon chemical and instrument technological fields. In pharmaceuticals and electrical equipment, the degree of specialization is even more marked in the same two fields at home and abroad in pharmaceuticals, and the same four fields in electrical equipment. Another noteworthy result is that the RTA index of foreign-owned electrical equipment firms in Switzerland is only 0.56 in the general electrical equipment technological field. The RTA of Swiss-owned firms at home or abroad in this field is over 1, indicating a positive technological specialization. Furthermore, this primary technological field is among those that show a large increase of international R&D. This may indicate a deterrent effect of a strong indigenous Swiss R&D position, which curtails foreign-owned firms in the same industry from locating research activities in the same primary technological field. Instead, it seems that foreign-owned electrical equipment firms seek to access other complementary technologies from their activities in Switzerland.

We turn now, then, to an examination of individual Swiss companies conducting inward and outward research resulting in US patents. We examine the share of US patents accounted for by domestic and foreign research, and the structure of the RTA distributions over the period of three key companies from the industries under closer investigation. The companies selected for this purpose are Ciba-Geigy, Roche/SAPAC and ABB. This selection is justified on the grounds that they all have a substantial research base that results in large numbers of US patents. In the case of ABB, which resulted from the merger of Brown-Boveri and Asea in 1987 (Zander 2002), only the independent data of Brown-Boveri was used for the years prior to its merger with Asea, so as to consider only the Swiss-owned part of the eventual cross-border merger.

Table 12 shows the share of the US patenting of these three companies attributable to research in foreign locations. Here, Ciba-Geigy saw increases in their foreign-origin patenting while Roche/SAPAC saw a net decline in foreign-origin patenting over the period. For Ciba-Geigy, from 1973–1977 the increase in the foreign research share was a consistent trend. Similarly, ABB has internationalized its research, as evidenced by the share of US patents attributable to research in foreign locations, by some 14.92% over the whole period. This trend is

Table 12. The Share of US Patents of Selected Leading Swiss-owned Firms Attributable to Research in Foreign Locations as a Proportion of Total US Patents Assigned to the Firm in Question, 1969–1995 (%)

	1969–1972	1973–1977	1978–1982	1983–1986	1987–1990	1991–1995
Ciba-Geigy	38.54	36.49	38.97	40.43	43.92	52.22
Roche/SAPAC	73.84	66.00	68.55	55.81	55.14	57.26
ABB	37.73	33.25	30.79	42.11	47.89	52.24

Source: As for Table 1.

attributable to increases from 1978–1982. Roche/SAPAC saw increases in the share of US patents from research conducted abroad between only two periods – 1973–1977 and 1978–1982 (2.55) and 1987–1990 and 1991–1995 (2.12). The total decline for Roche/SAPAC over the period as a whole was 16.58%.

Just how these companies exhibit similar or dissimilar patterns to those observed above can be demonstrated by looking at their RTA across fields of technological activity. This is shown in Table 13.

As with Tables 9 to 11, the picture presented here is one of a clear focus in specific and related technological fields. Ciba-Geigy had an RTA of greater than one in just four of the selected fields over the whole period: chemicals (1.20), organic chemicals (1.34), pharmaceuticals (1.97), and non-photographic instruments (1.12). These are the fields of specialization of all Swiss companies at home and abroad as represented in Tables 10 and 11. Similarly, the specializa-

Table 13. The Revealed Technological Advantage of Ciba-Geigy, Roche and ABB Across Fields of Technological Activity, 1969–1995

	Ciba Geigy	Roche/SAPAC	ABB
Chemicals	1.20	1.40	0.60
Chemical processes	0.67	0.57	0.72
Organic chemicals	1.34	1.65	0.20
Pharmaceuticals	1.97	0.77	n/a
Metals	0.20	0.09	2.16
Non-electrical machinery	0.34	0.39	1.65
Chemical and allied equipment	0.37	0.55	0.82
Specialised industrial equipment	0.41	n/a	0.56
Electrical equipment	0.09	n/a	0.97
Electrical systems	0.10	n/a	1.40
General electrical equipment	0.07	n/a	1.52
Professional and scientific instruments	0.90	0.60	0.78
Non-photographic instruments	1.12	0.60	0.90

Source: As for Table 1.
Notes: n/a = not applicable.
Sectoral headings in bold represent collective categories, while those not in bold represent sub-headings under the heading in bold immediately above them.

tion of Roche/SAPAC reflects that of all Swiss companies in chemicals (1.40) and organic chemicals (1.65). ABB also specializes in the same fields of technological activity as other Swiss companies: metals (2.16), non-electrical machinery (1.65), electrical systems (1.40), and general electrical equipment (1.52). The similarity of the pattern of focus of the three selected companies with those of other Swiss companies is notable. However, Switzerland is a small country and dominated by a few large companies that also do the bulk of R&D. Thus, the three companies selected themselves account for a good proportion of total large company research in Switzerland.

Finally, then, we examine the RTAs of these companies attributable to research in facilities located outside Switzerland between 1969 and 1995 across a range of technological fields.

Table 14 shows that Ciba-Geigy, in fact, had slightly wider specialization from its research abroad relative to the totality of its research (Table 13), but was again representative of all Swiss companies abroad (Table 11). Its RTA is greater than one in five fields: chemicals (1.08), organic chemicals (1.18), pharmaceuticals (2.25), professional and scientific instruments (1.45), and non-photographic instruments (1.77). Roche/SAPAC and ABB also exhibit similar specialisms to those covered in previous tables. Thus, Roche/SAPAC had specialization in just two of the selected fields: chemicals (1.40) and organic chemicals (1.72). ABB specialized in four fields abroad: metals (1.96), non-electric machinery (1.10), electrical systems (1.42), and general electrical equipment (1.67).

Table 14. The Revealed Technological Advantage of Ciby-Geigy, Roche and ABB from Their Research Facilities Outside Switzerland, Across Fields of Technological Activity, 1969–1995

	Ciba-Geigy	Roche/SAPAC	ABB
Chemicals	1.08	1.40	0.57
Chemical processes	0.81	0.30	0.68
Organic chemicals	1.18	1.72	0.27
Pharmaceuticals	2.25	0.79	n/a
Metals	0.36	0.12	1.96
Non-electrical machinery	0.46	0.34	1.10
Chemical and allied equipment	0.37	0.44	0.55
Specialised industrial equipment	0.83	n/a	0.33
Electrical equipment	0.08	n/a	0.97
Electrical systems	0.02	n/a	1.42
General electrical equipment	0.11	n/a	1.67
Professional and scientific instruments	1.45	0.57	0.79
Non-photographic instruments	1.77	0.57	0.92

Source: As for Table 1.
Notes: n/a = not applicable.
Sectoral headings in bold represent collective categories, while those not in bold represent sub-headings under the heading in bold immediately above them.

Concluding Remarks

Despite the variety of information on the internationalization of Swiss R&D presented here, the small scale and focus of this research compared to other larger country studies results in a few limitations that are important to keep in mind. Firstly, low levels of patents result in relatively few observations and can lead to difficulties in drawing unambiguous conclusions from the data. Secondly, the small number of large companies is reflected in the fact that the pattern of outward R&D and levels of specialization by the selected companies are very similar to those for all Swiss companies. However, despite these shortfalls it is possible to draw a first picture of the internationalization of Swiss research.

Generally, research is internationalizing and enhancing established specialisms by taking advantage of regional specialisms and innovation systems elsewhere (eg. by ABB using Fraunhofer structures in Germany). However, Roche/SAPAC's R&D over the period became more centralized, in contrast to the general trend in the industry and the other firms under investigation. Roche/SAPAC has been the most internationalized of the three companies with almost three quarters of its total R&D conducted abroad in the period 1969–1972. The decline we observe over the years down to a foreign share of 57.26% may be a reflection of an adjustment to a more balanced position, similar to the adjustment that the two other companies under investigation have achieved through an increase in their foreign R&D up to around 52%. It could also be a reflection of a similar trend to that which can be observed in the technological diversification of large firms, in which at a time of a generalized trend towards greater diversification, the very largest and most highly diversified firms have instead witnessed a refocusing in recent times (Cantwell/Santangelo 2000). Again, the initially very high degree of internationalization might have been a reflection of an over-dispersion for Roche/SAPAC, requiring a refocusing over the years, based partly on pressures in the pharmaceutical industry to cut costs in R&D spending while maintaining competitiveness in global markets (Blau 1995). It is also worth noting the similarity in the technological fields of focus of both the domestic and international research of Swiss-owned firms. In the case of ABB, this might be a reflection of the strong niche-character of the firm's R&D and its initial "... cautious movement out of the home base ..." (Zander 2002, p. 339), which meant maintaining and developing overlapping technological capabilities outside the home-country and only gradually expanding its technology base by adding peripheral technological capabilities (Zander 2002).

The internationalization of outward R&D is not met with a similar trend towards greater inward R&D into Switzerland by foreign-owned firms – Switzerland is becoming less attractive as location for overseas R&D overall and the inflow of R&D is becoming more polarized, concentrating in fewer industries and technological fields than at the beginning of the period under observation. This trend runs counter to the one we can observe in (for example) the Netherlands. Despite its also being a small country and even more internationalized in its firms' foreign R&D activity than is Switzerland, The Netherlands are becoming overall an increasingly attractive location for foreign-owned R&D (Cantwell/ Janne 1999a). However, we can see a similar pattern of increasing focus in the Netherlands as well, in that 8 out of 14 industries show an increasing share of foreign-owned R&D activity and the remaining 6 show a decline. Some factors that inhibit increasing foreign-owned R&D activity in the Dutch case are a small market, high wage costs and low investment bonuses (Cantwell/Janne 1999a). It is possible that similar factors may outweigh the benefits that Switzerland can offer foreign-owned firms and therefore contribute to a decline in attractiveness.

Another possible factor can be found in the dynamic processes associated with concentrated clusters of innovation that otherwise provide the stimulus to foreign participation in local R&D, namely to benefit from agglomeration externalities (as described earlier in the introduction). However, in some cases these positive spillover effects can be outweighed by negative congestion factors. If a local innovative system is dominated by a single major player or strong leader company then this leader may exercise a forceful gravitational pull on the best resources, implying a particular kind of congestion effect for any other entrant. There may also be more active competitive deterrence and policies on the part of other local actors that favor a local champion in such cases (Cantwell/ Kosmopoulou 2002, Cantwell/Piscitello 2004). As we have already noted, the Swiss innovation system is dominated by a few very large firms and such crowding out effects might seem plausible, particularly in the chemicals and metals industries, in which the observed patterns are consistent with that argument. At the same time, foreign-owned research effort has come into Switzerland to participate in the development of engineering and instrument technologies in which Switzerland has substantial local capabilities, even if not in the development of the primary technological fields of the strongest indigenous industries (namely chemicals and pharmaceuticals).

As we have noted above, the activities of large firms interact with the wider national system of innovation in a country, and so the general development on the national level may offer some explanation of the reduced attractiveness of Switzerland for foreign-owned R&D as well. The private sector accounted for almost 74% of national R&D spending in 2000, while government spending accounted for only 1% (BBW 2004). Compared to other countries the public involvement is amongst the lowest, and the overall spending on R&D has remained stagnant since 1990 compared to the generally rising trend observed in other leading OECD countries (BBW 2002). As a reaction to these developments, the Swiss government acknowledges the need to increase its support for the innovation system, has made education, research and technology into top political priorities, and has set up a plan for the years 2004–2007 to increase research spending and bolster Swiss competitiveness (BBW 2002). It is possible that the low level of the public support element of Swiss research has contributed to a lessening attractiveness of Switzerland as a potential location for foreign-owned R&D at a time when science-technology (university-industry) linkages have become increasingly critical, in addition to the other factors discussed above.

References

Archibugi, D./Pianta, M., Specialisation and Size of Technological Activities in Industrial Countries: The Analysis of Patent Data, *Research Policy*, 21, 1, 1992, pp. 79–93.
Audretsch, D. B./Feldman, M. P., Innovative Clusters and the Industry Life Cycle, *Review of Industrial Organization*, 11, 1996, pp. 253–273.
Baptista, R./Swann, G. M. P., Do Firms in Clusters Innovate More?, *Research Policy*, 27, 1998, pp. 525–540.
Bartlet, C./Ghoshal, S., *Managing Across Borders: The Transnational Solution*, Boston: Harvard Business School Press 1989.
BBW, *Education, Research, and Technology: Promoting Investment in Switzerland's Excellence*, Bern 2002, http://www.bbw.admin.ch/html/pages/bft/2002/bft-e.html.
BBW, *Statistics on R&D. 2004*, http://www.statistik.admin.ch/stat_ch/ber15/indic_st/ind20202d_210_synth.htm.
Blau, J., Collaboration, Cost-cutting Take Hold at European Chemical and Drug Companies, *Research Technology Management*, 38, 4, 1995, pp. 2–4.
Borner, S., *Internationalization of Industry: An Assessment in the Light of a Small Open Economy (Switzerland)*, Berlin: Springer-Verlag 1986.
Cantwell, J. A., *Technological Innovation and Multinational Corporations*, Oxford: Basil Blackwell 1989.
Cantwell, J. A., The International Agglomeration of R&D, in Casson, M. C. (ed.), *Global Research Strategy and International Competitiveness*, Oxford: Basil Blackwell 1991, pp. 104–132.
Cantwell, J. A., The Internationalisation of Technological Activity and its Implications for Competitiveness, in Granstrand, O./Håkanson, L./Sjölander, S. (eds.), *Technology Management and International Business: Internationalisation of R&D Technology*, Chichester: John Wiley&Sons 1992, pp. 117–135.
Cantwell, J. A., Corporate Technological Specialisation in International Industries, in Casson, M. C./Creedy, J. (eds.), *Economic Inequality and Industrial Concentration*, Aldershot: Edward Elgar 1993, pp. 216–232.
Cantwell, J. A., The Globalisation of Technology: What Remains of the Product Cycle Model?, *Cambridge Journal of Economics*, 19, 1, 1995, pp. 155–174.
Cantwell, J. A., Technological Lock-in of Large Firms Since the Interwar Period, *European Review of Economic History*, 4, 2, 2001, pp. 147–174.
Cantwell, J. A./Andersen, H. B., A Statistical Analysis of Corporate Technological Leadership Historically, *Economics of Innovation and New Technology*, 4, 3, 1996, pp. 211–234.
Cantwell, J. A./Barrera, M. P., The Localisation of Corporate Technological Trajectories in the Interwar Cartels: Cooperative Learning Versus an Exchange of Knowledge, *Economics of Innovation and New Technology*, 6, 2–3, 1998, pp. 257–290.
Cantwell, J. A./Harding, R., The Internationalisation of German Companies R&D, *National Institute Economic Review*, 163, 1998, pp. 99–115.
Cantwell, J. A./Hodson, C., Global R&D and UK Competitiveness, in Casson, M. C. (ed.), *Global Research Strategy and International Competitiveness*, Oxford: Basil Blackwell 1991, pp. 133–182.

Cantwell, J. A./Janne, O. E. M., The Internationalisation of Technological Activity: The Dutch Case, in van Hoesel, R./Narula, R. (ed.), *Multinational Enterprises from the Netherlands*, London: Routledge 1999a, pp. 84–137.
Cantwell, J. A./Janne, O. E. M., Technological Globalisation and Innovative Centres: The Role of Corporate Technological Leadership and Locational Hierarchy, *Research Policy*, 28, 2–3, 1999b, pp. 119–144.
Cantwell, J. A./Kosmopoulou, E., What Determines the Internationalisation of Corporate Technology?, in Havila, V./Forsgren, M./Håkanson, H. (eds.), *Critical Perspectives on Internationalization*, Oxford: Pergamon 2002, pp. 305–334.
Cantwell, J. A./Kotecha, U., The Internationalisation of Technological Activity: The French Evidence in a Comparative Setting, in Howells, J./Michie, J. (eds.), *Technology, Innovation and Competitiveness*, Aldershot: Edward Elgar 1997, pp. 126–173.
Cantwell, J. A./Piscitello, L., Accumulating Technological Competence – Its Changing Impact on Corporate Diversification and Internationalization, *Industrial and Corporate Change*, 9, 1, 2000, pp. 21–51.
Cantwell, J. A./Piscitello, L., The Recent Location of Foreign-owned R&D Activities by Large MNCs in the European Regions: The Role of Spillovers and Externalities, *Regional Studies*, 38, 2004, forthcoming.
Cantwell, J. A./Santangelo, G. D., Capitalism, Profits and Innovation in the New Techno-economic Paradigm, *Journal of Evolutionary Economics*, 10, 1–2, 2000, pp. 131–157.
Dosi, G., The Nature of the Innovative Process, in Dosi, G./Freeman, C./Nelson, R./Silverberg G./Soete L. L. G. (eds.), *Technical Change and Economic Theory*, London: Frances Pinter Publishers 1988, pp. 221–238.
Dunning, J. D., *Multinational Enterprises and the Global Economy*, Chichester: Addison-Wesley 1993.
Dunning, J. D./Pearce, R. D., *The World's Largest Industrial Enterprises, 1962–1983*, Franborough: Gower 1985.
Duysters, G./Hagedoorn, J., Internationalization through Strategic Technology Partnering: The Role of Multinationals in the Netherlands, in Van Den Bulcke, D./Verbeke A. (eds.), *Globalization and the Small Open Economy*, Cheltenham, UK and Northampton, MA, USA: Edward Elgar 2001, pp. 113–126.
Feldman, M. P., An Examination of the Geography of Innovation, *Industrial and Corporate Change*, 2, 3, 1993, pp. 451–470.
Freeman, C., The National System of Innovation in Historical Perspective, *Cambridge Journal of Economics*, 19, 1, 1995, pp. 5–24.
Griliches, Z., Patent Statistics as Economic Indicators: A Survey, *Journal of Economic Literature*, 28, 4, 1990, pp. 1661–1707.
Howells, J./Michie, J., Technological Competitiveness in an International Arena, in Howells, J./Michie, J. (eds.), *Technology, Innovation and Competitiveness*, Aldershot: Edward Elgar 1997, pp. 222–228.
Katzenstein, P. J., *Small States in World Markets: Industrial Policy in Europe*, Ithaca: Cornell University Press 1985.
Kogut, B./Chang, S. J., Technological Capabilities and Japanese Foreign Direct Investment in the United States, *Review of Economics and Statistics*, 73, 1991, pp. 401–413.
Lundvall, B. A., Innovation as an Interactive Process: From User-producer Interaction to the National System of Innovation, in Dosi, G./Freeman, C./Nelson, R./Silverberg G./Soete L. L. G. (eds.), *Technical Change and Economic Theory*, London: Frances Pinter 1988, pp. 349–369.
Macharzina, K., Innovationsdynamik der Globalisierung, in Peske, Th./Schrank, R. (eds.), *Strategie, Innovation und Internationalisierung*, Köln: EUL Verlag 2003, pp. 305–311.
Macharzina, K./Engelhard, J., Paradigm Shift in International Business Research. From Partist and Eclectic Approaches to the GAINS Paradigm, *Management International Review*, 31, Special Issue 1991, pp. 23–43.
Mariotti, S./Piscitello, L., The Role of Territorial Externalities in Affecting Internationalisation of Production by SMEs, *Entrepreneurship and Regional Development*, 13, 2001, pp. 65–80.
Patel, P./Pavitt, K. L. R., Large Firms in the Production of the World's Technology: An Important Case of "Non-globalisation", *Journal of International Business Studies*, 22, 1, 1991, pp. 1–21.

Pavitt, K. L. R., Uses and Abuses of Patent Statistics, in van Raan, A. (ed.), *Handbook of Quantitative Studies of Science and Technology*, Amsterdam: North Holland 1988, pp. 504–536.
Pavitt, K. L. R./Robson, M./Townsend, J., Technological Accumulation, Diversification and Organisation in UK Companies, 1945–1983, *Management Science*, 35, 1, 1989, pp. 1–19.
Pearce, R. D., *The Internationalisation of Research and Development by Multinational Enterprises*, London: McMillan 1989.
Pearce, R. D./Singh, S., *Globalizing Research and Development*, London: MacMillan 1992.
Torrisi, S./Granstrand, O., Technological and Business Diversification: A Survey of Theories and Empirical Evidence, in Cantwell, J. A./Gambardella A./Granstrand O. (eds.), *The Economics and Management of Technological Diversification*, New York: Routledge 2004, forthcoming.
Vertova, G., Stability in National Patterns of Technological Specialisation: Some Historical Evidence from Patent Data, *Economics of Innovation and New Technology*, 8, 1999, pp. 331–354.
Zander, I., The Formation of International Innovation Networks in the Multinational Corporation: An Evolutionary Perspective, *Industrial and Corporate Change*, 11, 2, 2002, pp. 327–353.

Marian Beise/Hans Georg Gemünden

Lead Markets: A New Framework for the International Diffusion of Innovation

Abstract

- This article attempts to explain why countries lead the international diffusion of specific innovations.

- It can often be observed that the global diffusion of innovations can be characterised by the competition of several innovation designs, each favoured by a different country, and that finally one becomes the globally dominant design. Lead markets are national or regional markets that are first to adopt a global dominant design of an innovation.

- It is suggested that the demand side can play a decisive role for the international competitiveness of the companies of a country and not only their technological competencies.

- This article presents a framework for country-specific factors on the market side that are responsible for the global success of innovations.

Key Results

- In analysing several globally successful innovations, we find a number of mechanisms why innovations that are favoured by a country become successful worldwide. We present attributes of the national market grouped into a system of five lead market advantages that render a country a lead market.

- It is suggested that a company that is eager to develop internationally standardised innovations can leverage the lead market role of a country by responding to the users in the lead market for each innovation project. If an innovation design is successful in the lead market it can be commercialised world wide.

Authors

Dr. Marian Beise, Researcher, Research Institute for Economics and Business Administration, University of Kobe, Kobe, Japan.
Hans Georg Gemünden, Professor of Production Management, Faculty of Business and Management, Technical University of Berlin, Berlin, Germany.

Marian Beise/Hans Georg Gemünden

Introduction

One of the most valuable assets of a multinational company is an internationally successful innovation. However, most innovations emerge in response to local markets. Research on user-producer relationships in the innovation process has shown that domestic demand gives local firms an advantage over foreign firms in perceiving local demand preferences and developing innovations because user-producer interaction are more efficient within countries.[1] But local demand for innovations and efficient interactions between domestic users and producers do not always lead to export success. A firm normally faces a variety of demand preferences and market contexts from country to country that hampers the development of an internationally standardised product or process. Despite the apparent homogenisation of world demand, the difficulties experienced by multinational firms in developing globally standardised innovations demonstrates that demand preferences still vary from country to country when new technologies and innovations are introduced (see e.g., Kotabe/Helsen 1998, Bartlett/Ghoshal 1995). This article discusses the success factors of the international diffusion of innovation designs, in particular the question of why a local market context supports the adoption of domestic innovations in foreign countries.

Over time, various scholars have suggested strategies of how to develop a global innovation (e.g. Keegan 1969, Livingstone 1989, Takeuchi/Nonaka 1986). Based on our analysis we follow the approach suggested by Bartlett and Ghoshal (1990). Firms can harness the forces that drive the global diffusion of an innovation in order to develop internationally standardised innovations. Central to this strategy is the observation that the adoption of most globally successful innovations starts in one country or region, the lead market. In concentrating customer interaction on this market, a company can increase the chances for its innovations to be successful internationally.

The International Diffusion of Innovation

National preferences for particular specifications of an innovation vary because of different economic, social, cultural and environmental conditions. These international differences result in the emergence of a variety of nation-specific innovation designs when firms respond to local market preferences.[2] Nation-specific standards also emerge when there are strong local externalities of adoption.[3] In contrast to strong incentives for localisation of innovation designs, one can observe that many innovation designs became internationally successful after they have been preferred and adopted by a single country. For instance, the mass market for cellular mobile telephony emerged in the Nordic countries before a joint-European cellular system became the world standard in mobile telephony (Beise 2001). The internet is today embraced by all countries in the world [originally adopted in the US.] The United States are also leading the usage of PCs and as a result, the IBM-Microsoft-Intel specification prevailed on the world market as the global dominant design of personal computers. Many innovations in the automobile industry such as the anti locking brake, the airbag and the high pressure diesel direct injection became international standard equipment after they were adopted widely in Germany.

As a rule, an innovation is normally accepted by countries at different points in time. The ranking of countries by penetration rate is often preserved over a long time during the whole diffusion cycle. The frequently observed pattern of the international diffusion of an innovation by country is depicted by Figure 1. The country that first adopts an innovation can be called a lead market, those that follow are lag markets.

Several studies have either tried to explain the lag between countries or discuss the effect of the lag on the shape of the diffusion curve.[4] Most studies interpret the ranking of countries by time to adoption as the *innovativeness*[5] of a country (e.g. Lee 1990, Dekimpe et al. 2000b, Albach et al 1989). Yet, Porter (1990) finds that country demand for innovations can be idiosyncratic or antici-

Figure 1. An International Diffusion Pattern of an Innovation Design

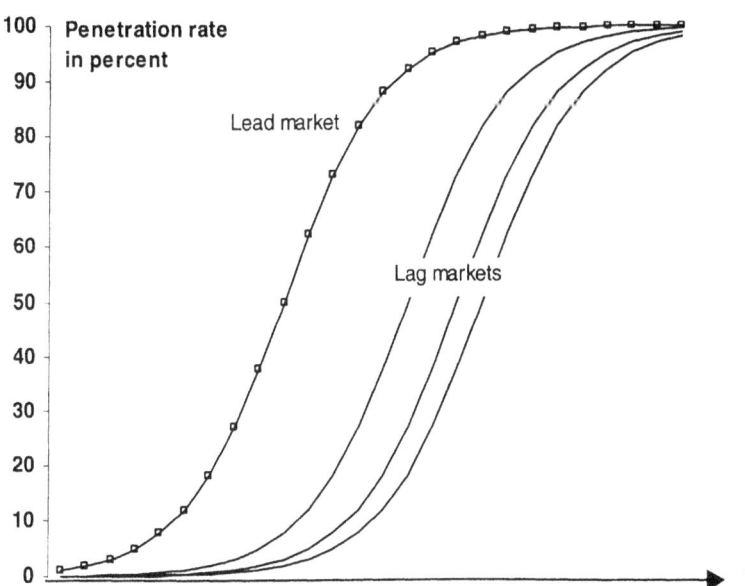

patory. Demand is idiosyncratic if users prefer innovation designs that will not be demanded in other countries, while countries with anticipatory demand prefer innovation designs which are subsequently demanded worldwide. Countries can be defined as *idiosyncratically innovative* if they adopt new ideas early which no other country ever finds worthy of adopting. We suggest that this distinction is more important than the innovativeness of national demand. Often, lag markets have adopted a different design of an innovation before the lead market, but later switch to the lead market design to their own nation-specific designs. Nation-specific designs compete against each other on the world market, since there are often worldwide standardisation advantages as well as changes in the market context that make specific designs more advantageous over time. Finally, as happened in many cases, a global dominant design[6] emerges as most countries choose the lead market design or switch from the initially preferred design to the lead market design. Including rivalry among national innovation designs, Figure 2 exhibits the extended model of the international diffusion of an innovation design. If only the innovation design B is observed, the pattern of Figure 1 is derived. In Figure 2, the lag market adopts a different innovation design A even before the lead market adopts the design B, but later switches to B, which becomes the globally dominant design.

The lead market is not the country that first adopts any innovation design, but the country that first adopts an innovation design that becomes adopted by other

Figure 2. International Diffusion Patterns of Competing Innovation Designs

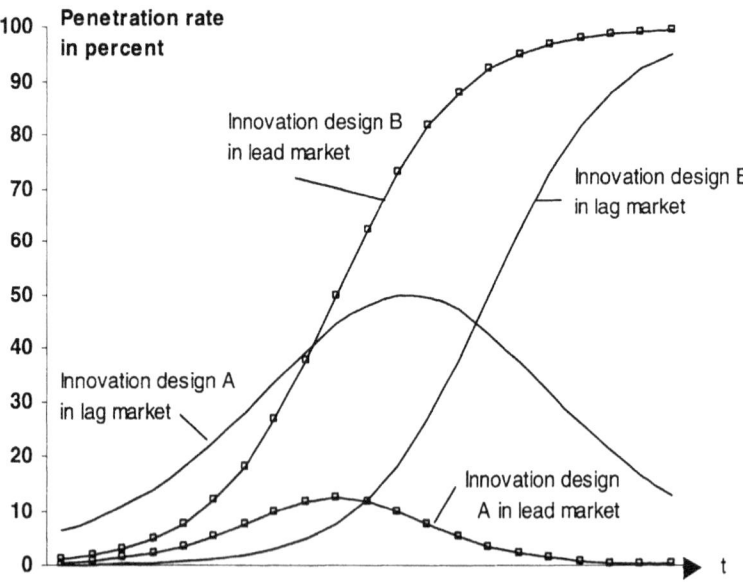

countries as well. A cellular mobile telephone system was adopted in Japan as early as in 1979, but neither the Japanese system nor their handphones were accepted in other countries. In France, an online system, called Minitel was tremendously successful before most people in the US have heard of the Internet, but it was never accepted outside France. As well, a variety of PC standards competed until the IBM compatible PC began to dominate. Likewise, the international adoption pattern is not determined by the pattern of scientific and technological inventions. It is often observable that the innovation was invented and designed in one country, but first accepted in another country from where it spread to other countries. In all examples mentioned so far there were no technology gaps between the United States, Europe and Japan before the diffusion of the innovation took off.[7]

We suggest that anticipatory innovativeness of a country is constituted by nation-specific attributes of the local market and not by scientific or technical discoveries, the decisions of firms or by chance. We will discuss these attributes based on theoretical models. Examples will illustrate each of our arguments. We have studied the observed pattern of diffusion for many internationally successful products and processes. In this article, the facsimile machine shall be given as the main example.

Figure 3. The International Diffusion of the Facsimile Machine

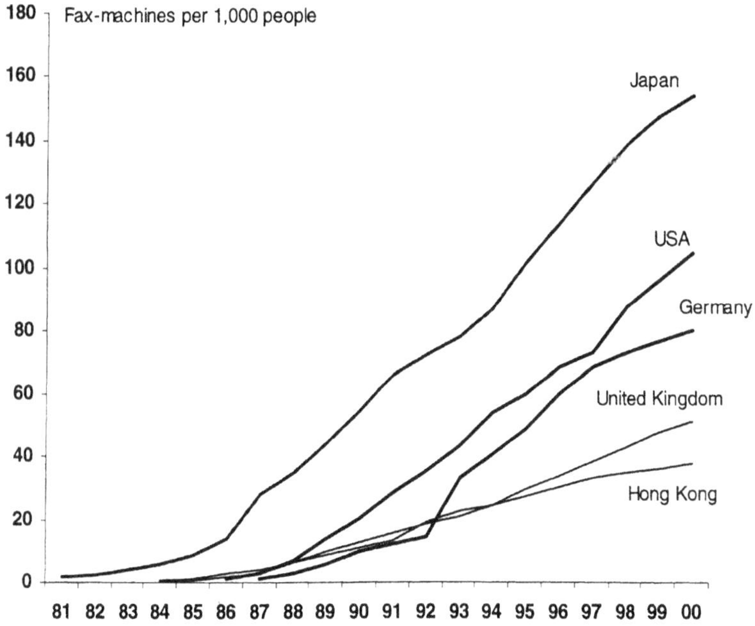

Source: ITU

In the history of the facsimile machine the diffusion pattern of a lead market is clearly visible (Figure 3). The fax machine was a failure in the US and Europe until it was adapted to the Japanese market. The fax machine was invented in principal in 1843 and in 1924 AT&T presented the first prototype of an electric telephotography device. Since then the machine has been improved continuously by firms in many advanced countries such as Siemens of Germany. However, the fax machine remained stuck in niche applications until a mass market emerged in Japan in the early 1980s (Peterson 1995, Coopersmith 1993). Yet, once the fax machine was widely used in Japan, it spread over to the United States and to Europe within a few years. Previously, a competing technology like the teletypewriter or telex was favoured by European and US users. This market preference had the effect that most companies in Europe and the US focussed on developing the teletypewriter and abandoned the fax technology. Yet, although the teletypewriter was superior to the fax machine it was later referred to minor applications. Today, the fax machine is seen worldwide as an indispensable means of text communication. Figure 4 magnifies the diffusion process of the fax machine in Germany and Japan and exhibits the effect the success of the facsimile had on the rivalling teletypewriter in Germany: it squeezed out the telex system within few years.

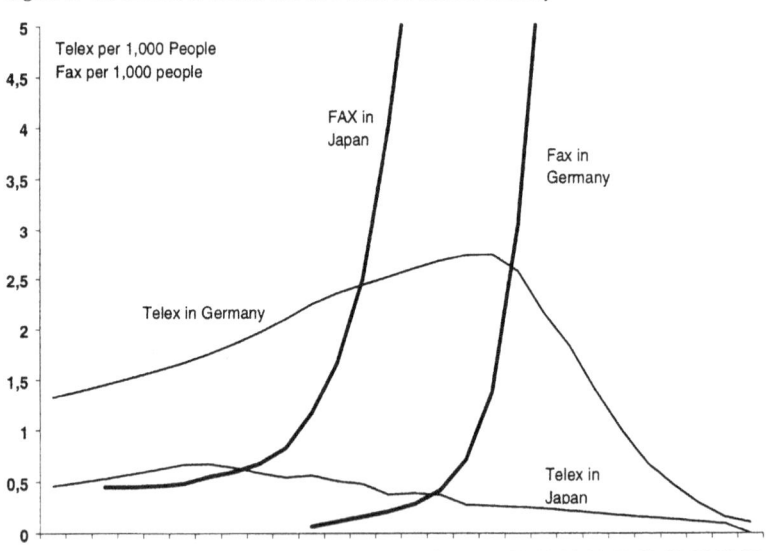

Figure 4. The Success of the Fax and the Demise of Telex in Germany

Source: Estimations based on Scherer (1992), Yoffie (1997), ITU

The Origins of the Lead Market Role of Nations

Why do innovation designs spread to other national markets although the same design failed in these countries before? Bartlett and Ghoshal (1990) suggest that lead markets exist, because "local innovations in such markets become useful elsewhere as the environmental characteristics that stimulated such innovations diffuse to other locations" (Bartlett/Ghoshal 1990, p. 243). Other authors have concluded that nation-specific attributes can support the lead market role of a nation (Takeuchi/Porter 1986, Johansson, Roehl 1994, Gerybadze et al. 1997). The lead market hypothesis should therefore be defined as:

There are nation-specific demand and market conditions (market context) that increase the possibility that an innovation design that is favoured locally is subsequently adopted in other countries as well.

The national market context is defined here as the sources of stimuli for the adoption of an innovation design. We assume that lead markets do not exist because an innovation just happened to be first available in a country. Local availability of an innovation depends on market side factors such as profitability, demand articulation and local competition as well (Griliches 1957). The initial regional bias of adoption is caused by internationally varying adoption stimuli. For example, users in one country adopt an innovation design first because they have a higher benefit from adopting an innovation design than users in other countries, which often initially prefer a different innovation design. The stimuli for the adoption of innovations include demand preferences formed by tastes and environmental conditions, the budgets of possible adopters, the relative prices of innovation designs and prices of complementary goods and local externalities. In order to follow the country that first adopted the design, the stimuli for adopting the same innovation design must increase in other countries. We have assigned all nation-specific attributes for the lead market role into five groups of lead market advantages, which we will now discuss in detail.

Demand Advantage

A national demand advantage results from a global trend in which specific innovations become increasingly beneficial or preferable worldwide. Changes in the market context result in new needs and this induces innovation. Countries at the forefront of an international trend are lead markets for innovations that are induced by the trend. This anticipatory demand is a feature of international competitiveness mentioned by Porter (1990, p. 91) and it is the main argument for lead users suggested by von Hippel (1986). To avoid misinterpretation we define a trend independent from the actual adoption in the lead market. The case in which firms of one country actively influence foreign user or "transfer" domestic needs abroad will be defined as *transfer advantage* below.

The most influential trend until the 1970s was the rise of per-capita-income. The international product-life-cycle suggests that many commercially successful innovations were developed in the United States because the per-capita-income in the United States was the highest in the world and the rising middle class established the demand for convenience products (Vernon 1966, Franko 1976). As other countries caught up and reached the previous levels of per-capita-income of the US, demand for the same new products emerged in these markets as well. In general, the wealth of a nation has frequently been empirically proven to have a positive effect on the rate and time of adoption (see the literature review by Dekimpe et al. 2000b). Although the convergence between many industrialised countries has left very small differences in per-capita-income, the income of certain user groups can still considerably vary between countries, for example, the disposable income of young persons, the elderly, the unemployed, the wealthy, women and chronically ill persons.

However, more relevant are trends within the technological, economical, social and environmental contexts. For instance, population growth or the increase of population density in cities are global trends and affect some countries earlier than others. Population density problems occur in highly populated regions early and foreshadow a global problem. Demand for innovations that ease problems caused by high population density, such as traffic congestion and the high cost of real estate is greatest in highly populated regions. Other global trends that occur in certain countries first are the cost of environmental pollution, an increase in life expectancy and thus in the number of elderly people, individual mobility, and information needs and the number of diseases caused by civilisation. Global trends can be consumer trends or mere fads as well. For instance, there are global trends towards fat-free food, high quality pet food (Cvar 1986) or herbal extracts in shampoos. Personal computers are suggested to have been induced by individualism, a social trend which the US leads (Freiberger/Swain 1984).

The availability of collateral assets can be a trend as well that constitutes a lead market. The benefit of an innovation design is highest in the country that offers the largest stock of collateral assets. The innovation is therefore more likely to be adopted in the country with the largest collateral asset stock. If other countries increase their stock of collateral assets over time to the same level, the innovation adopted more widely there as well. A new motor vehicle design, for example an electric vehicle or a car powered by hydrogen, requires a network of recharge stations. As these networks are created the benefit of the new vehicle design increases. Easy access to and the variety of videocassettes for VCRs together with new content such as aerobics were responsible for the diffusion of

VCRs in the United States (Rosenbloom/Cusamano 1987). As videocassettes became available in other countries through the creation of a retail infrastructure, the benefit of VCRs increased there too. Purchases via the internet are facilitated by the use of credit cards. Countries in which credit cards are more common have a lead in the adoption of e-commerce services over other countries in which credit cards are slowly taking off.

Price Advantage

When different designs compete on the world market, a design that becomes relatively cheaper compared to other designs can become the globally dominant design. This price mechanism is the centrepiece of Levitt's (1983) globalisation hypothesis, in which the consumers in foreign markets "capitulate" to the attraction of lower prices of foreign products and abandon their initial endowments of domestic goods. Countries can gain a price advantage when the relative price of the nationally preferred innovation design decreases so that differences in demand preference to foreign countries can be compensated. In Tilton's (1971) study of the semiconductor industry, the large cost reduction of semiconductor devices proved to be the main driver of the internationalisation. Price reductions are mainly due to cost reductions based on static and dynamic economies-of-scale and decreases in the prices of input factors. Nation-specific factors of economies-of-scale are market size and market growth. Another price advantage results from price changes of input factors and goods complementary to the innovation design that anticipate global price changes.

Size of Demand

The size of the home market at an early stage of the technology cycle provides the basis for economies-of-scale in production and early amortisation of large R&D investments. For instance, the large Japanese market for facsimile machines made it easier for Japanese producers to exploit static and dynamic economies-of-scale (Scherer 1992, p. 101). The cost of machines dropped thirty-fold from 1980 until 1992 (Coopersmith 1993, p. 48). Only when the fax machine became available at a low price, did other countries follow in its adoption (Figure 5). A sufficiently large domestic market enables innovations to be profitable for specialised high-tech products with few applications (Kravis/Lipsey 1971). The country with the largest demand is not always the largest country. The customer industry can be large in a small country, e.g. the watch industry in Switzerland. The size of the segment of the population for which the good is designed can vary internationally, for instance the age structure of a population.

Figure 5. The Price of the Fax Machine and Global Adoption

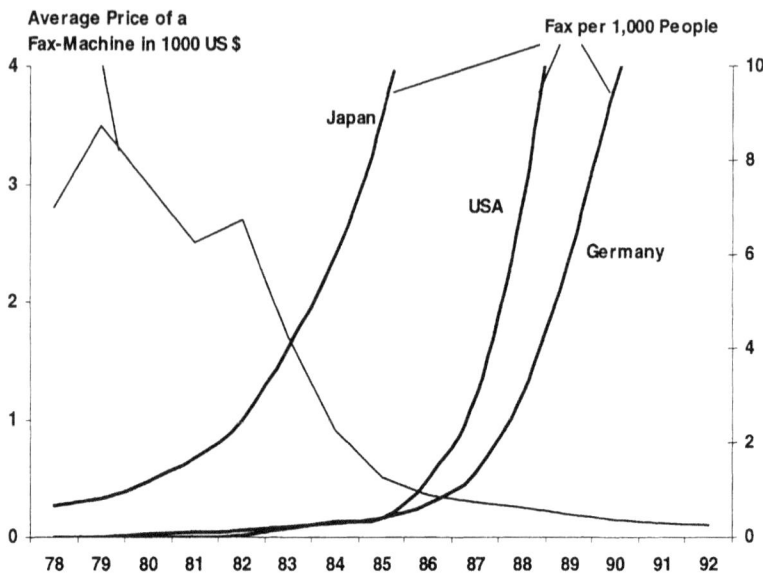

Source: Prices: Economides, Himmerlberg (1995), penetration: ITU

Finally, a mass market can emerge in a small country and exceed the market in a large country where the innovation is still refined to a niche. For instance the cellular mobile telephony markets in Finland and Sweden in the beginning of the 1980s were the largest in the world. For many electronic applications such as digital cameras or flat panel TV sets, the Japanese market is the largest for the long introduction period in which manufacturing capacity is being built up before the US becomes the biggest market.

The price reduction of an innovation design can also result from the falling prices of complementary goods. The adoption of an innovation in one country can drive down the cost of complementary goods and make the usage of the innovation cheaper without price changes of the core good.

Anticipatory Factor Costs

The second price advantage is the price lead effect: prices of innovation designs converge to the price pattern initially present in the lead market. The most important reason for the price lead advantages is a time lag in global changes of factor prices of input factors of production of a technological design or for the use of a good such as the fuel to power a vehicle. Different degrees of domestic competition can cause internationally varying prices as well (see below). When global changes in factor prices first occur in one country, the country "anticipates" global price trends. According to the induced innovation theory, factor changes induce new products and processes that economise the factor that became relatively more expensive or use more of the factor that became relatively cheaper. A lead market is often the country where an innovation is cheaper in the introduction period. When its price falls in other countries demand picks up there as well. For instance, from the 1980s on handphones and mobile calls were already sufficiently cheap in the Nordic countries to enable a mass market, long before telecom liberation pushed prices in other countries down to same low levels (see Beise 2001).

Transfer Advantage

The adoption of an innovation design in one country can influence the adoption decisions of users in other countries when the perceived benefit of the design that was adopted in the lead market increases for users in other countries. For instance the perceived benefit increases when information on the usability of the innovation design is made available. Therefore a country has a transfer advantage if its market context increases the perceived benefit of a nationally preferred innovation design for users in foreign countries. There are several mechanisms for this effect.

The International Demonstration Effect

An innovation is associated with uncertainty about the usefulness of the innovation and a risk of failure. The adoption of an innovation design in one country increases awareness and reduces the uncertainty surrounding new innovation designs. This "demonstration effect" (Mansfield 1968) has been suggested as the main driver of diffusion of innovation.

The reduction of uncertainty about the benefit of a new technology has been identified as a factor leading to a dominant design (Cowan 1991). Uncertainty and risk is lowered the more users adopt the innovation and prove its benefit and reliability. In the international context, the choice of the proven foreign technology would be rational even if the foreign design does not fit the domestic context as much as a domestic technology. A tested foreign design becomes preferred against an untested design that better suits the local context, but for which the benefit is uncertain. Reliability of a design can therefore compensate for initial international differences in preferences.

As a result, the international diffusion of innovations depends on the intensity of communication between countries (Takada/Jain 1991). If several countries adopt different innovation designs at the same time, a higher international observability of a country's adoption is therefore a lead market attribute. For instance, a country that is intensively covered by mass media or whose lifestyles are often present in television series and motion pictures is more liesely to be followed by users in other coutries.[8]

The uncertainty reduction behaviour of lag countries is especially relevant when the risk and complexity of a new technology is high. The light-water nuclear reactor, which was favoured in the US because of its defence applications, prevailed in many other countries despite the fact that more experimental designs are theoretically superior (Cowan 1990).

Global Externalities

The benefit of many innovation designs increases with the number of adopters. Externalities generated by the adoption process of an innovation design are normally strong within countries. These local externalities often lead to nation-specific standards and the lock-in of a country to a national – and often idiosyncratic – innovation design. A national transfer advantage is gained when the diffusion process in a country generates global externalities. Global externalities, however, were hardly ever apparent in the cases we have studied so far. For instance the adoption of the facsimile machine by users in Japan did not increase the benefit of a facsimile machine for a potential adopter in Europe or the US. Only in the case of the internet, did global externalities play a role in its global success over the French Minitel system. In cases in which language is a central product feature (internet, software, entertainment), English speaking countries have an lead market advantage, because English is the most commandly spoken language around the world.

Proprietary Technologies and Governmented Support

Property rigths are often detrimental to the international diffusion of an innovation design. First of all, non-proprietary standards can be imitated by other firms and therefore disseminated broader (Anderson/Tushman 1990). Second, proprietary standards are expected to improve less over time than non-proprietary or "open" designs. Open designs can easily be improved by many other producers and users, not only by the firm that owns the property rights of a design. Third, the willingness to adopt a foreign design often decreases with an increasing degree of private ownership of the technology. Governmental institutions are often reluctant to support a standard that is seen as the property of foreign firms. Public subsidies are often interpreted as international rent-shifting behaviour of governments (Brander/Spencer 1985). For instance, for a long time the Franco-German relationship was marked by the choice of different national standards (colour televisions, trains, nuclear reactor types) because of a mutual reluctance to choose the standards of the other country. One of the advantages of the European cellular mobile telephone system, GSM, is that it is a non-proprietary standard. A country has a transfer advantage if it prefers a design that is more non-proprietary in character or that is not backed by one government alone. Countries that prefer to adopt designs that are standardised by international standardisation bodies or intergovernmental agreements gain a transfer advantage.

Multinational Firms and Mobile Users

Multinational firms often transfer products and technologies abroad through massive worldwide marketing investments and internal technology transfers. Multinational firms are regarded as *cross-cultural change agents* (Fayerweather 1969, p. 216). Their large marketing investments often have the purpose of changing consumption patterns in order to establish a standardised product in foreign countries. Multinational firms support the diffusion of industrial products as well, because they have an incentive to employ the same components and other input factors in foreign affiliates. Multinational firms can exploit economies-of-scale by using the same input factors and processes worldwide. For instance, using the same software is necessary for an internal communication network and the exchange of standardised corporate information. In addition, multinational firms train local employees to represent a coherent firm philosophy (Kreutzer 1989, p. 47) often reflecting the home market preference context (e.g., a preference for quality, reliability, individualism). A country therefore has a transfer advantage if it is the home country of many multinational firms. On the contrary, a country is disadvantaged if it is predominantly a host country for multinational firms.

Not only do multinational firms transfer preferences abroad, but also mobile users. Mobile buyers who travel extensively to other countries, such as businessmen, tourists and military personnel, can transfer their home-specific demand to foreign countries (Porter 1990, Douglas/Wind 1987) and initiate the adoption by domestic users. Examples are business hotels, credit cards or the McDonald's restaurant chain which often targeted US American tourists and military personnel when it entered a foreign country.

Export Advantage

Firms in a country have an advantage over foreign competitors of other countries if their innovations can easily be exported. Innovations can be exported more easily if the environment and market conditions of foreign countries are similar to the market the innovation was designed for. Dekimpe et al. (2000a) support the hypothesis already suggested by Vernon (1979) that the higher the similarity of cultural, social and economic factors between two countries, the greater the likelihood that an innovation design adopted by one of two countries will be adopted by the other country as well.

In addition, expert are supported, if features are included in an innovation design that make the design suitable for a variety of environments.

Therefore a country constitutes a lead market if it lies in the middle within the variety of country preferences or the market context pressures domestic firms to develop innovation designs that are exportable.

With these "dual-use" or "robust" innovation designs[9] a firm can catch up with a foreign firms' innovations in their home markets at an early stage to preempt the international competition of nation-specific technologies.

The pressure for including foreign preferences can directly come from suppliers and customers even if a local idiosyncratic version would technically fit their own environment better. Customers, for instance, gain from exports of their suppliers through lower prices or because it increases their own exports. Suppliers of components can also profit from the export orientation of product manufacturers through own exports. Furthermore, exporting customers have knowledge about the requirements for components of global products. An export intensive industry in a country therefore increases the export success of its suppliers.[10] A strong world-market orientation of firms often derives from the small home market which does not suffice in amortising the investment in R&D and is therefore more export oriented (Walsh 1988). This is the case, for instance, for Swiss, Dutch and Swedish firms.[11]

Furthermore, exportability of innovation can be triggered by domestic demand that is sensitive to the problems and needs of foreign countries. Even if the domestic environment is not at the front of a global trend, domestic users can be more sensitive to global problems and needs than potential adopters in countries where the problem is more advanced. This sensitivity of demand can push domestic firms into a global perspective and increase its ability to meet global problems before firms in other countries. For instance, consumers in a country can be sensitive to the effects of worldwide climatic change even if their domestic environment is not affected as much as in other countries. Other examples are wildlife protection (e.g. fur), deforestation in the tropics (e.g. wood products) and pollution of raw material extraction.[12]

Market Structure Advantage

The last attribute of a lead market is a high degree of competition. Competition and entrepreneurial effort is one of the main determinants of international patterns of innovations from Posner (1961) to Dosi et al. (1990). A competitive market is characterised by more and a higher variety of innovation designs offered and tested in the market. Often, preferences are not perfectly known either because users are not aware of or do not effectively articulate their preferences. The high variety of innovation designs tested can lead to the selection of an innovation design that is superior to innovation designs that have been chosen in a less competitive market and therefore becomes the global dominant design even if preferences vary from country to country. In a less competitive market the initial selection of innovation designs may not reflect the local preferences when too few alternatives are offered in the market to uncover the latent preferences and determine the locally most beneficial design. A country with more local competitors or tougher competition is therefore more likely to find a design that is more beneficial to users in other countries as well.

A high degree of competition is marked by a high number of competitors or low barriers to entry. Low barriers to entry are especially essential for lead markets because new products and technologies are frequently brought about by new firms (see e.g., Audretsch 1995). Because of this openness new firms can enter the market and test the reception of new designs by users. This makes the process of finding the best product design, i.e. the product that is most profitable for the users, by means of search and selection more efficient.

In addition, a high number of independent buyers, together with an early saturation of a market, urges a reduction of prices and an improvement in product performance (Porter 1990). This gives buyers an incentive to replace an old product with the new version. Competition drives costs down and makes a new technology more competitive in replacing the old technologies. The liberalisation of the communication equipment market in Japan initiated intense competition among Japanese companies and caused the cost of fax machines to decrease (Coopersmith 1993). The United States lead in express package transportation was supported by its lead in the deregulation of the heavily regulated postal sector. Deregulation of air cargo and interstate trucking in 1980 led to new carriers, increased competition and lowered prices and as a result US express carriers dominat the world market in share and technology employed (Council on Competitiveness 1998, p. 116).

Discussion

We have argued in this article that the international diffusion of innovation often follows a lead market pattern and that the reason why a country leads the world in adopting a specific innovation design is not initially based on a technological knowledge lead but originates from nation-specific attributes of the local market. The importance of national market conditions as a competitive advantage of nations is based on three hypotheses: (1) innovation designs are nation-specific when market contexts vary from country to country, (2) nation-specific demand and the national market context needs can be perceived more efficiently by domestic firms and (3) particular characteristics of a nation's market context increase the probability that innovation designs that are initially adopted in this country are adopted worldwide. We have presented several internationalisation mechanisms that can be responsible for the worldwide spread of a specific innovation design adopted in one country first. It does not imply that a lead market pattern exists for each innovation that becomes internationally successful. A regionally unbiased diffusion of innovation is possible when market contexts do not vary considerably. On the other hand, when market contexts vary so much that they cannot be compensated by the internationalisation mechanisms different region-specific innovation designs can prevail for a long time.

Lead markets can be utilised for the development of global innovation designs. Once a specific innovation design has been adopted by users in the lead market chances are that it subsequently becomes adopted by users in other countries as well. By focusing on the design of the innovation which is preferred within the lead market, a company can leverage a success experienced in the lead market for a global market launch. In order to follow a lead market strategy of new product development, however, it is necessary to assess the lead market potential of countries before an innovation is developed and tested in the market. In a related paper Beise and Cleff (2003) suggest a methodology for estimating the lead market potential of countries for a new innovation idea. Their method is based on a detailed list of possible nation-specific indicators that can constitute a lead market. The method for identifying potential lead markets has several steps. After a discussion on whether one can expect a lead market to exist at all, one must derive the lead market factors specific to the innovation project. Third, one must find quantitative indicators for the lead market factors for every country that could be a lead market. Fourth, the values of the indicators for each country are to be aggregated into a small set of factor values. Finally, the set of factor values leads to a ranking of countries according to their lead market potential. The prediction of lead markets is a matter of further research that can be of great interest for multinational firms that have the capacity to select an affiliate in a foreign country for developing and first market entry of a new innovation as well as for governments intending to promote the international competitiveness of the domestic economy.

Endnotes

1. The home market advantage of firms was first suggested by Linder (1961) and later refined by Lundvall (1988). In management science, customer interaction has been identified as one of the most important success factors of innovation, see e.g. Gemünden, Heydebreck and Herden (1992), Cooper and Kleinschmidt (1987), Gruner and Homburg (2000).
2. An innovation design is a specification or configuration of an innovation idea. Different designs of an innovation fulfil the same function with different technical features or technology (see Utterback 1994, p. 18). For instance, the facsimile machine and the teletypewriter are different innovation designs for a communication device transmitting written information. An IBM and an Apple computer are different designs of a personal computer. The GSM cellular telephone and pagers are different designs of mobile communication.
3. Local externalities are beneficial to adopters within a regional entity or within a specific user group only, such as friends, colleagues and relatives. In contrast, global externalities enhance the benefit for all potential users worldwide. In the presence of strong local externalities, countries are likely to adopt different innovation designs even if all other local conditions are equal. Models of technological adoption with local externalities such as Arthur (1989), David (1993), David, Foray and Dalle (1998) have demonstrated that regional islands of standardisation occur determined by random initial selections of innovation designs and small historical accidents. If all stimuli are equal among most countries and there are no local externalities an innovation would diffuse internationally in an interspersed pattern, the adopters are scattered geographically and no regional pattern would emerge.
4. For instance, Redmond (1994), Chen and Takada (1994) study the inter-regional variance of the pattern of diffusion, Helsen, Jedidi, and DeSarbo (1993) international differences of diffusion curve parameters. For studies that considered the national order of adoption see Gatignon et al. (1989), Dekimpe et al. (2000a), Poznanski (1983), Takada and Jain (1991), Antonelli (1986) Ihde (1996), Ganesh et al. (1997).
5. An appropriate definition of 'innovativeness' is "the degree to which an individual makes innovation decisions independently of the communicated experience of others" (Midgley/Dowling 1978, p. 235).
6. A dominant design is defined as a design that is adopted by a majority of users, a design that wins the "allegiance of the marketplace" (Utterback 1994, p. 24). A global dominant design is the design that is adopted by most countries, in contrast to national dominant designs, which are only widely adopted within a country.
7. For instance, the cellular mobile telephone system was not invented in the Nordic countries, the lead market, but in the US by Bell laboratories of AT&T. At the advent of the computer industry both the US and Europe had equal scientific competence (Bresnahan/Malerba 1999). The first personal computer was not invented in the United States but in France. The Boston computer museum officially declared the *Micral* the first microprocessor-based personal computer invented by the Vietnamese-born André Thi Truong in 1973 using a US processor chip, the Intel 8008 processor. The "personal" computer that followed were not technological superior innovations but assembled by hobbyists who started their own firm using electronic parts available for all firms (Freiberger/Swaine 1984). All computer firms around the world were certainly competent enough to have designed a personal computer at that time. Yet, the US-designs became an instant success with hobbyists and mass market users, attracting new firms to build mass-produced, consumer-friendly models.
8. Putsis et al. (1997) show that the number of cross-country communication ties are not equally distributed among nations and are not symmetrical. A case study presented by Nabseth and Ray (1974, p. 115) demonstrates that users get information on new innovations of a product domain from preferred countries. In the case study on special presses for the paper industry information flowed from the United States to Sweden, from Sweden to Germany and from Germany to Austria, resulting in a similar international rank of adoption.
9. The term "dual-use" is often used for products that are designed for the military but can be used in civil applications as well. Robust design is a term suggested by Urban and Hauser

(1993, p. 350) for design concepts that can be used for a variety of potential uses and under a variety of conditions. For instance, baking powder mix is a product that can be used under a variety of national environmental conditions (climate, oven temperatures, altitude).

10 For empirical evidence see Beise and Rammer (2003).

11 The argument of export orientation is similar to what Ohmae (1995) calls a port of entry: a region state that is shaped by the demands of the global economy and characterised by large export shares. A strong export orientation of local firms shapes the political, social and cultural system of a nation, the education of its engineers and managers, export competence of employment and its supporting institutions (governmental agencies). This shapes the firms' development activities towards innovations that are beneficial for users in foreign countries as well as for local users. These regions are also centres of a communications network between several large economies because firms that serve foreign markets "develop a high-level intelligence gathering capability in order to identify world trends in output, demand, market potential and scientific and technological constraints" (Walsh 1988, p. 53). The latter reverses the former argument – that other countries would subsequently adapt to the local demand preferences – and understands the lead market as a regional information centre of a global market's preferences.

12 An example of how this mechanism works is the boycott of Shell in Germany and other European countries to protest a plan to sink an oil platform in the North sea. Shell UK was persuaded by Shell Germany to abandon the plan (Scherler 1996, Hecker 1997). Shell has since strengthened its strategy to prevent environmental problems.

References

Albach, H./de Pay, D./Rojas, P., Der Innovationsprozeß bei kulturspezifisch unterschiedlich innovationsfreudigen Konsumenten, *Zeitschrift für Betriebswirtschaft, Ergänzungsheft*, 1, 1989, pp. 109–129.

Anderson, P./Tushman, M. L., Technological Discontinuities and Dominant Designs: A Cyclical Model of Technological Change, *Administrative Science Quarterly*, 35, December 1990, pp. 604–633.

Antonelli, Ch., The International Diffusion of New Information Technologies, *Research Policy*, 15, 1986, pp. 139–147.

Arthur, B., Competing Technologies, Increasing Returns and Lock-in by Historical Events, *Economic Journal*, 99, 1989, pp. 116–131.

Audretsch, D. B., *Innovation and Industry Evolution*, Cambridge: MIT Press 1995.

Bartlett, Ch. A./Ghoshal, S., Managing Innovation in the Transnational Corporation, in Bartlett, Ch./Doz, Y./Hedlund, G. (eds.), *Managing the Global Firm*, London/New York: Rontledge 1990, pp. 215–255.

Bartlett, Ch. A./Ghoshal, S., *Transnational Management: Texts, Cases and Readings in Cross-Border Management*, 2nd edition, Chicago: Irwin 1995.

Beise, M., *Lead Markets: Country-Specific Success Factors for the Global Diffusion of Innovations*, Heidelberg: Physica 2001.

Beise, M./Cleff, T., Assessing the Lead Market Potential of Countries for Innovation Projects, RIEB Discussion paper No. 142, Kobe 2001.

Beise, M./Rammer, C., Local User-Producer Interaction in Innovation and Export Performance of Firms, ZEW Discussion paper No. 03-51, Mannheim 2003

Brander, J./Spencer, B., Export Subsidies and International Market Share Rivalry, *Journal of International Economics*, 18, 1985, pp. 83–100.

Bresnahan, T. F./Malerba, F., Industrial Dynamics and the Evolution of Firms' and Nations' Competitive Capabilities in the World Computer Industry, in Mowery, D./Nelson, R. (eds.), *Sources of Industrial Leadership*, Cambridge: Cambridge University Press 1999, pp. 79–132.

Chen, Y.-M./Takada, H., Estimating the Geographical Diffusion of the Video Cassette Recorder Market, *Empirical Economics*, 19, 1994, pp. 451–472.

Cooper, R. G./Kleinschmidt, E. J., Success Factors in Product Innovation, *Industrial Marketing Management*, 16, 1987, pp. 215–223.
Coopersmith, J., Facsimile's False Starts, *IEEE Spectrum*, February 1993, pp. 46–49.
Council on Competitiveness, Going Global: The New Shape of American Innovation, Washington, D.C. 1998.
Cowan, R., Nuclear Power Reactors: A Study in Technological Lock-in, *Journal of Economic History*, 50, 3, 1990, pp. 541–567.
Cowan, R., Tortoise and Hares: Choices among Technologies of Unknown Merit, *Economic Journal*, 101, 1991, pp. 801–814.
Cvar, M. R., Case Studies in Global Competition: Patterns of Success and Failure, in Porter, M. E. (ed.), *Competition in Global Industries*, Boston: Harvard Business School Press 1986, pp. 483–516.
David, P. A., Path-Dependencies and predictability in Dynamic Systems with Local Externalities: A Paradigm for Historical Economics, in Foray, D./Freeman, C. (eds.), *Technology and the Wealth of Nations: the Dynamics of Constructed Advantage*, London: Pinter 1993, pp. 208–231.
David, P. A./Foray, D./Dalle, J.-M., Marshallian Externalities and the Emergence and Spatial Stability of Technological Enclaves, *Economic Innovation of New Technologies*, 8, 1998, pp. 147–182.
Dekimpe, M. G./Parker, P. M./Sarvary, M., "Globalisation": Modeling Technology Adoption Timing across Countries, *Technological Forecasting and Social Change*, 63, 2000a, pp. 25–42.
Dekimpe, M. G./Parker, P. M./Sarvary. M., Multi-Market and Global Diffusion, in Mahajan, V./ Muller, E./Wind, Y., *New-Product Diffusion Models*, Boston et al.: Kluwer 2000b, pp. 49–74.
Dosi, G./Pavitt, K./Soete, L., *The Economics of Technical Change and International Trade*, New York: Harvester Wheatsheaf 1990.
Douglas, S. P./Wind, Y., The Myth of Globalisation, *Columbia Journal of World Business*, 22, Winter 1987, pp. 19–29.
Economides, N./Himmelberg, Ch., Critical Mass and Network Size with Application to the US FAX Market, Working Paper 95-11, New York University 1995.
Fayerweather, J., *International Business Management: A Conceptual Framework*, New York: McGraw-Hill 1969.
Franko, L. G., *The European Multinationals*, London: Harper & Row 1976.
Freiberger, P./Swaine. M., Fire in the Valley: *The Making of the Personal Computer*, Berkeley: Osborne/McGraw-Hill 1984.
Ganesh, J./Kumar, V./Subramaniam, V., Learning Effects in Multinational Diffusion of Consumer Durables: An Exploratory Investigation, *Journal of the Academy of Marketing Science*, 25, 3, 1997, pp. 214–228.
Gatignon, H./Elishberg, J./Robertson, T. S., Modelling Multinational Diffusion Patterns. An Efficient Methodology, *Marketing Science*, 8, 3, 1989, pp. 231–247.
Gemünden, H. G./Heydebreck, P./Herden, R., Technological Interweaverment: A Means of Achieving Innovation Success, *R&D Management*, 22, 4, 1992, pp. 359–376.
Gerybadze, A./Meyer-Krahmer, F./Reger, G., *Globales Management von Forschung und Innovation*, Stuttgart: Poeschel 1997.
Griliches, Z., Hybrid Corn: An Exploration of the Economics of Technological Change, *Econometrica*, 25, 4, 1957, pp. 501–522.
Gruner, K. E./Homburg, Ch., Does Customer Interaction Enhance New Product Success?, *Journal of Business Research*, 49, 2000, pp. 1–14.
Hecker, S., *Kommunikation in ökologischen Unternehmenskrisen: Der Fall Shell und Brent Spar*, Wiesbaden: DUV 1997.
Helsen, K./Jedidi, K./DeSarbo, W. S., A New Approach to Country Segmentation Utilizing Multinational Diffusion Patterns, *Journal of Marketing*, 57, October, 1993, pp. 60–71.
Hippel, E. v., Lead users: A Source of Novel Product Concepts, *Management Science, 32*, 7, 1986, pp. 791–805.
Ihde, O., *Internationale Diffusion von Mobilfunk*, Wiesbaden: DUV 1996.
Johansson, J. K./Roehl, T. W., How Companies Develop Assets and Capabilities: Japan as a Leading Market, in Beechler, S./Bird, A. (eds.), *Research in International Business and International Relations: Emerging Trends in Japanese Management*, Vol. 6, Greenwich, CT: JAI Press 1994, pp. 139–160.
Keegan, W. J., Multinational Product Planning: Strategic Alternatives, *Journal of Marketing, 33*, 1, 1969, pp. 58–62.

Kotabe, M./Helsen, K., *Global Marketing Management*, New York: Wiley 1998.
Kravis, I. B./Lipsey, R. E., *Price Competitiveness in World Trade*, New York: National Bureau of Economic Research 1971.
Kreutzer, R., *Global Marketing – Konzeption eines länderübergreifenden Marketing: Erfolgsbedingungen, Analysekonzepte, Gestaltungs- und Implementierungsansätze*, Wiesbaden: DUV 1989.
Lee, C., Determinants of National Innovativeness and International Market Segmentation, *International Marketing Review*, 7, 5, 1990, pp. 39–49.
Levitt, T., The Globalisation of Markets, *Harvard Business Review*, 61, 3, 1983, pp. 92–102.
Linder, S. B., *An Essay on Trade and Transformation*, Uppsala: Almquist & Wiksells 1961.
Livingstone, J. M., *The Internationalisation of Business*, Houndmills: Macmillan 1989.
Lundvall, B.-Å., Innovation as an Interactive Process – from User-producer Interaction to the National System of Innovation, in Dosi, G./Freeman, Ch./Nelson, R./Silverberg, G./Soete, L. (eds.), *Technical Change and Economic Theory*, London: Pinter 1988, pp. 349–369.
Mansfield, E., *Industrial Research and Technological Innovation: An Econometric Analysis*, New York: Norton 1968.
Midgley, D. F./Dowling, G. R., Innovativeness: The Concept and its Measurement, *Journal of Consumer Research*, 4, March 1978, pp. 229–242.
Nabseth, L./Ray, G. F. (eds.), *The Diffusion of New Industrial Processes: An International Study*, London: Cambridge University Press 1974.
Ohmae, K., *The End of the Nation State: The Rise of Regional Economies*, New York: Free Press 1995.
Peterson, M. J., The Emergence of a Mass Market for Fax Machines, *Technology in Society*, 17, 4, 1995, pp. 469–482.
Porter, M. E., *The Competitive Advantage of Nations*, New York: Free Press 1990
Posner, M. V., International Trade and Technical Change, *Oxford Economic Papers*, 30, 1961, pp. 323–341.
Poznanski, K. Z., International Diffusion of Steel Technologies: Time lag and the Speed of Diffusion, *Technological Forecasting and Social Change*, 23, 1983, pp. 305–323.
Putsis, W. P./Balasubramanian, S./Kaplan, E. H./Sen, S., Mixing Behavior in Cross-Country Diffusion, *Marketing Science*, 16, 1997, pp. 354–369.
Redmond, W. H., Diffusion at Sub-National Levels: A Regional Analysis of New Product Growth, *Journal of Product Innovation Management*, 11, 1994, pp. 201–212.
Rosenbloom, R. S./Cusamano, M. A., Technological Pioneering and Competitive Advantage: The Birth of the VCR Industry, *California Management Review*, 29, 1, 1987, pp. 51–76.
Scherer, F. M., *International High-Technology Competition*, Boston: Harvard University Press 1992.
Scherler, P., *Kommunikation mit externen Anspruchsgruppen als Erfolgsfaktor im Krisenmanagement eines Konzerns*, Basel, Frankfurt a. M.: Helbing & Lichtenhain 1996.
Takada, H./Jain, D., Cross-National Analysis of Diffusion of Consumer Durable Goods in Pacific Rim Countries, *Journal of Marketing*, 55, April 1991, pp. 48–54.
Takeuchi, H./Porter, M. E., Three Roles of International Marketing in Global Strategy, in Porter. M. E. (ed.), *Competition in Global Industries*, Boston: Harvard Business School Press 1986, pp. 111–146.
Tilton, J. E., *International Diffusion of Technology: The Case of Semiconductors*, Washington, D.C.: The Brookings Inst. 1971.
Urban, G. L./Hauser, J. R., *Design and Marketing of New Products*, 2nd edition, Englewood Cliffs: Prentice Hall 1993.
Utterback, J. M., *Mastering the Dynamics of Innovation*, Boston: Harvard University Press 1994.
Vernon, R., International Investment and International Trade in the Product Cycle, *Quarterly Review of Economics*, 88, May 1966, pp. 190–207.
Vernon, R., The Product Cycle Hypothesis in a New International Environment, *Oxford Bulletin of Economics and Statistics*, 41, 4, 1979, pp. 255–267.
Walsh, V., Technology and the Competition of Small Countries: Review, in Freeman, C./Lundvall, B.-Å. (eds.), *Small Countries Facing the Technological Revolution*, London: Pinter 1988, pp. 37–66.
Yoffie, D. B. (ed.), *Competing in the Age of Digital Convergence*, Boston: Harvard Business School Press 1997.

Management
International Review
© Gabler Verlag 2004

Alexander Gerybadze

Knowledge Management, Cognitive Coherence, and Equivocality in Distributed Innovation Processes in MNCs

Abstract

- This study examines structural changes in innovation: continuous globalization of R&D and changes towards more distributed innovation processes. MNCs have continuously extended their network of R&D locations and knowledge centers. They are moving away from a single, self-contained, in-house center of knowledge towards a more distributed and open architecture of knowledge generation and use.

- Managing distributed innovation processes means orchestration of capabilities, multiple centers of excellence, and cross-cultural knowledge exchange. The paper differentiates between two issues: configuration and communication. The first issue deals with the tangible, hard and "objective" side, while the second issue is more concerned with interpretation, and this is often considered as "soft" or intangible.

- Most existing studies have concentrated on tangible and "hard" aspects. We argue more in favour of the "soft" issues: processes of social communication, and the sharing of knowledge between diverse groups in a cross-cultural setting.

Key Results

- Based on our own empirical research on innovation projects within 50 MNCs, the paper differentiates between two orthogonal variables: (1) the degree to which knowledge is explicit or implicit, and (2) the degree to which knowledge is canonical or equivocal.

- For geographically distributed innovation to succeed, managers in MNCs have to make sure that knowledge is interpreted and used in a coherent way. Situations of strong interpretive coherence and a dominance of canonical knowledge are favourable for knowledge sharing across locations. Great problems arise for equivocal knowledge and in situations of interpretive divergence, even if a significant part of the knowledge base is explicit.

Author

Alexander Gerybadze, Professor of International Management, Faculty of Economics and Social Sciences, University of Hohenheim, Stuttgart, Germany.

Alexander Gerybadze

Trends in International R&D and Knowledge Management

Managing innovation and building and leveraging knowledge have become core activities for attaining competitive advantage. Multinational Corporations (MNCs) as the prime engines of growth account for the largest share of industrial R&D in most OECD countries, and they have continuously extended their network of R&D locations and knowledge centers across the world. Three significant trends characterize international innovation activities:

1. the increasing *intensity and speed* of the innovation process;
2. continuous *globalization* and the increased international dispersion of innovation activities;
3. the core of value-added changes and there is a *downstream movement* of innovation towards the application and user spectrum.

Industrial R&D expenditure has increased considerably in most technology-intensive industries. In high-tech industries (e.g. information technology (IT), pharmaceuticals, biotechnology and semiconductors), new product warfare is the name of the game, and participating firms have to invest high percentages of revenues in R&D.[1] Even more "traditional" medium-tech industries such as automobiles, chemicals, and engineering & machinery have been changed and now place much greater emphasis on product development and innovative restructuring. The speed at which new products are introduced and at which former generations of products become obsolete has intensified considerably.

R&D has become heavily concentrated in large MNCs in only few dynamic sectors, in which speed of innovation and size and effectiveness of R&D investments have become the most critical parameters. As can be seen in Figure 1, three industrial sectors (pharmaceuticals & biotechnology, automobiles and information technology) account for almost half of global industrial R&D expenditure. Each of these three sectors is strongly dominated by a few large MNCs involved in fierce Schumpeterian type creative destruction. New product warfare and cycle-time management is particularly characteristic of telecommunications, electronics and software & IT-services. Together this "six-pack" of technology-intensive and speed-oriented sectors accounts for more than three quarters of industrial R&D, outpacing some other sectors that were traditionally considered as innovative, such as chemicals, aerospace and engineering & machinery, which remain under persistent threat of restructuring.

Innovation in most of these industries has become a highly *globalized* activity. Increasing investment in R&D and faster rates of obsolescence have forced managers of MNCs to design products for global markets and to launch new products worldwide. Many nation states have developed advanced innovation systems, and this leads to a further incentive for MNCs to build up globally dis-

Figure 1. Concentration of Industrial R&D Expenditures in a few Globalized Sectors

Industry / Sector	R&D-Expenditures in million $ 2001	R&D as %- of Revenues 2001	Extent of R&D Globalization
Pharmaceutical, Biotechnology & Health	54,661	12.1	***
Automobiles & Parts	49,451	4.0	**
Information-Technology (IT)-Hardware	39,657	9.4	***
Telecommunication (Equipment&Services)	35,444	N.A.	***
Electronics & Electrical	30,985	5.3	**
Software & IT-Services	19,987	10.2	***
Chemicals	14,567	4.2	***
Aerospace & Defense	11,755	4.3	*
Engineering & Machinery	9,001	2.6	*
Packaged Consumer Goods	7,879	N.A.	**
Other Industries (Sum of 12 Sectors)	26,345		*
All Companies / Total of 600 Co.	299,376	4.3	**

*** High Degree of R&D Globalization
** Medium Degree of R&D Globalization
* Low Degree of R&D Globalization

Sources: INTERIS-Database / University of Hohenheim; The 2002 R&D Scoreboard

persed portfolios of innovation activities. The increased globalization of R&D has become a prime topic in management research (see the special issues on "International Management of Technology" in Management International Review 2000 and on the "Globalization of R&D" in Research Policy 1999).

Globalization indicators have been rising continuously for the large technology-intensive MNCs. The Global Benchmark Survey on Strategic Management of Technology, probably the most comprehensive analysis of foreign R&D expenditure within a sample of 209 large MNCs, shows that the share of R&D spending outside the home region rose continuously between 1992 and 2001, with similar patterns being observed for corporations from North America, Europe and Japan.[2] The top six R&D-intensive sectors in Figure 1 are also at the forefront of globalizing R&D activities. As can be seen in the right-hand column in Figure 1, R&D has become most globalized in pharmaceuticals & biotechnology, computers, software, telecommunications and chemicals.

Another pertinent feature of global innovation is the reversal of the classical sequence of R&D. Most existing studies still emphasize linear, technology-push processes where basic research is followed by applied R&D, product development,

Figure 2. The Core of Value Added in the Innovation Process Moving Downstream

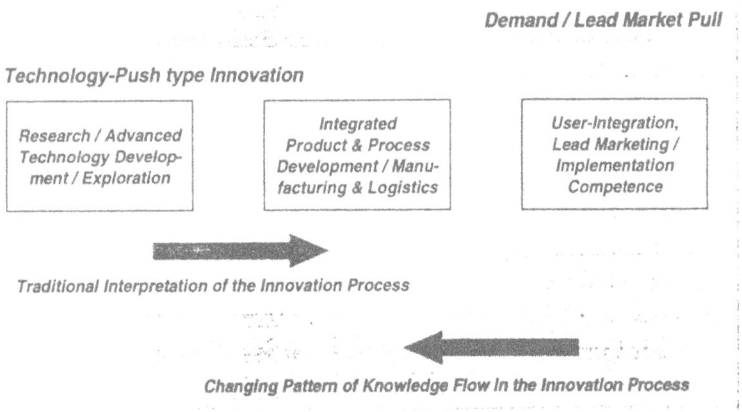

Demand / Lead Market Pull

Technology-Push type Innovation

| Research / Advanced Technology Development / Exploration | Integrated Product & Process Development / Manufacturing & Logistics | User-Integration, Lead Marketing / Implementation Competence |

Traditional Interpretation of the Innovation Process

Changing Pattern of Knowledge Flow In the Innovation Process

manufacturing and market launch (see the shaded sequence on the left-hand side in Figure 2).[3] In many of the aforementioned R&D-intensive sectors, the sequence and focus of activities is changing. Fast and responsive innovation requires early involvement of potential users, proximity to lead markets and strengthening the front-end of the innovation process. The core of value-added in the innovation process moves downstream, towards the application system and end-user side of the spectrum. This can be observed in more and more industries: automobile manufacturers increasingly differentiate through new "trend cars", for which design and manufacturing need to be close to most advanced markets. Telecommunication firms have to follow design trends, regulatory changes and new forms of integration with related components (Internet, personal computing etc.).

The new pattern of innovation is illustrated by the shaded zone on the right-hand side in Fig. 2. Close proximity to lead markets, interactive networks with users and complementary service providers, and the ability to integrate with suppliers and manufacturing are becoming more and more important. As a result, downstream network externalities drive the innovation process and this often leads to changing patterns of knowledge flows (Gerybadze 1999 and 2003, Iansiti 1998, Thomke 2003).

The Fallacy of Knowledge Sharing in Distributed Innovation Processes

Due to these trends management of knowledge has become a much more dispersed and complicated activity. Greater user-orientation, interactivity and cross-cultural learning have resulted in a new paradigm of globally dispersed innovation that is significantly different from the more traditional view of international technology transfer. From the linear-sequential process of process innovation, which is synonymous with a one-way technology transfer (typically a flow of knowledge from the center to the periphery), MNCs have moved towards a new paradigm of distributed and globally dispersed innovation (Gupta/Govindarajan 1991, 2000, Gerybadze 2003, Doz/Santos/Williamson 2001).

MNCs are moving away from a single, self-contained, in-house center of knowledge towards a more distributed and open architecture of knowledge production and application. Managing distributed innovation processes means orchestration of capabilities, intense market and technology interaction, multiple centers of knowledge at dispersed locations, cross-functional integration and interactive knowledge exchange.[4] This requires highly flexible organizational capabilities embracing a variety of forms of distributed knowledge management:

- managing distributed knowledge centers and locations within the same MNC;
- managing across business units and managing cross-divisional teams within firms;
- integrating dispersed capabilities across firms, involving suppliers, partner firms and complementors for different parts of the value chain;
- integrating knowledge and managing diverse networks with external research units and universities.

These distributed processes of innovation and knowledge management were traditionally seen as merely involving a problem of information exchange and synthesis. Bits and pieces of information are scattered around and have to be rearranged like a puzzle. The basic problem was seen in interconnectivity and in the reduction of asymmetric information. Information is "already there", it is located somewhere within a large MNC, from where the required bits of information just have to be transferred to the right places and units. New information technologies (distributed personal computing, the Internet, satellite communication etc.) were seen as suitable tools for reducing information asymmetries and for responding to information requirements of distributed agents.

Asymmetric Information and Sensemaking

More recent studies of knowledge management in MNCs appear to be less optimistic and discuss more openly the pros and cons involved in distributed innovation processes. It is not merely a matter of bringing bits and pieces of information together which are "objectively there" and which only need to be collected and integrated into a meaningful whole. The process of collection and integration is not merely a matter of information transfer and of overcoming asymmetric information. It is much more a *social communication* process and requires dealing with *asymmetric understanding*. Knowledge is distributed between groups of agents with diverse cultures and identities, with often incompatible value systems, who may interpret and respond to the same type of information quite differently. In most studies on knowledge management, we tend to overemphasize the rational, objective and content aspects of information, and we underestimate the interpretive, social and subjective aspects and the social process of knowledge sharing. "Information and insight are created in the hearts and minds of individuals, and information seeking and use are a dynamic and disorderly social process that is unfolded in layers of cognitive, affective and situational contingencies" (Choo 1998, p. 29).

Developing new technologies, finding user support and commercialising an innovation requires a complex process of *socio-technical construction of meaning*. Separate bits and pieces of information may be distributed between agents, but the integration process and the construction of a meaningful whole is very difficult and costly. Even though it may become meaningful to one agent (e.g. the innovator) or a small group, this does not represent shared knowledge or shared meaning for a larger group of distributed agents as user communities.

> *"New technologies ... create unusual problems in sensemaking for managers and operators. ... The central idea is captured by the phrase technology as equivoque. An equivoque is something that admits of several possible or plausible interpretations and therefore can be esoteric, subject to misunderstandings, uncertain, complex and recondite. ... Because new technologies are equivocal, they require ongoing structuring and sensemaking if they are to be managed. ... New technologies are fascinating because, in their complex equivocality, they force us to grapple with a key issue in technology – namely, how to apply perceptual perspectives to a material world"* (Weick 2001, pp. 148 and 172).

Social processes of consensus building and knowledge sharing are particularly important for user-driven or user-centered innovation. Finding out what is valuable for a potential user group in a particular national market is basically a process of social construction of meaning: understanding what works and what does not work in a particular national context or in a regulatory environment, understanding the use of new technology and its acceptance in everyday life. Close physical proximity is critical, since information is unstructured and needs to be articulated. The innovator and information provider has to ask questions in order to specify information needs, while the potential users and information seekers cannot readily express what they do not know or what is missing.[5]

Knowledge Sharing and Interpretation across Locations

Management of global R&D and knowledge management in MNCs has to address two strongly interdependent issues. The first issue addresses the tangible, hard and "objective" side, while the second issue is more concerned with the construction of meaning and interpretation, and is often considered as "soft" or "intangible", but nonetheless very important. The first issue is often addressed when managers have to decide where to do what: where to locate an R&D unit and where to establish or support an infrastructure. In studies on global R&D, this issue is typically addressed under the heading "*International configuration of R&D*/Location decisions for R&D units and competence centers". Most existing studies concentrate on these tangible and "hard" issues and some of our past studies have concentrated on these configuration and location issues as well.[6]

Knowledge management in MNCs also has to deal with soft and intangible issues, with subjective elements and interpretation. This involves processes of social communication, the construction of meaning and the sharing of knowledge among diverse groups within MNCs. These aspects are much more difficult to analyze and to understand, but if neglected, will result in hidden problems and project breakdowns. It is our intent in this paper to focus more on these soft factors and on the tacit dimension in international knowledge management. In Figure 3 this issue is addressed on the left-hand side. Here, we have to study *processes of international (social) communication*. We need to analyze preconditions for effective knowledge flows between different units and locations. This does not simply involve exchanging information or "objective content"; it has more to do with interpretation and meaning. How do we make sure that people in different units and at different locations develop a coherent understanding of a project? To what extent is knowledge shared, interpreted and acted upon by distributed agents? Important elements for this are global teamwork, team cohesion and integration. Furthermore, for communication and global teams to be effective, they need to be supported by appropriate mechanisms and platforms, including a supportive IT-infrastructure.

Critical Knowledge Characteristics and Effective Social Communication Processes

Our paper concentrates on the international communication issue and on the subjective aspects of knowledge management, as outlined on the left-hand side in Figure 3. Getting people from different locations and business units within

Figure 3. Key Issues to be Addressed in Global R&D and Knowledge Management

```
                Management of Global R&D
                and Knowledge Management
                in Multinational Corporations
                    /              \
                   /                \
    International Communication,    International Configuration /
    Knowledge Management and        Location Decisions for R&D Units
    Effective Global Teams          and Competence Centers
         /         |         \
        /          |          \
  Understanding   Managing        Mechanisms
  Knowledge Characte-  Effective Global  for Effective Com-
  ristics / Preconditions  Teams         munication / IT-
  for Cognitive                           Support
  Coherence
    /    \           /    \           /    \
  Explicit  Canonical  Team    Team    Modularity  Effective
  vs. Implicit  vs. Equivocal  Compo-  Leader-  of Know-  IT-Support
  Know-   Know-   sition &  ship &   ledge
  ledge   ledge   Formation  Integration
```

Focus of our paper

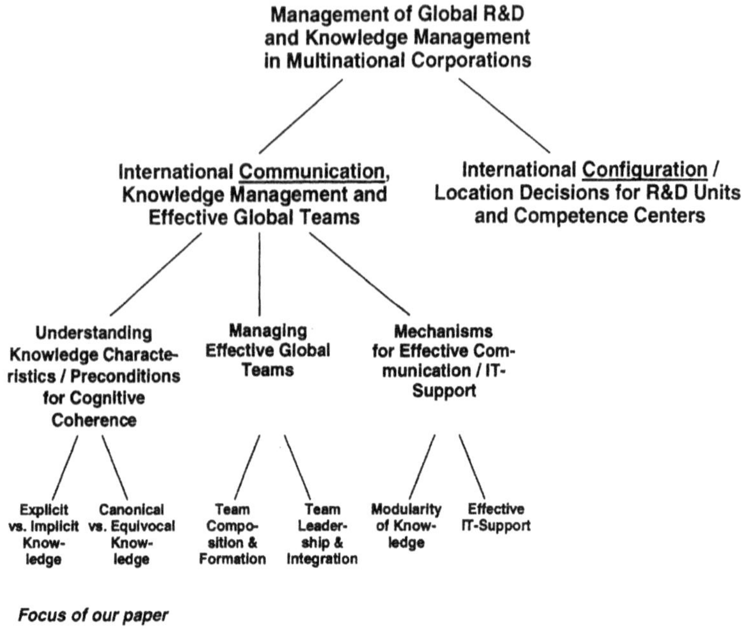

MNCs to work on joint projects and to share knowledge, requires dealing with three sub-issues:

1. We have to understand *knowledge characteristics* and the intrinsic difficulties and the hidden problems of sharing knowledge in a cross-cultural setting.
2. The second sub-issue deals with the management of *effective global teams*. Under which conditions can people from different locations and often with a diverse professional background work together and share knowledge?
3. How can we design and implement communication mechanisms and platforms? This sub-issue also involves decisions about information and communication technology, even though the technical side represents only one (sometimes overemphasized) aspect.

Let us begin with the first topic: understanding knowledge characteristics. What kind of knowledge needs to be transferred and shared between different entities? Given a certain configuration of competencies which are distributed across geographical locations, what are the preconditions for effective interaction and knowledge exchange? What motivates people often working for different organizational units, who may or may not have the same professional background and who may or may not share a common language, to effectively share knowledge? Most existing studies on international R&D and knowledge management in MNCs overemphasize the *objective, rational and declarative aspects* of information transmission between agents and/or locations. They underestimate the intrinsic difficulties of social communication processes within the firm. Critical knowledge to be exchanged and shared has a *subjective, interpretative and procedural* component. This interpretative aspect does not receive enough attention in managerial studies within MNCs, and this is what complicates most studies on geographically distributed innovation projects.

Based on our own empirical research on innovation projects within multinational corporations,[7] we have found it useful to differentiate between two important and distinct knowledge characteristics:

- the degree to which knowledge is *explicit or implicit*;
- the degree of *interpretative coherence*, i.e. the extent to which knowledge is interpreted and used in a coherent way.

Explicit vs. Implicit Knowledge

Research on knowledge management has strongly emphasized the first dimension, the degree of tacitness and the differentiation between explicit and implicit knowledge. This aspect is very important and "tacitness" is a rich concept for understanding knowledge management and problems of technology transfer within MNCs. Based on the conceptualisation of tacit knowledge, originally introduced by Polanyi (1966) and operationalized by Winter (1987), Nonaka and Takeuchi (1995) have further refined empirical studies of explicit vs. implicit knowledge. Kogut and Zander (1993) have adapted this approach to the study of knowledge transfer within MNCs, and they have emphasized that this degree of tacitness is the most critical variable for understanding knowledge exchange across locations. This dimension of tacitness can be measured by (1) the degree of codifiability, (2) the ease of teachability, (3) the observability in use and (4) by the degree of complexity (Winter 1987, Kogut/Zander 1993).

Knowledge transfer across geographical locations within MNCs works smoothly for explicit knowledge, i.e. as long as information is codified, easily teachable, observable in use and not too complex. The cost of transferring knowledge across locations will increase if one or more of these four criteria cannot be satisfied. Highly-complex knowledge which is difficult to codify and/or which cannot be observed and taught, by contrast, represents implicit knowledge, and this is much more difficult to transfer across locations.

This proposed metric of explicitness emphasizes the objective characteristics of knowledge as an item to be transferred. Knowledge is "objectively there"; it may be closely tied to individuals or to local practices. At least one or a few people in the MNC control the information even though "they know more than they can tell" (in the case of tacitness). This situation may be described as *uncertainty*: information is asymmetrically distributed between agents, but the less informed agents can learn from the better informed agents. One way of transferring involves documentation and making knowledge available in a more explicit form to other units. The distinction between explicit and implicit knowledge is helpful for studying the objective or "content" aspects of the transfer process, but there is also a subjective or ontological aspect to be taken into consideration. Knowledge cannot be reduced to its objective form, it also has an important interpretive component.[8]

Canonical vs. Equivocal Knowledge

In our empirical studies of innovation projects, we have encountered many situations in which knowledge appears to be highly explicit but does not get transferred and turns out to be extremely difficult to communicate and share between locations or between independent organizational units within a firm. What appears to be obvious or explicit to one side of the transfer (typically the source), may be difficult to understand or absorb by another entity or group. This has to do with framing, understanding or interpreting issues. For knowledge about innovation to become effective, it requires cognitive frames (Tversky/Kahnemann 1981) and conceptions of control (Fligstein 1990). These cognitive frames and conceptions of control are locally bound, they are linked to particular groups of actors and they are also embedded in particular locations and national cultures.

In order to study knowledge transfer and knowledge sharing between independent units or geographical locations within MNCs, we find it useful to distinguish between different degrees of *interpretive coherence* and cognitive coherence. The same element of explicit information (i.e. a document, a manual or a standard operating procedure) can have a quite different meaning to different groups of agents within a firm. This phenomenon is described as equivocality, or, alternatively, by the term ambiguity. Ambiguous situations with equivocal knowledge are described in the upper two boxes in Figure 4. Equivocal knowledge involves asymmetric understanding and often leads to interpretation difficulties. Information may be there and highly explicit, but not interpreted coherently by different agents working in a cross-cultural setting.

Figure 4. Knowledge Characteristics: "Objective" Content vs. "Subjective" Interpretation

	Explicit Knowledge	Implicit Knowledge
Equivocal Knowledge	*Equivocal, explicit Knowledge* • Problems of Misunderstanding • Hidden, indirect costs of information transfer • International knowledge exchange difficult	*Equivocal, implicit Knowledge* • Very serious communication problems • Prohibitive cost of information transfer • Location very important
Canonical Knowledge	*Canonical, explicit Knowledge* • Ease of communication • Very low cost of information transfer • Global distribution of activities	*Canonical, implicit Knowledge* • Problems of transfering tacit Knowledge • Information transfer through people • International transfer feasible but costly

Explicit though equivocal knowledge will lead to considerable problems of misunderstanding and to hidden and indirect costs of information transfer, and typically results in great difficulties in cross-cultural knowledge transfer. Equivocality or ambiguity is what makes international knowledge management in MNCs so troublesome. Both terms are often used as synonyms, even though we prefer the word "equivocality". "Ambiguity refers to a lack of clarity or consistency in reality, causality or intentionality. Ambiguous situations are situations that cannot be coded precisely into mutually exhaustive and exclusive categories" (March 1994, p. 178). "Ambiguity is more about unclear meaning and equivocality is more about the confusion created by two or more meanings, as in a pun or equivoque" (Weick 1995, p. 92). Increasing the rate and intensity at which explicit information is exchanged does not reduce problems of cognitive incoherence: "The problem of ambiguity is not that the real world is imperfectly understood and that more information will remedy that. The problem is that information may not resolve misunderstandings" (Weick 1995, p. 92).

Alexander Gerybadze

Equivocality, Canonical Knowledge and Interpretive Coherence

Based on our studies of knowledge management and group interaction within MNCs we have developed a metric of interpretive coherence and knowledge sharing. We differentiate between

- *canonical knowledge* for which all members of a group share the same frame of reference and interpret problems, processes and outcomes in a similar way (*strong interpretive coherence*), and
- *equivocal knowledge*: in group interaction across different locations within an MNC participating members use different frames of reference, and they interpret problems, processes and outcomes of projects differently, even if they have access to the same knowledge base. This situation may be described as *weak interpretive coherence* or as interpretive divergence.

Canonical knowledge is based on social communication processes, through which members of a group agree on a joint frame of reference and on ways of seeing

Figure 5. Effective Ways for Communicating across Locations

Equivocal Knowledge	• Joint meetings to develop group identity and coherent frame of understanding • Locally distributed work in intermediate phases • Exchange of explicit information through IT • Joint workshops for coordination and project review	• Highly-specialized, locally concentrated activities and workgroups • Highly-interactive face-to-face communication • Long-term transfer of people / teams to develop capabilities at other locations
Canonical Knowledge	• Internationally distributed work at best locations • Extensive use of information technology • Short, infrequent intermediate meetings of coordinators	• Temporary visits to other locations to learn about best practices • Transfer through sending people and teams to other locations • Information technology and written documents not very effective
	Explicit Knowledge	*Implicit Knowledge*

things, on interpreting knowledge, on working together and on implementing projects. Precisely defined instructions, manuals, contracts or other types of written documents "may be there", but they are often not used in a canonical way.

Both dimensions, the aforementioned distinction between explicit knowledge and implicit knowledge, and the differentiation between canonical and equivocal knowledge, represent orthogonal variables; they should thus be measured along two separate axes, as outlined in Figures 4 and 5. Along the horizontal axis, we differentiate between explicit knowledge (on the left-hand side) and implicit knowledge (right-hand side). With "explicit" or "implicit" we characterize the object or content of knowledge. Content *per se*, using the appropriate object and "getting the right information", does not necessarily result in a successful, implemented project.

For effective knowledge sharing and innovation to succeed, we have to make sure that knowledge is interpreted and used in a coherent way. Along the vertical axis in Figure 5, we differentiate between canonical knowledge (lower segment) and equivocal knowledge (upper segment). Situations of strong interpretive coherence and a dominance of canonical knowledge are favourable for internationalisation and knowledge sharing across locations. Great problems arise for equivocal knowledge and in situations of interpretive divergence, even if a significant part of the knowledge base is explicit. Explicit content is taken for granted, and managers in MNCs tend to underestimate the tedious processes required for different units and locations to understand and share knowledge, and to act accordingly.[9]

Group Cognition Processes and Knowledge Sharing within Global Teams

Knowledge management and globalization of R&D is crucially dependent on the existence of functioning global teams. MNCs set up development projects with team members located in different countries. Sub-teams or individual members may work independently and they need to exchange and share information and intermediate results with other members working at distant locations. Based on a rich tradition of research on the effectiveness of teams, we know quite well under which conditions groups can become effective and highly productive. This research has been extended to study heterogeneous groups and boundary-spanning groups. This includes cross-divisional groups, cross-cultural groups and multi-location work teams. Any type of boundary-spanning leads to complications for group work and tends to undermine group cohesion, identity, and shared understanding.

"Suppose that a group has just been assigned (or identified for itself) a task with high equivocality. What do they do? The group begins a mode of inception: the group must come to shared agreements of goals for the assigned task (i.e. the production function). With high equivocality there are multiple and possibly conflicting interpretations of the situation. Participants are not certain about what questions to ask, and if questions are posed, the situation is ill-defined to the point where a clear answer will not be forthcoming" (Dennis, Valacich 1998, 10).

Any group is a form of social capital, and it takes a lot of time and effort to build and sustain a well-functioning team. Each group has to pass through a lifecycle of forming, storming and norming, and has to arrange complex modes of group interaction (Hackman 1987, 1990). We know quite well what it takes to build up effective teams and we know under which conditions global teams can work effectively across locations. The only problem is that executives in MNCs persistently neglect these well-established principles of effective team management. Global teams are often established on an ad-hoc basis, hardly enough time and effort is made available to build effective teams, participants come and go, and reward systems are often counterproductive to effective teamwork.

The characteristics of knowledge described in the preceding sections are useful for structuring effective global teams and also for identifying situations in which globally distributed work will not be feasible. In general, the global distribution of activities is easy if there is a high share of *canonical, explicit knowledge*. Relevant information is made explicit and easy to understand and will be interpreted coherently. In this case, information can easily be transferred through formal channels (e.g. through e-mail or intranet) and activities can be divided up globally. The other extreme would be a project with a high percentage of *implicit and equivocal knowledge*. Serious communication problems will necessarily arise. Information is linked to people or local practices and is very difficult to transfer. Effective work requires building up highly-specialized practices and workgroups at particular locations in the world. Co-location is extremely important in such a case, and companies are well-advised to concentrate their activities in this particular field at one, single location.

Globally distributed work is feasible for the other two combinations of knowledge characteristics in Figures 4 and 5. Development projects for automobiles, electronic equipment or software use a high share of explicit knowledge; still, team members in different countries will often interpret the same type of codified information differently, due to differences in priority setting, work experience and local cultures. *Explicit but equivocal knowledge* may complicate the effective interaction of team members and will often result in hidden, indirect costs of information transfer. Multinational companies have developed effective routines to reduce asymmetric understanding in global teams. One important means of forming effective teams is to have team members meet face-to-face at the outset of the project. Joint meetings help to clarify purpose and goals while developing group identity and trust, and they result in a coherent frame of understanding. After building sufficient team-specific social capital, sub-teams can work in different locations and organize workshops for coordination and project review at certain intervals.[10]

Global teams may work for other combinations of knowledge characteristics, but require appropriate routines for transferring knowledge across locations. If knowledge is *canonical but implicit*, MNCs encounter problems of transferring tacit skills and practices. International transfer in such cases is feasible but costly. Critical knowledge is embedded in teams that work effectively in a certain geographic context. MNCs will organize temporary visits to the most advanced locations in order to learn more about best practices. Transfer works primarily through people, by sending teams to other locations for certain periods. Global team arrangements may be feasible if the overall project can be modularized into subteams with complementary tacit skills. Highly-sophisticated subteams with special locally-embedded expertise can work side-by-side, while being integrated into a larger global network or project within the MNC.

Another very important topic in global R&D deals with the *role of information and communication technology*. New technologies, like the Internet, distributed personal computing and satellite technology, have been characterized as drivers of the globalization processes. Throughout the 1990s, MNCs invested strongly in their IT-infrastructure, and a significant part of these investments was used for facilitating global design and development. The role of virtual, IT-supported teams and round-the-clock development via Internet and satellites has been overemphasized though. Information and communication technology reduces both costs and speed for projects relying on explicit, canonical knowledge (as illustrated in the lower left-hand box in Figure 5). For implicit knowledge, there are limits to the use of formal IT channels. The sharing of equivocal knowledge requires highly-interactive face-to-face communication, and even the most sophisticated IT-based solutions have not met the expectations for advanced development work.[11] Overall, information technology is extremely helpful for the exchange and transfer of explicit, canonical information and may reduce information asymmetries at low cost. Problems of equivocality and asymmetric understanding, by contrast, are very difficult to deal with in IT-supported distributed work.[12]

International Configuration of Competence Centers and R&D Units

So far, we have not addressed the international configuration issue, the question of where to locate R&D units and how to organize distributed competence cen-

Figure 6. International Configuration/Location Decisions for R&D Units and Competence Centers

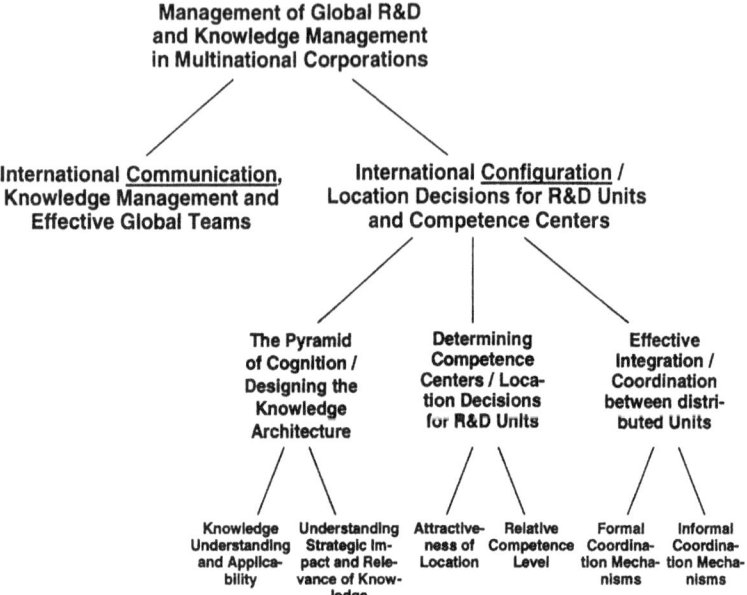

ters within an MNC. This *configuration/location issue* has been strongly emphasized by scholars studying the globalization process of R&D. Bartlett and Ghoshal (1998) have formulated an "ideal type" of the Transnational solution and have highlighted international configuration issues. Gupta and Govindarajan (1991, 2000) have analysed knowledge flows within distributed federations of highly-competent subsidiaries of MNCs. Fisch (2001, 2003) has developed an interesting model and an entropy-measure for a multi-center structure of R&D. Gerybadze (1999, 2003) and Gerybadze and Reger (1998, 1999) have developed a resource-based framework for analyzing location decisions for R&D and the configuration of competence centers. Most of these studies have emphasized *efficiency* considerations and have designed idealized structures that MNCs would choose if they could built up their global structure from scratch. Most existing large corporations, however, remain cautious in implementing a multi-center transnational framework. In our empirical studies we have reported several cases in which companies had serious difficulties in implementing the "transnational solution".[13] It appears that a multi-center architecture of knowledge centers is difficult to manage, and this is due to communication breakdown and problems of misunderstanding, the issues emphasized in the preceding parts of the paper.

In spite of these managerial and communication difficulties, forces remain strong for increasing foreign R&D and for building up distributed competence centers in several countries of the world. The following model was developed on the basis of empirical studies of location decisions in 50 MNCs and describes some important criteria which managers use in evaluating R&D locations and alternative modes of organization. In order to solve the international configuration issue on the right-hand side in Figure 6, the following topics need to be addressed:

1. What does the overall design of the *corporate knowledge architecture* look like? Is there a predisposition for a centralized structure within the firm, or is a multi-center architecture more appropriate? Which parts of the knowledge domain tend to be centralized and which parts are shared among locations?
2. The second topic addresses *location decisions* for R&D units and selection criteria for the number of competence centers and for determining their specific roles and responsibilities within the MNC.
3. Finally, we also have to deal with *effective integration* and the design of *coordination mechanisms* for managing distributed R&D units and competence centers.

In the following we will concentrate on the first topic, the overall design of the corporate knowledge architecture. We will describe important criteria which managers in MNCs use for choosing alternative institutional regimes. Based on both our empirical and conceptual studies, we will describe a three-layered structure for corporate competence portfolios, which we have labelled the *pyramid of cognition*.

Based on in-depth studies in MNCs in which we have analysed how competence centers are formed, how companies coordinate distributed competence centers and which criteria are used for R&D location and resource allocation, we have developed the following analytical framework. The aim is to explain the international configuration and location of R&D units and competence centers within a particular MNC. We call this the *knowledge architecture* of the firm and it can be used to explain which factors are most influential in determining generic configuration decisions. In Figure 7 this is illustrated by arrows pointing to the core issue to be addressed. Four determinants were identified that have a strong influence on international configuration decisions:

- the *strategic role of the business unit* or product group which uses a particular capability exerts a very strong influence;[14]
- it is also very important whether the competence in question is *generic or specific*;
- *maturity and life cycle* considerations also have a strong influence on configuration decisions;
- a fourth factor describes *knowledge characteristics* and whether tasks are easily decomposable or not.[15]

Figure 7. Factors influencing the International Configuration and Location Decisions

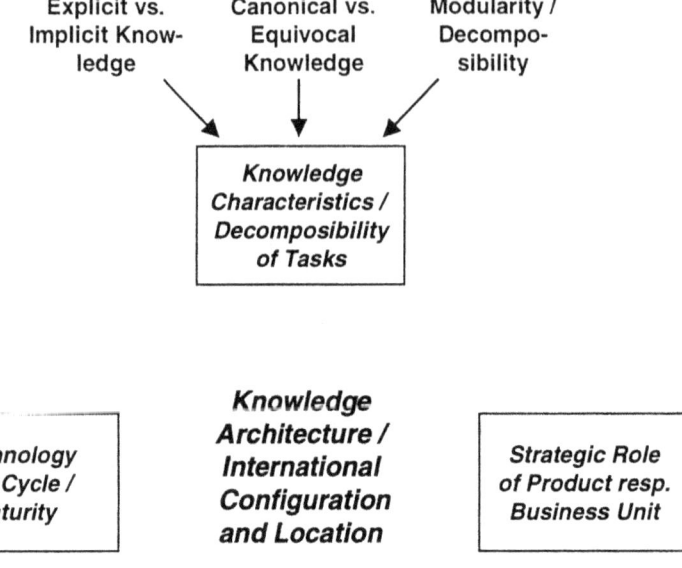

The strategic role of the business unit or a particular product group has become most influential in driving configuration decisions for R&D. Highly innovative and dynamic business units exert a strong influence on R&D resource allocation. R&D people need to understand the dynamics in this particular line of business and they want to be close to the most dynamic users of knowledge. A business unit closely tied to and supported by corporate strategy will also receive stronger support for R&D. Location decisions for core activities of that business unit also strongly influence the location of related R&D units.[16]

Knowledge can be *generic or specific* and this has a strong influence on international configuration decisions. A generic competence is widely applicable to a number of business units and products. Many companies have identified selected core competencies, i.e. critical areas of expertise with a strong impact on competitive advantage across a range of business units.[17] Location decisions for core competencies of the corporation tend to be much more centralized and linked to headquarter control. More specific competencies, by contrast, that are only tied to one or a few products, and competencies that are of particular value only in selected country markets, will often be supported and leveraged at foreign R&D units.

Maturity and the life cycle of a technology or a competence have a strong influence on international configuration decisions. Potentially useful technologies may appear at the horizon and will be considered as embryonic or as pacing technologies. During later stages they may become key technologies with high competitive impact.[18] There is a tendency in MNCs to decentralize sensing capabilities for competencies during early phases, but to exert stronger centralized control for key technologies.

In order to study international configuration decisions, one has to develop a profound understanding of *knowledge characteristics* and the decomposability of tasks in the development process. A more decentralized, multi-center configuration is only feasible for areas of expertise and for projects with a high percentage of explicit knowledge, for which cognitive coherence can be maintained across locations, and for which modularization and the decomposability of subtasks is feasible.

Managing Competence Portfolios and the Pyramid of Cognition in MNCs

Earlier studies of innovation and knowledge management in MNCs were too optimistic concerning the "transnational solution": they overestimated the extent of global dispersion and the reduction of hierarchical control. The transnational model (Bartlett/Ghoshal 1998, Hedlund 1993) emphasizes the tendency towards (1) multiple geographical centers of learning, (2) managerial autonomy of subsidiaries, (3) open, non-hierarchical knowledge exchange between globally dispersed units, (4) a strong role of global projects and teams and (5) the widespread use of information and communication technologies to facilitate global R&D.

More recently, scholars have become somewhat sceptical about the feasability and the virtues of the transnational solution.[19] Our own research has demonstrated that MNCs tend to remain centralized and hierarchical and that very few firms are really in favour of the "transnational solution".

1. Increases in the geographical spread of innovation activities and a larger number of foreign R&D units do not necessarily mean a decentralization of control. On the contrary, there are tendencies of greater concentration of control in spite of ongoing geographical dispersion of knowledge-generating activities.
2. We observed a ranking into first tier, second tier and third tier units concerning managerial influence, decision-making power and control over resources. Managerial competence and resource allocation decisions are still concentrated in very few centers in most of the large MNCs.
3. Subsidiaries and R&D units in different locations tend to be much less networked and interlinked than suggested by the "transnational solution". A few, leading first tier units often act as network nodes or gateways, and strategic information is still channelled through this central node.[20]
4. Development work is much less distributed across locations than believed. Global teams are only effective for certain kinds of development projects with favourable knowledge characteristics. Many strategically important and highly-innovative projects still require co-location and intensive personal interaction.
5. The use of advanced information technologies as a driver of globalized development work has been overemphasized. Close, interactive work and spontaneous face-to-face communication is still very critical for innovation in MNCs.[21] Some subtasks and certain phases in innovation projects are facilitated by IT-solutions (e.g. e-mail for supporting project teams, video-conferencing etc.). Most often, however, they only serve to complement more direct, interactive and personal forms of communication.

It appears that management research has underemphasized the important influence of strategic direction, interpretation and knowledge sharing in designing appropriate organizational solutions for MNCs. The four factors outlined in Figure 7, namely knowledge characteristics, the evaluation of strategic roles and different maturity classes of technology, as well as the question of ownership and intra-corporate dispersion of knowledge are still very critical.

Management research has somewhat neglected the role of sensemaking, asymmetric understanding, and the process of reaching shared agreement within managerial groups. This is the reason this paper has emphasized the role of the equivocality of knowledge and of cognitive coherence within MNCs. Multiple and geographically distributed centers of learning are troubled by problems of equivocality and asymmetric understanding. Because reaching a consensus on innovation projects is so difficult, MNCs build up a sheltered model of knowledge domains. This may be called the *Portfolio of Knowledge* or the *Pyramid of Cognition*. The first tier of the knowledge base (as illustrated by the darkly shaded inner circle in Figure 8) tends to be concentrated in one prime location, often very close to corporate headquarters. This core asset base comprises all projects

Figure 8. Competence Portfolios and the Pyramid of Cognition in MNCs

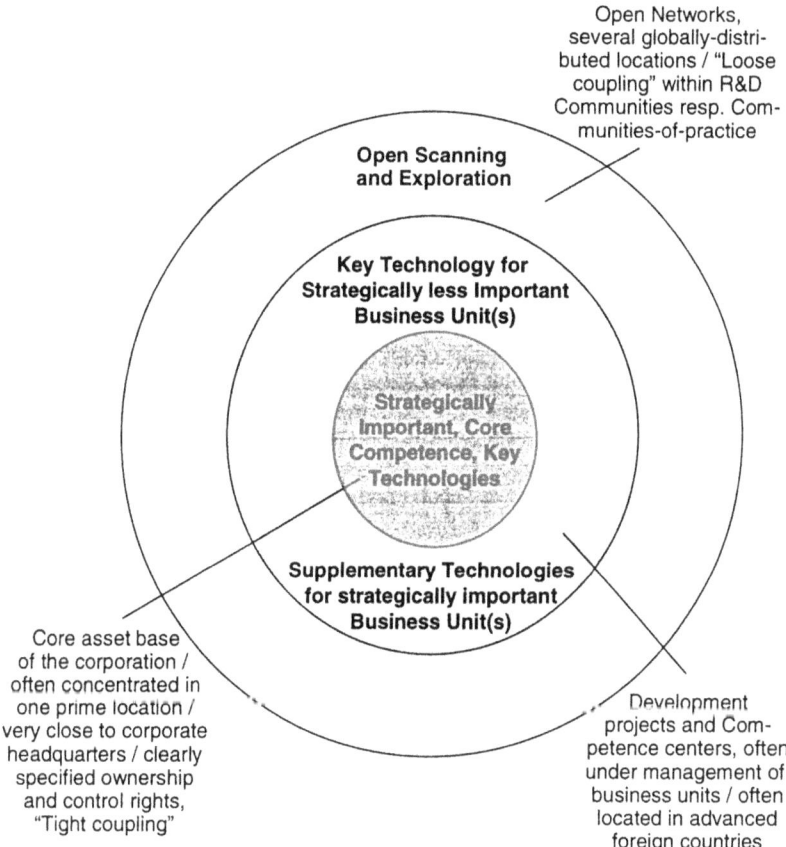

and technologies characterized by equivocality and cognitive divergence and the requirement to integrate tasks. For everything considered of high relevance for corporate strategy, and evaluated as core competence, large MNCs tend to remain very hierarchical, and they prefer "tight coupling" and clearly specified ownership and control rights.

For the second-tier layer in the pyramid of cognition (as illustrated by the lightly shaded zone in Figure 8), MNCs develop strategically directed multi-center strategies. Projects are less troubled by equivocality and cognitive convergence, sub-tasks may be modularised and clear responsibilities may be assigned to business units. Companies invest in important development projects and set up competence centers, which are often managed by strong global business units.

Some of these R&D units and competence centers are located in the most advanced foreign countries, while some critical activities still remain centered in the home country. MNCs from the largest, most advanced countries (e.g. American and Japanese firms) choose foreign locations for supplementary technologies within strategically important business units or, alternatively, for separable key technologies within strategically less important business units.

There is a third layer of distributed knowledge, for which MNCs accept more open, heterarchical modes of *scanning and exploration* (illustrated by the more peripheral zone in Figure 8). Open network arrangements are chosen at several globally-distributed locations. This is the area where "weak ties" and "loose coupling" are important and large MNCs are interlinked with R&D communities and communities-or-practice in numerous fields of expertise in order to generate options for future growth. As soon as business prospects become more promising and real, however, large MNCs tend to shift knowledge domains and projects towards the inner circles of the pyramid of cognition in Figure 8.

Summary

This paper describes three significant trends that characterize international innovation activities in MNCs: (1) the increasing *intensity and speed* of R&D, (2) continuous *globalization* and (3) changes towards more distributed innovation processes with greater emphasis on users. MNCs as the prime engines of growth account for the largest share of R&D in most OECD countries, and they have continuously extended their network of R&D locations and knowledge centers across the world. They are moving away from a single, self-contained, in-house center of knowledge towards a more distributed and open architecture of knowledge production and application. Managing distributed innovation processes means orchestration of capabilities, multiple centers of knowledge at dispersed locations, and cross-cultural knowledge exchange.

Knowledge management needs to address two interrelated issues: configuration and communication. The first issue deals with the tangible, hard and "objective" side, while the second issue is concerned more with interpretation and the construction of meaning, and this is often considered as "soft" or "intangible". The first issue, configuration, is addressed when managers have to decide where to do what: where to locate R&D and where to establish or support an infrastructure. So far, most existing studies have concentrated on these tangible and "hard" issues.

We argue that knowledge management studies in MNCs should also take into consideration the "soft" and intangible issues, sensemaking and interpretation. This involves studying processes of social communication, the construction of meaning and the sharing of knowledge between diverse groups in a cross-cultural setting. Based on our own empirical research on innovation projects within 50 MNCs, we have found it useful to differentiate between two important and distinct knowledge characteristics:

- the degree to which knowledge is *explicit or implicit*, and
- the degree to which knowledge is *canonical or equivocal*.

While research on knowledge management in MNCs has emphasized the first dimension, the degree of tacitness and the differentiation between explicit and implicit knowledge, the second dimension has not received enough attention. In our empirical studies of innovation projects, we have encountered many situations in which knowledge appears to be highly explicit but does not get transferred and turns out to be extremely difficult to communicate and share between locations or between independent organizational units within MNCs. The paper thus differentiates between canonical knowledge and equivocal knowledge, and provides a metric for studying different arrangements for knowledge sharing in MNCs.

The paper develops an empirically-grounded method for studying knowledge management in MNCs and provides an analytical framework for structuring international configuration decisions for R&D units and geographically distributed competence centers. Four determinants are identified that are most critical for the design of the knowledge architecture within MNCs: (1) the strategic role of the business unit, (2) generic vs. specific competence, (3) maturity and life cycle considerations and (4) knowledge characteristics and the decomposability of tasks. Based on these criteria, MNCs build up a sheltered model of knowledge domains, and they define priority classes and a portfolio of knowledge. Based on this portfolio of knowledge, MNCs rearrange their international network of R&D units and competence centers in a way that knowledge sharing can be facilitated.

Endnotes

1 Firms in high-tech industries have to invest between 10 and 15% of revenues on R&D. For some companies in pharmaceuticals and biotechnology, these percentages are in the range of 15 to 25%.
2 See Roberts (2001). European firms attain levels of 35% (for investments outside of Europe), North American firms move beyond 33%, while Japanese firms are approaching 10%. The Global Benchmark Survey on Strategic Management of Technology is based on a collaborative project of MIT, Fraunhofer, the Center of International Management and Innovation at University of Hohenheim and NISTEP (Japan).
3 For a detailed comparison of the linear-sequential model and the chain-link model of innovation see OECD (1997) and Kline and Rosenberg (1986).

4 For a similar description of distributed knowledge production see Gibbons, Limoges, Nowotny et al. (1994) and Nowotny, Scott, and Gibbons (2001). The authors distinguish between *Mode 1* and *Mode 2* of knowledge production. *Mode 1* describes a linear, research-driven, sequential and self-contained process. *Mode 2* of knowledge production is socially distributed, often problem- or user-driven and involves shifting patterns of connectivity between large numbers of agents, often located at different places.
5 The Anomalous State of Knowledge (ASK) hypothesis formulated by Belkin (1980) describes situations in which information seekers do not precisely know what they want to know or how to express their need.
6 Most publications on the globalization of R&D focus on configuration and location issues. See the special issues in Research Policy (1999) and in Management International Review (2000), as well as our own publications in Gerybadze (1999, 2003) and Gerybadze and Reger (1999).
7 See Gerybadze and Reger (1999) and Gerybadze (1999, 2003). Most of our published studies have so far also emphasized the international configuration aspects and the "hard and measurable" side of R&D globalization. During our more recent in-depth case studies, however, we have learnt that social communication processes and asymmetric understanding are extremely important. Our more recent studies thus emphasize more the interpretive or epistemic aspects of international technology transfer.
8 See Blackler (1995), Burell and Morgan (1997) and Berger and Luckmann (1966) for this subjectivist and interpretive view of "knowledge".
9 For an illustrative description of communication problems arising in networks of R&D units within MNCs see Haworth and Savage (1989) and Fisch (2001, 87 ff.).
10 See Barczak and McDonough (2003) for a detailed description of effective routines for global teams in MNCs. The authors emphasize three actions that are particularly critical: holding initial face-to-face meetings that typically last three days, frequent communication over distance in the meantime and periodic progress update meetings.
11 There are techniques like video-conferencing and interactive 3-D design which are very helpful for some selected R&D tasks. Similar to our own findings on the use of IT in global development work in MNCs, Barczyk and McDonough (2003, 17) report that "many companies have discovered that video-conferencing does not live up to its billing as a substitute for face-to-face meetings".
12 See the excellent book on Distributed Work edited by Hinds and Kiesler (2002), particularly the contribution of Armstrong and Cole (2002) and Kiesler and Cummings (2002). For a balanced assessment of different hard and soft technologies in global product development see McDonough and Kahn (1996).
13 There are also cases where companies have re-centralized due to serious difficulties in maintaining a multi-center structure. Typical examples are ABB, Aventis, Bayer and DaimlerChrysler. For a similar description of weaknesses of the transnational MNC see Sölvell (2003).
14 This again shows what we emphasized in the first section of this paper, that the core of knowledge creation moves downstream, in this case towards the most influential and dynamic internal customer within a MNC.
15 This fourth factor is closely tied to the variables described in the preceding: tacitness vs. explicitness, canonical vs. equivocal knowledge and modularity/decomposability.
16 As an example: If a European pharmaceutical company locates its business unit for a certain indication in New Jersey, a significant part of R&D in this field will be located in the US.
17 For the concept of core competence see Prahalad and Hamel (1990) and Sanchez (2001, 2003). An operationalization and a metric for analyzing core competencies and distributed competencies within MNCs is described in Gerybadze (2001) and Gerybadze et al. (1997, Chap. 6).
18 This concept of the technology life cycle was originally developed by Arthur D. Little. See Roussel, Saad and Erikson (1991), Floyd (1997) and Gerybadze (2001) for a more detailed description.
19 See Sölvell (2003) Patel and Pavitt (1994), Patel (2003) and Gerybadze (2003), for a more differentiated view of configuration and location decisions within large MNCs.
20 See the interesting findings on communication flows within German MNCs in Welge and Holtbrügge (2000).
21 For an excellent description of the advantages and disadvantages of information and communication technology in distributed cooperative work see Hinds and Kiesler (2002).

References

Armstrong, D. J./Cole, P., Managing Distances and Differences in Geographically Distributed Work Groups, in Hinds, P. M./Kiesler, S. (eds.), *Distributed Work*, Cambridge, MA: MIT Press 2002, pp. 168–189.

Barczak, G./McDonough, E. F., Leading Global Product Development Teams, *Research Technology Management*, November–December 2003, pp. 14–19.

Bartlett, C. A./Ghoshal, S., *Managing across Borders: The Transnational Solution*, 2. edition, Boston, MA: Harvard Business School Press 1998.

Belkin, N. J., Anomalous States of Knowledge as a Basis for Information Retrieval, *The Canadian Journal of Information Science*, 5, May 1980, pp. 133–143.

Berger, P. L./Luckmann, T., *The Social Construction of Reality*, New York: Doubleday 1966.

Blackler, F., Knowledge, Knowledge Work and Organizations: An Overview and Interpretation, *Organization Studies*, 16, 6, 1995, pp. 1021–1046.

Burrell, G./Morgan, G., *Sociological Paradigms and Organizational Analysis*, London: Heinemann 1979.

Choo, C. W., *The Knowing Organization: How Organizations use Information to Construct Meaning, Create Knowledge and Make Decisions*, New York: Oxford University Press 1998.

Dennis, A./Valacich, J., Rethinking Media Richness: Towards a Theory of Media Synchronicity, Working Paper, Georgia Institute of Technology, Atlanta, GA 1998.

Doz, Y./Santos, J./Williamson, P., *From Global to Metanational: How Companies Win in the Knowledge Economy*, Boston, MA: Harvard Business School Press 2001.

Fisch, J. H., *Structure Follows Knowledge: Internationale Verteilung der Forschung und Entwicklung in multinationalen Unternehmen*, Wiesbaden: Gabler 2001.

Fisch, J. H., Optimal Dispersion of R&D Activities in Multinational Corporations with a Genetic Algorithm, *Research Policy*, 32, 2003, pp. 1381–1396.

Fligstein, N., *The Transformation of Corporate Control*, Cambridge, MA: Harvard University Press 1990.

Floyd, C., *Managing Technology for Corporate Success*, Aldershot: Gower 1997.

Gerybadze, A., *Managing Technology Competence Centers in Europe*, The Role of European R&D for Global Corporations, Nijmegen Lectures on Innovation Management, Antwerpen-Apeldoorn: Maklu 1999.

Gerybadze, A., Technological Competence Assessment within the Firm: Applications of Competence Theory to Managerial Practice, in Sanchez, R./Heene, A. (eds.), *Implementing Competence-Based Strategy: Advances in Applied Business Strategy*, Vol. 6 B, Stamford, CT: JAI Press 2001.

Gerybadze, A., Resource-based Strategies for Global Research and Development, in Dankbaar, B. (ed.), *Innovation Management in the Knowledge Economy*, London: Imperial College Press 2003, pp. 185–208.

Gerybadze, A./Meyer-Krahmer, F./Reger, G. (eds.), *Globales Management von Forschung und Innovation*, Stuttgart: Schäffler Poeschel 1997.

Gerybadze, A./Reger, G., Managing Globally Distributed Competence Centers within Multinational Corporations: A Resource-Based View, in Scandura, T. A./Serapio, M. G. (eds.), *Research in International Business and International Relations*, Vol. 7, Stanford, CT: JAI Press 1998, pp. 183–217.

Gerybadze, A./Reger, G., Globalization of R&D: Recent Changes in the Management of Innovation in Transnational Corporations, *Research Policy*, 28, 1999, pp. 252–274.

Gibbons, M./Limoges, C./Nowotny, H. et al., *The New Production of Knowledge*, London: Sage 1994.

Gupta, A. K./Govindarajan, V., Knowledge Flows and the Structure of Control within Multinational Corporations, *Academy of Management Review*, 16, 1991, pp. 768–792.

Gupta, A. K./Govindarajan, V., Knowledge Flows within Multinational Corporations, *Strategic Management Journal*, Vol. 21, 2000, pp. 473–496.

Hackman, J. R. (ed.), *Groups that Work (and Those That Don't): Creating Conditions for Effective Teamwork*, San Francisco: Jossey Bass 1990.

Hackmann, R., The Design of Work Teams, in Lorsch, J. W. (ed.), *Handbook for Organizational Behaviour*, Englewood Cliffs, NJ: Prentice Hall 1987, pp. 315–342.

Haworth, D. A./Savage, G. T., A Channel Ratio Model of Intercultural Communication, *Journal of Business Communication*, Vol. 26, 1989, pp. 231–254.
Hedlund, G. (ed.), *Organization of Transnational Corporations*, The United Nations Library on Transnational Corporations, Vol. 6, London: Routledge 1993.
Hinds, P. M./Kiesler, S. (eds.), *Distributed Work*, Cambridge, MA: MIT Press 2002.
Iansiti, M., *Technology Integration: Making Critical Choices in a Dynamic World*, Boston, MA: Harvard Business School Press 1998.
Kiesler, S./Cummings, J. N., What do we Know about Proximity and Distance in Work Groups? A Legacy of Research, in Hinds, P. M./Kiesler, S. (eds.), *Distributed Work*, Cambridge, MA: MIT Press 2002, pp. 57–80.
Kline, S. J./Rosenberg, N., An Overview of Innovation, in Landau, R./Rosenberg, N. (eds.), *The Positive Sum Strategy*, Washington, DC: National Academy Press 1986, pp. 275–305.
Kogut, B./Zander, U., Knowledge of the Firm, Combinative Capabilities and the Replication of Technology, *Organization Science* 3, 1992, pp. 383–397.
Kogut, B./Zander, U., Knowledge of the Firm and the Evolutionary Theory of the Multinational Corporation, *Journal of International Business Studies*, 24, 1993, pp. 625–645.
March, J. G., *A Primer on Decision Making: How Decisions Happen*, New York: Free Press 1994.
McDonough, E. F./Kahn, K. B., Using 'Hard' and 'Soft' Technologies for Global New Product Development, *R&D Management*, 26, 1996, pp. 241–253.
Nonaka, I./Takeuchi, H., *The Knowledge-Creating Company: How Japanese Companies Create the Dynamics of Innovation*, New York: Oxford University Press 1995.
Nowotny, H./Scott, P./Gibbons, M., *Re-Thinking Science. Knowledge and the Public in an Age of Uncertainty*, Oxford: Blackwell 2001.
OECD, *The Oslo Manual: Proposed Guidelines for Collecting and Interpreting Technological Innovation Data*, Organization for Economic Cooperation and Development, Paris 1997.
Patel, P., What are Advantages in Knowledge Doing to the Large Industrial Firm in the New Economy?, in Christensen, J. F./Maskell, P. (eds.), *The Industrial Dynamics of the New Digital Economy*, Cheltenham: Edward Elgar 2003.
Patel, P./Pavitt, K., Technological Competencies in the World's Largest Firms: Characteristica, Constraints and Scope for Managerial Choice, Presentation at the Prince Bertil Symposium, Stockholm School of Economics, June 1994.
Polanyi, M., *The Tacit Dimension*, London: Routledge 1966.
Prahalad, C. K./Hamel, G., The Core Competencies of the Corporation, *Harvard Business Review*, 68, 3, 1990, pp. 79–93.
Research Policy, *Special Issue on the Internationalization of Industrial R&D*, Vol. 28, Nos. 2–3, March 1999.
Roberts, E. B., Benchmarking Global Strategic Management of Technology, *Research Technology Management*, March-April 2001, pp. 25–36.
Roussel, P. A./Saad, K./Erickson, T. J., *Third Generation R&D: Managing the Link to Corporate Strategy*, Boston, MA: Harvard Business School Press 1991.
Sölvell, Ö., The Multi-Home-Based Multinational: Combining Global Competitiveness and Local Innovativeness, in Birkinshaw, J./Ghoshal, S. et al. (eds.), *The Future of the Multinational Company*, New York: Wiley 2003, pp. 34–44.
Taggart, J. H./Pearce, R. D. (ed), *International Management of Technology: Theory, Evidence and Policy*, Management International Review, 40, Special Issue 1/2000.
Thomke, S., *Experimentation Matters: Unlocking the Potential of New Technologies for Innovation*, Boston, MA: Harvard Business School Press 2003.
Tversky, A./Kahnemann, D., The Framing of Decisions and the Psychology of Choice, *Science*, January 1981, pp. 453–458.
Weick, K., Technology as Equivoque: Sensemaking in New Technologies, in Weick, K., *Making Sense of the Organization*, Oxford: Blackwell 2001, pp. 148–175.
Weick, K., *Sensemaking in Organizations*, Thousand Oaks, CA: Sage 1995.
Welge, M. K./Holtbrügge, D., Wissensmanagement in multinationalen Unternehmungen: Ergebnisse einer empirischen Untersuchung, *ZfbF*, 12, 2000, pp. 762–777.
Winter, S. G., Knowledge and Competence as Strategic Assets, in Teece, D. J. (ed.), *The Competitive Challenge: Strategies for Industrial Innovation and Renewal*, New York: Ballinger 1987, pp. 159–184.

Management
International Review
© Gabler Verlag 2004

Dirk Holtbrügge/Nicola Berg

Knowledge Transfer in Multinational Corporations: Evidence from German Firms

Abstract

- In recent years, several theoretical and empirical studies in the field of organizational knowledge management were published. With rare exceptions, however, little attention has been paid to the specific aspects of knowledge transfer within MNCs.

- The purpose of this article is to overcome this limitation and to explore how knowledge is transferred across organizational and national boundaries.

Key Results

- Based on an analysis of theoretical and empirical studies two dimensions of knowledge management are distinguished: source and content.

- An empirical study of 142 subsidiaries of German MNCs shows that the sources and characteristics of knowledge flows are affected by different firm-specific and country-specific variables.

Authors

Dirk Holtbrügge, Professor of International Management (Head of Department), University of Erlangen-Nuremberg, Germany.
Nicola Berg, Assistant Professor of Business Administration, University of Dortmund, Germany.

Dirk Holtbrügge/Nicola Berg

Introduction

The globalization of markets and growing international competition have caused a fundamental change of corporate strategy in many companies. The main challenge is not only to manage the growth of foreign activities but also to operate simultaneously under different economic, legal, political, and cultural conditions. Especially multinational corporations (MNCs) attempt to respond to these challenges by integrating their domestic and foreign operations into a transnational corporate strategy.

The core idea of a transnational strategy is the simultaneous exploitation of two main sources of competitive advantage that have been mostly understood as opposite in the past, namely advantages of local responsiveness and of global integration (Prahalad/Doz 1987). To harmonize these two goals, the subsidiaries of an MNC can no longer be treated as a portfolio of largely independent companies like most MNCs did in the past. Instead, they have to be seen as integral parts of a complex configuration of value-creating activities across national borders. As a consequence, each subsidiary becomes not only responsible for its position on the local market (*atomistic perspective*) but must also increasingly be concerned with the contribution it makes to the competitive position of the MNC as a whole (*holistic perspective*) (Porter 1986).[1]

From an organizational point of view the concept of transnational strategy is associated with a high need for cross-border coordination between interdependent domestic and foreign operations. According to Bartlett/Ghoshal (1989), this need can be coped with most efficiently by the transition to integrated transnational networks. Integrated networks are characterized by a changing role of the headquarters away from hierarchical control of foreign subsidiaries to decentralized decision processes. Simultaneously, there is a shift in the spectrum of organizational coordination and control mechanisms from structural and technocratic instruments to informal and personal instruments (e.g., Martinez/Jarillo 1989).

In this context of transnational network management the collection, development and exploitation of organizational knowledge is often characterized as the main success factor of MNCs. Organizational knowledge can be defined as context-specific, relational and action-oriented network of information that organizations develop in order to interact with their environment (Nonaka/Takeuchi 1995, p. 57). As Bartlett/Ghoshal (1987, p. 37) recognize, knowledge management, that is "the ability to learn – to transfer knowledge and expertise from one part of the organization to others worldwide – became more important in building durable competitive advantage". Similarly, Gupta/Govindarajan (1991, p. 772) argue that, in addition to capital and product flows, "knowledge flows across subsidiaries become particularly significant". The main reason for this is that knowledge is very difficult to imitate and to adopt, thus, compared to products, technologies and other resources, building a more reliable and sustainable source of competitive advantage (e.g. Grant 1996, Meso/Smith 2000, Adams/Lamont 2003). As a consequence of this growing importance several theoretical and empirical studies in the field of organizational knowledge management were published in the last years. These studies develop, for example, knowledge taxonomies (e.g., Kogut/Zander 1992), explore how knowledge is managed in international joint ventures and strategic alliances (e.g., Inkpen 1997, Simonin 1999), describe knowledge enablers (e.g., von Krogh 1997, von Krogh et al. 2000), and identify different models of knowledge management in various countries of the world (e.g., Hedlund/Nonaka 1993). However, only few studies (e.g., Gupta/Govindarajan 1991, 1995, 2000, Kogut/Zander 1993, Asakawa 1995, Arvidsson 2000, Grant et al. 2000, Sölvell/Birkinshaw 2000) pay attention to the specific aspects of knowledge management in MNCs. Especially, there is a lack of empirical studies of the determinants of intra-MNC knowledge flows. With some notable exceptions (e.g., Zander/Kogut 1995, Inkpen/Dinur 1998, Foss/Pedersen 2002, Martin/Salomon 2003), "very little systematic empirical investigation in the determinants of intra-MNC knowledge transfers has so far been attempted" (Gupta/ Govindarajan 2000, p. 474).

The purpose of this study is to overcome this limitation and to explore the factors that influence transnational knowledge flows in MNCs. The paper proceeds as follows. After reviewing the literature on knowledge management in MNCs the research hypotheses are derived. In the following section, the research methodology is described. We then report the findings of an empirical study among 142 subsidiaries of German MNCs. In the final section, conclusions, limitations, and implications for future research are presented.

Literature Review

One of the first theories in international management to recognize the relevance of knowledge is the learning theory of internationalization developed by Johanson/Vahlne (1977, 1990, 2003).[2] According to Johanson/Vahlne, the internationalization process of a firm evolves in an interplay between the development of knowledge about foreign markets and operations on one hand and an increasing commitment of resources to foreign markets on the other. Following Penrose (1959), two kinds of knowledge are distinguished: objective knowledge (e.g. market data, legislation, export regulations) which can be taught, and experiential knowledge which can only be acquired through personal experience.

A main assumption of the learning theory is that the internationalization process of a firm is primarily driven by experiential knowledge. This is needed in order to understand the political, economic, cultural and technological conditions of foreign markets and to overcome the psychic distance to these markets. Potential sources of experiential knowledge are managers in sales departments, representative offices and foreign subsidiaries. Only after both the uncertainty and the transaction costs of operating in a foreign market are reduced through the acquisition of experiential knowledge firms will proceed in the establishment chain from simple internationalization forms with low market commitment to more advanced forms which imply an increasing commitment of resources to the market. Moreover, experiential knowledge is necessary to reduce the perceived psychological distance between the host and the home country, to advance on the cultural distance chain and to enter markets with greater differences to the home market. As Macharzina et al. (2001, p. 639) state, each step in the cultural distance chain "may be considered a learning cycle that provides an opportunity to improve the ability to absorb the relevant information from the external environment and to process it."

While the learning theory of internationalization directs its attention primarily to external sources of knowledge such as customers, suppliers, and consultants, network approaches to MNCs emphasize the importance of internal transfers of knowledge between headquarters and subsidiaries (e.g., Hedlund 1986, Hedlund/Rolander 1990, Nohria/Ghoshal 1997, Bartlett/Ghoshal 1989). The basic premise of these approaches is that competitive advantages can be achieved from the capability of transferring knowledge to those MNC sub-units where it will increase value added. A precondition for this is that the geographically dispersed units are able to transfer knowledge to other MNC units as well as to adopt knowledge generated there. Especially subsidiaries with reference knowledge that is valuable world-wide have to assure that this knowledge is available for the entire MNC (Boettcher/Welge 1994). This capacity of worldwide knowledge transfer becomes essential to support transnational organizational learning and to enhance the holistic perspective of MNCs.

To support the transnational collectivization of individual knowledge, Cerny (1996) suggests the institutionalization of global knowledge and best-practice sharing systems. Their aim is to enhance the systematic collection of knowledge about customers, suppliers, competitors, technologies and products, its distribution about national borders, and its exploitation in the entire MNC. Through this permanent process of "world-wide organizational information creation" (Nonaka 1990, p. 70) MNCs should be enabled to use the knowledge acquired locally by their various subsidiaries for transnational organizational learning.

Most prominently, this idea of MNCs as knowledge networks has been elaborated by Gupta/Govindarajan (1991). The key idea of their concept is that MNCs can be thought of as a network of multidirectional knowledge transactions among units located in different countries.[3] For each type of transaction subsidiaries can differ regarding the volume and criticality of knowledge flows. To the extent that subsidiaries engage in intra-corporate transactions, they can differ also regarding whether they are either the receivers or the providers of what is being transacted. Combining these two factors, any subsidiary of an MNC can be distinguished according to the extent to which it engages in knowledge inflows from and the extent to which it engages in knowledge outflows to other units of the MNC. In terms of knowledge flow patterns this leads to a typology of four generic subsidiary roles: global innovator (high outflow, low inflow), integrated player (high outflow, high inflow), implementor (low outflow, high inflow), and local innovator (low outflow, low inflow).

Hypothesis Development

Sources of Knowledge Flows

Summarizing the key arguments of both the learning theory of internationalization and of network theories of MNCs, two basic dimensions of knowledge flows can be distinguished: sources and characteristics. Concerning the *source of knowledge flows*, it can be further distinguished between *external knowledge* that is to a large extent created on the basis of knowledge inputs from local sources (customers, suppliers, workforce, consultants, etc.), and *internal knowledge* that is primarily created on the basis of knowledge inputs from internal network relations with other MNC units and transferred across national borders.[4]

In line with previous studies we argue that the use of *external knowledge* is to a high degree influenced by the cultural distance between the subsidiary and the home country of the MNC.[5] As stated by Hofstede (2001), knowledge is largely embedded in its local environment, that is knowledge which is appropriate in one cultural context may not be relevant in others. Cultural distance may also impede the knowledge transfer process. Different languages, business cultures, and institutions increase the perceived psychic distance and make it less likely that knowledge is transferred across borders (Johannson/Vahlne 1977). Another reason for the difficulties of knowledge transfers across cultural borders may be the "not-invented-here" syndrome (Allen 1977). As Macharzina et al. (2001, p. 647) put it: "Ethnocentrism, skepticism of the credibility of remote sources, suspicion of the unknown, and resistance to change can lead organizational units to reject proposals." Consequently, Bhagat et al. (2002) propose that the transfer of internal knowledge is most effective when the transacting organizations are located in national contexts with identical cultural patterns. Similarly, Barkema et al. (1996) found that learning effects are more likely to occur in countries that are culturally similar to the home country of the MNC. This leads to the following hypothesis:

Hypothesis 1. The larger the cultural distance between a subsidiary and the home country of the MNC, the more important the inflow of external knowledge.

It is widely accepted that the inflow of external knowledge does not only depend on external, country-specific factors such as the cultural distance between the host and home country but also on MNC-specific variables. E.g., Cohen/Levinthal (1990) argue that a firm's absorptive capacity, that is its ability to value, assimilate, and apply new external knowledge depends on its prior investment in research and development. Andersson et al. (2002) found a subsidiary's absorptive capacity positively related to its global mandate and to the attention it receives from the headquarters. We argue that the inflow of external knowledge is also influenced by the level of local resources and capabilities (Bartlett/Ghoshal 1989). Subsidiaries with large personal and organizational resources have higher organizational slack (Bourgeois 1981) which allows them to implement new technologies and routines more easily than subsidiaries without these resources. This argument is in line with other studies which underline that a firm's human and organizational capital is an important precondition of its ability to acquire and exploit external knowledge (for an overview see Zahra/George 2002). Thus,

Hypothesis 2. The higher a subsidiary's level of local resources and capabilities, the more important the inflow of external knowledge.

With regard to *internal knowledge*, it can be argued that its transfer is mainly dependent on the strategic importance of a subsidiary for the entire MNC (Bartlett/Ghoshal 1989). Strategically important subsidiaries will receive more attention from the headquarters and will play a more important role for the entire MNC than subsidiaries in remote markets. They may be granted, for instance, a mandate to carry out certain activities for other units' operations (Birkinshaw 1996). In terms of corporate coordination and control, the subsidiary will be evaluated based not only for its success on the local market but also on the results of the other units for which it carries responsibility, thereby motivating the subsidiary to contribute to the competence development of those units (Andersson et al. 2002). Consequently, we hypothesize that the integration into the transnational strategy requires close communication and the exchange of knowledge with other MNC units.

Hypothesis 3. The higher the strategic importance of a subsidiary for the entire MNC, the more important the inflow and outflow of internal knowledge.

Figure 1. Conceptual Framework (Part 1)

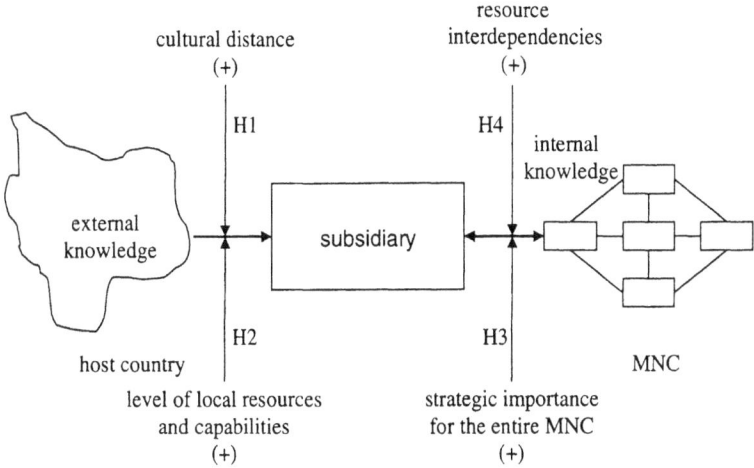

Previous studies reveal that the development and transfer of internal knowledge is also stimulated by the transfer of goods and services between MNC units, that is by intra-MNC trade (e.g., Subramaniam/Venkatraman 2001, Foss/Pedersen 2002). The underlying argument behind this finding is that a part of internal knowledge is embodied in products and services. Their transfer to other units of the MNC is likely to enhance the MNC-wide communication about possible modifications to the goods and services, so that these may be better adapted to the needs of the receiving MNC unit (Foss/Pedersen 2002, p. 100). Thus, we hypothesize that:

Hypothesis 4. The higher the resource interdependencies between a subsidiary and other units of the MNC, the more important the inflow and outflow of internal knowledge.

The first four hypotheses concerning potential country-specific and firm-specific influences on the preferred sources of knowledge we want to test in our study are presented in Figure 1.

Characteristics of Knowledge Flows

With reference to the *characteristics of knowledge flows* it can be distinguished between objective vs. experiential knowledge (Penrose 1959) respectively explicit vs. tacit knowledge (Polanyi 1966). Objective or explicit knowledge, on the one hand, refers to knowledge that can be articulated either verbally or in writing (e.g., in manuals or mathematical expressions) and thus can be transmitted in formal, systematic language (e.g., in mails or reports). Experiential or tacit knowledge, on the other, is implicit, non-verbalized and therefore difficult to formalize and to communicate since it is embedded in individual experiences and involves personal beliefs, perspectives and value systems (Hedlund/Nonaka 1993, Nonaka/Takeuchi 1995).[6]

Several studies underline that these two forms of knowledge require different mechanisms of transfer. Experiential or tacit knowledge can be best exploited through personal transfer mechanisms like the international transfer of managers and global teams. Parent-country and third-country nationals, for example, may use their experiences made during previous assignments for decisions in their current host country (Almeida/Kogut 1996). Foreign delegations also allow transfer of knowledge that the sender may be unaware of, that requires trust-creation between the sender and the receiver, and that needs to be adapted to different cultures, laws, and business practices (Pedersen et al. 2003). Moreover, global teams may act as interfaces and boundary-spanners between different MNC units (Cohen/Levinthal 1990). Composed of managers from different countries they are argued to be efficient mechanisms to exchange tacit knowledge between geographically dispersed subsidiaries and to translate it into a form that is appropriate to the specific local conditions (Ghoshal et al. 1994). These considerations lead to the following hypothesis:

Hypothesis 5. Tacit or experiential knowledge will be transferred primarily through personal transfer mechanisms.

On the contrary, explicit or objective knowledge is more likely to be transferred through written or electronic media (Pedersen et al. 2003, p. 76). One reason for this is that personal transfer mechanisms are costly (e.g., travel expenses, foreign delegations). Moreover, written and electronic modes are able to transfer large amounts of data which is not possible through face-to-face interaction. Knowledge transfer through written and electronic media is also more precise because information may be digitalized and selective perceptions of individuals are less likely. Finally, the storage of information in an electronic form allows permanent access irrespective of space, time and context. This leads to the following hypothesis:

Hypothesis 6. Explicit or objective knowledge will be transferred primarily through written or electronic transfer mechanisms.

The last two hypotheses concerning the preferred mechanisms of knowledge transfer that we want to test in our study are presented in Figure 2.

Figure 2. Conceptual Framework (Part 2)

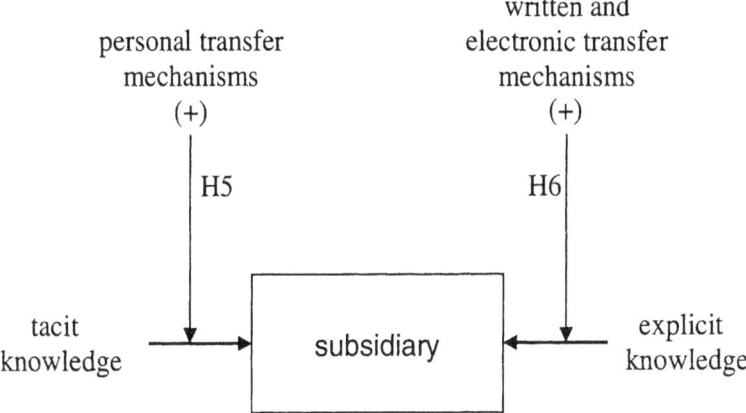

Methodology

Sample

To test the hypotheses developed in the previous paragraph, an empirical study among German MNCs was conducted. In a first step the largest 200 German manufacturing companies (in terms of turnover) were identified by using the Hoppenstedt Directory of German Firms. From this group those companies which belong to a parent firm that has its headquarters outside of Germany were excluded.[7] Secondly, the sample was limited to companies with at least eight foreign subsidiaries and a foreign share in turnover of at least 30 percent.[8] These criteria were met by 60 of the original 200 companies.

From these 60 MNCs the largest 8–12 foreign subsidiaries that are owned at least by 50 percent by the German parent firm were selected by using company reports and internet materials. The highest-ranking German expatriates of these 600 foreign subsidiaries were mailed a three-pages questionnaire. This choice of respondents is motivated by the assumption that foreign delegates have experiences in both headquarters and subsidiaries and therefore are the best to make an overall judgment of transnational knowledge flows.[9]

The mailing yielded 147 responses and 142 completed questionnaires, for an overall response rate of 25.4 percent. Compared to the other empirical studies in international management, this is remarkable high. Statistical analyses of firm characteristics that were assumed to influence knowledge transfer (industry, corporate parent, and size) revealed no significant differences between the responding and the non-responding firms. However, regarding home countries, subsidiaries in China, India and Russia are slightly overrepresented in the sample.

Dirk Holtbrügge/Nicola Berg

Measures

To measure the dominant *source of knowledge* the respondents were asked to indicate how important to their decisions are external sources of knowledge such as employees, customers, consultants, etc., or internal sources such as knowledge from the headquarters or other subsidiaries on 5-point Likert scales, with $1 =$ not important at all and $5 =$ very important. Similarly, the respondents were asked to assess outflows of knowledge to other units of the MNC.

Following Pedersen et al. (2003, p. 81), the *characteristics of knowledge* were measured by asking the respondents to indicate to what extent the knowledge needed for their current assignment was acquired through own, practical experience or via purchase of external expertise. Thereby, the respondents indicated tacitness or explicitness, respectively, of the acquired knowledge. Both variables were measured on 5-point Likert scales with $1 =$ own practical experience and $5 =$ purchase of external expertise.

The applied *mechanism of knowledge transfer* was measured by asking the respondents to indicate the extent to which (i) foreign delegates and (ii) global decision teams (proxy for personal mechanisms of knowledge transfer) and to which (i) manuals, reports or other written media and (ii) electronic modes such as the intranet (proxy for written and electronic mechanisms of knowledge transfer) are used. All variables were measured on 5-point Likert scales going from $1 =$ not important at all to $5 =$ very important.

Resource interdependencies were calculated according to Gupta et al. (1999) as the percentage of the subsidiary's total cost of goods sold accounted for by imports from (input interdependencies) and exports to (output interdependencies) other sub-units of the MNC. *Strategic importance of the local market* and *level of local resources and capabilities*: Both variables were measured on 5-point Likert scales, with $1 =$ very low importance (very weak position) and $5 =$ very high importance (very strong position).

Cultural distance between the home and the host country was measured according to the study of Hofstede (1980), who found that cultures differ substantially on four dimensions: power distance, uncertainty avoidance, masculinity, and, individualism. Later, Hofstede (2001) developed a fifth dimension, namely long-term orientation. Because no data are available, for several countries in our study we concentrate on the original four dimensions. Based on this study, Kogut/Singh (1988) developed a composite index for each headquarters-subsidiary country pair based on their deviations along each of the four cultural dimensions. The cultural distance between Germany, as the home country, and the respective host country was calculated using the following equation:

$$CD_{jk} = \ln\{(D_{ij} - D_{ik})2/V_i\}/4,$$

where CD_{jk} stands for the cultural distance between countries j and k, D_{ij} is the score for parent country j (Germany) on cultural dimension i, D_{ik} indicates the score for subsidiary in country k on cultural dimension i, and V_i is the variance of the index for cultural dimension i.

Results and Discussion

The means, standard deviations and correlation coefficients of all variables are presented in Table 1. A descriptive analysis of our findings reveals that inputs from local sources such as customers, suppliers and workforce are the most important source of knowledge (mean = 3.04), followed by internal knowledge that is transferred from other MNC (mean = 2.64). The outflow of knowledge to other parts of the MNC is less relevant (mean = 2.37).

Surprisingly, no significant correlation between external inflows and internal outflows of knowledge was found. This means that, contrary to our expectations, external learning is not associated with the transfer of new knowledge throughout the MNC. It has to be taken into account, however, that our findings might be biased by home-country influences; as explained earlier, subsidiaries in countries with large cultural distance to the home country Germany (China, India, and Russia), which are argued to be less integrated into intra-MNC knowledge flows, are overrepresented in our sample.

Another remarkable result is the negative correlation between external and internal inflows of knowledge ($r = -0.22$, $p < 0.05$). This means that subsidiary managers base their decisions either on local knowledge or on international knowledge which is transferred from other units of the MNC but do not use both sources of knowledge simultaneously. Thus, no transnational combination of knowledge from different sources which is argued to be a main characteristic of integrated networks (Nonaka/Takeuchi 1995) can be observed.

Our data reveal no significant correlation between inflow and outflow of knowledge. According to the typology of Gupta/Govindarajan (1991), 20.4 percent of the subsidiaries in our sample can be characterized as global innovators, 20.4 percent as integrated players, 26.1 percent as implementors and 33.1 percent as local innovators. Compared to Gupta/Govindarajan (2000), our findings show a slightly higher proportion of global innovators and implementers and a slightly lower proportion of integrated players and local innovators.

As proposed in *Hypotheses 1 and 2*, the inflow of external knowledge is positively influenced by both the cultural distance between the subsidiary and the home country ($r = 0.25$, $p < 0.01$) and the subsidiary's level of local resources and capabilities ($r = 0.23$, $p < 0.05$). This finding is in line with Johann-

Table 1. Descriptive Statistics and Correlation Matrix

Variable	Mean	SD	1	2	3	4	5	6	7	8	9	10	11	12
1. External Inflow	3.04	1.09												
2. Internal Inflow	2.64	1.33	−0.22*											
3. Internal Outflow	2.37	1.08	0.06	−0.01										
4. Explicitness	3.19	1.02	0.04	0.05	−0.06									
5. Foreign Delegates	3.20	0.75	−0.03	0.06	0.13	−0.28**								
6. Global Teams	2.23	1.15	−0.02	−0.06	0.05	−0.35***	0.23*							
7. Manuals, Reports	3.45	1.10	0.07	−0.11	−0.04	0.40***	−0.25**	−0.09						
8. Intranet	3.34	1.17	−0.03	−0.12	0.04	0.15	−0.18	0.12	0.27**					
9. Input Interdependencies	20.60	12.52	0.12	0.20*	0.06	−0.08	0.06	0.11	−0.05	−0.10				
10. Output Interdependencies	18.23	10.47	−0.07	0.09	0.26**	−0.10	0.10	0.07	−0.18*	0.05	−0.04			
11. Strategic Importance of Local Market	2.74	1.55	−0.27**	0.19*	−0.02	−0.13	−0.03	−0.06	−0.15	−0.01	−0.03	0.07		
12. Level of Local Resources and Capabilities	3.33	0.91	0.23*	−0.07	−0.06	−0.03	0.04	−0.26**	−0.15	−0.08	0.03	−0.00	−0.06	
13. Cultural Distance	1.98	1.06	0.25**	−0.08	−0.00	0.11	0.04	0.05	0.17	0.13	0.13	−0.03	0.04	−0.06

N = 142
*** = $p < 0.001$
** = $p < 0.01$
* = $p < 0.05$

son/Vahlne (1977) and others who found that knowledge is to a high degree embedded in its cultural context and difficult to transfer across large cultural distances. Moreover, our findings give strong support for the hypothesis saying that the absorptive capacity of a subsidiary depends on its level of human and organizational capital. External knowledge can be best acquired and exploited when the subsidiary is equipped with strong personal and organizational resources.

Hypothesis 3 can be confirmed only partially. While the correlation between the strategic importance of the local market and the inflow of internal knowledge is significantly positive ($r = 0.19$, $p < 0.05$), no significant correlation with the outflow of internal knowledge was found. One reason for this interesting finding may be that headquarters perceive subsidiaries which operate in strategically relevant markets primarily as receivers but not as providers of internal knowledge. According to Gupta/Govindarajan (1991) these subsidiaries might be labeled as implementors. Obviously, most MNCs perceive a strong need to control subsidiaries in strategically important markets by providing them with internal knowledge and do not recognize them as important sources of transnational learning.

In *Hypothesis 4*, we proposed a positive relationship between resource interdependencies and knowledge flows. Interestingly, this hypothesis can be confirmed only when the direction of intra-firm trade respectively knowledge flows is considered. While we found significant correlations between input interdependencies and internal knowledge inflows ($r = 0.20$, $p < 0.05$) as well as between output interdependencies and internal knowledge outflows ($r = 0.26$, $p < 0.01$), the correlations between input interdependencies and knowledge outflows as well as between output interdependencies and knowledge inflows are not significant. Thus, knowledge flows are not stimulated by the level of transferred goods and services per se but depend on direction of intra-MNC trade to or from the subsidiary.

As proposed in *Hypothesis 5*, tacit or experiential knowledge is transferred primarily through personal transfer mechanisms such as foreign delegations and global teams. Although the overall relevance of the latter is only low (mean = 2.23), global teams are very specifically used to exchange knowledge between MNC units that is difficult to formalize and involves personal beliefs, perspectives and experiences. The same can be said for foreign delegations. Thus, our data confirm the findings of other studies (e.g. Welge/Holtbrügge 2000, Harzing 2001) that expatriates are not only seen as an instrument to control foreign subsidiaries but also as a mechanism to transfer technical and management know-how as well as organizational culture.

Finally, *Hypothesis 6* is confirmed only partially. While we found, as expected, a highly significant correlation between the explicitness of knowledge and the use of written transfer mechanisms such as manuals and reports, no significant correlation between explicitness and the use of electronic media such as the intranet can be observed. Although the relevance of the intranet is higher than that of all other mechanisms of knowledge transfer (mean = 3.34), this media is still relatively new. Obviously, many firms test the possibilities of the intranet for data exchange across national borders without having already enough experiences and a clear idea of its strengths and weaknesses.

Limitations and Implications for Future Research

This paper contributes to our understanding of transnational knowledge flows in MNCs, an issue that has thus far received relatively limited attention in international management literature. It shows especially, that the sources and characteristics of knowledge flows in MNCs are affected by different firm-specific and country-specific variables.

The results of our study, however, should be interpreted in consideration of some inherent limitations. First, the findings might be biased due to the use of single-source data. Sources and characteristics of knowledge flows were reported by German expatriates. As such the study is limited to the individual perceptions of these single respondents which is, however, a very common problem in international management research. Since it is felt that expatriates are best placed to make an overall judgment of transnational knowledge flows they are perceived as the best source of information that is available.

Second, the study is limited to German MNCs, which show a strong tendency toward hierarchical control (e.g., Holtbrügge 2002). It would be interesting therefore to replicate the study in MNCs from smaller countries such as the Netherlands, Switzerland or Sweden, which are supposed to have a stronger transnational orientation. It could be expected that in MNCs from these home countries internal inflows and outflows will play a more important role.

Third, we used a rather broad definition of knowledge in our study. An interesting issue for further research would thus be to analyze whether variations in knowledge transfer is related to specific activities such as R&D, marketing, or production. A recent study of Egelhoff et al. (2003) gives support to this hypothesis.

Finally, our findings are descriptive in the sense that we did not measure the efficiency of various forms of knowledge transfer. Consequently, we cannot say whether or not the described ways of knowledge transfer are able to enhance competitive advantages. Therefore, future studies should integrate efficiency measures into the analysis of knowledge transfers in MNCs. This can be done by using either objective performance criteria such as of profitability, competitiveness and business volume (Holmström 2003) or subjective perceptions of satisfaction with knowledge transfer (Pedersen et al. 2003).

Endnotes

1 The distinction between the atomistic and the holistic perspective in international management is extensively explained in Welge/Holtbrügge (2003).
2 The relevance of knowledge in various internationalization theories is intensively discussed in Macharzina et al. (2001).
3 Gupta/Govindarajan (1991) recognize that MNCs are also characterized by intra-corporate transactions of capital and products. However, they focus on knowledge flows because the latter are seen as particularly important.
4 As Foss/Pedersen (2002, p. 97) argue, no knowledge is entirely internally accumulated, and the ability to absorb local knowledge is likely to be a result of previous knowledge transfer from other MNC units. Nevertheless, it makes sense to say that some knowledge is largely locally produced, while some other knowledge is strongly based on transfer from MNCs units located in other countries.
5 We recognize that cultural differences exist also within countries. This, however, is not a concern of our paper.
6 As Pedersen et al. (2003, p. 75) note, knowledge is never completely tacit or explicit and will often consist of inseparable components with different characteristics. Typically, however, one form of knowledge is dominant.
7 This applies to companies such as IBM, Opel or Ford.
8 This excludes companies with only limited foreign operations like Deutsche Telekom or VEW.
9 Local managers are also important subjects and sources of organizational knowledge. Since their corporate socialization is mostly restricted to their particular home country they may be neglected, however, in a study that is aimed to better understand the process of *transnational* knowledge management.

References

Adams, G. L./Lamont, B. T., Knowledge Management Systems and Developing Sustainable Competitive Advantage, *Journal of Knowledge Management*, 7, 2, 2003, pp. 142–151.
Allen, L., *Managing the Flow of Technology*, Cambridge, MA: MIT Press 1977.
Almeida, P./Kogut, B., The Exploration of Technological Diversity and the Geographic Localization of Innovation, *Small Business Economics*, 9, 1996, pp. 21–31.
Andersson, U./Björkman, I./Furu, P., Subsidiary Absorptive Capacity, MNC Headquarters' Control Strategies and Transfer of Subsidiary Competencies, in Lundau, S. M. (ed.), *Network Knowledge in Multinational Business*, Cheltenham-Northhampton, MA: Edward Elgar 2002, pp. 115–136.
Arvidsson, N., Knowledge Management in the Multinational Enterprise, in Birkinshaw, J./Hagström, P. (eds.), *Capability Management in Network Organizations*, Oxford: Oxford University Press 2000, pp. 176–193.
Asakawa, K., *Managing Knowledge Conversion across Borders: Toward a Framework of International Knowledge Management*, INSEAD Working Paper 1995.
Barkema, H. G./Bell, J. H. J./Pennings, J. M., Foreign Entry, Cultural Barriers, and Learning, *Strategic Management Journal*, 17, 1996, pp. 151–166.
Bartlett, C. A./Ghoshal, S., Managing across Borders: New Strategic Requirements, *Sloan Management Review*, 1987, pp. 37–47.
Bartlett, C. A./Ghoshal, S., *Managing across Borders. The Transnational Solution*, second edition, Boston, MA: Harvard Business School Press 1989.
Bhagat, R. S./Kedia, B. L./Harveston, P. D./Triandis, H. C., Cultural Variations in the Cross-border Transfer of Organizational Knowledge: An Integrated Framework, *Academy of Management Review*, 27, 2, 2002, pp. 204–221.

Birkinshaw, J., How Global Subsidiary Mandates are Gained and Lost, *Journal of International Business Studies*, 37, 3, 1996, pp. 467-495.
Boettcher, R./Welge, M. K., Strategic Information Diagnosis in the Global Organization, *Management International Review*, 34, 1, 1994, pp. 7-24.
Bourgeois, J., On the Measurement of Organizational Slack, *Academy of Management Review*, 36, 1, 1981, pp. 29-39.
Cerny, K., Making Local Knowledge Global, *Harvard Business Review*, 74, 3, 1996, pp. 22-26.
Cohen, W. M./Levinthal, D. A., Absorptive Capacity: A New Perspective on Learning and Innovation, *Administrative Science Quarterly*, 35, 1990, pp. 128-152.
Egelhoff, W. G./Gorman, L./McCormick, S., Causes of Knowledge Flows in MNCs, Paper presented at the Annual Conference of the European International Business Academy, Copenhagen 2003.
Foss, N. J./Pedersen, T., Sources of Subsidiary Knowledge and Knowledge Transfer in MNCs, in Lundau, S. M. (ed.), *Network Knowledge in Multinational Business*, Cheltenham-Northhampton, MA: Edward Elgar 2002, pp. 91-114.
Ghoshal, S./Korine, H./Szulanski, G., Interunit Communication in Multinational Corporations, *Management Science*, 40, 1, 1994, pp. 96-110.
Grant, R. M., Toward a Knowledge-based Theory of the Firm, *Strategic Management Journal*, 17, 1996, pp. 109-122.
Grant, R. M./Almeida, P./Song, J., Knowledge and the Multinational Enterprise, in Millar, C. C. J. M./Grant, R. M./Choi, C. J. (eds.), *International Business. Emerging Issues and Emerging Markets*, Basingstoke-London: MacMillan 2000, pp. 102-129.
Gupta, A. K./Govindarajan, V., Knowledge Flows and the Structure of Control within Multinational Corporations, *Academy of Management Review*, 16, 4, 1991, pp. 768-792.
Gupta, A. K./Govindarajan, V., Organizing for Knowledge Flows within MNCs, *International Business Review*, 3, 1995, pp. 443-457.
Gupta, A. K./Govindarajan, V., Knowledge Flows within Multinational Corporations, *Strategic Management Journal*, 21, 2000, pp. 473-496.
Gupta, A. K./Govindarajan, V./Malhotra, A., Feedback-seeking Behavior within Multinational Corporations, *Strategic Management Journal*, 20, 1999, pp. 205-222.
Harzing, A.-W., Of Bears, Bumble-Bees, ad Spiders: The Role of Expatriates in Controlling Foreign Subsidiaries, *Journal of World Business*, 36, 4, 2001, pp. 366-367.
Hedlund, G., The Hypermodern MNC - A Heterarchy?, *Human Resource Management*, 25, 1986, pp. 9-35.
Hedlund, G./Rolander, D., Action in Heterachies - New Approaches to Managing the MNC, in Bartlett, C. A./Doz, Y./Hedlund, G. (eds.), *Managing the Global Firm*, London/New York: Routledge 1990, pp. 15-46.
Hedlund, G./Nonaka, I., Models of Knowledge Management in the West and Japan, in Lorange, P. et al. (eds.), *Implementing Strategic Process, Change, Learning, and Cooperation*, London: Basil Blackwell 1993, pp. 117-144.
Hofstede, G.: *Culture's Consequences: International Differences in Work-Related Values*, Beverly Hills-London: Sage 1980.
Hofstede, G.: *Culture's Consequences. Comparing Values, Behaviors, Institutions, and Organizations Across Nations*, seond edition, Thousand Oaks/London/New Delhi: Sage 2001.
Holmström, C., Internal versus External Knowledge Sourcing in Subsidiaries and the Effect on Knowledge Transfer and MNC Performance, Paper presented at the Annual Conference of the European International Business Academy, Copenhagen 2003.
Holtbrügge, D., *Configuration and Coordination of Multinational Corporations*, Working Paper 1/2002, University of Erlangen-Nuremberg, Department of International Management, Nuremberg 2002.
Inkpen, A. C., An Examination of Knowledge Management in International Joint Ventures, in Beamish, P./Killing, J. (eds.), *Cooperative Strategies. North American Perspectives*, San Francisco, CA: New Lexington Press 1997, pp. 337-369.
Inkpen, A.C./Dinur, A., *The Transfer of Management of Knowledge in the Multinational Corporation: Considering Context*, Carnegie Bosch Institute 98-16: Working Paper 1998.
Johanson, J./Vahlne, J.-E., The Internationalization Process of the Firm - A Model of Knowledge Development and Increasing Foreign Market Commitments, *Journal of International Business Studies*, 8, 1, 1977, pp. 23-32.

Johanson, J./Vahlne, J.-E., The Mechanism of Internationalization, *International Marketing Review*, 7, 4, 1990, pp. 11-24.
Johanson, J./Vahlne, J.-E., Building a Model of Firm Internationalisation, in Blomstermo, A./Sharma, D. D. (eds.), *Learning in the Internationalisation Process of Firms*, Cheltenham-Northampton, MA: Edward Elgar 2003, pp. 3-15.
Kogut, B./Singh, H.: The Effect of National Culture on the Choice of Entry Mode, *Journal of International Business Studies*, 19, 3, 1988, pp. 411-432.
Kogut, B./Zander, U., Knowledge of the Firm, Combinative Capabilities, and the Replication of Technology, *Organization Science*, 3, 3, 1992. pp. 383-397.
Kogut, B./Zander, U., Knowledge of the Firm and the Evolutionary Theory of the Multinational Corporation, *Journal of International Business Studies*, 24, 2, 1993, pp. 625-646.
Macharzina, K./Oesterle, M.-J./Brodel, D., Learning in Multinationals, in Dierkes, M./Berthoin Antal, A./Child, J./Nonaka, I. (eds.), *Handbook of Organizational Learning and Knowledge*, Oxford: Oxford University Press 2001, pp. 631-356.
Martin, X./Salomon, R., Knowledge Transfer Capacity and its Implications for the Theory of the Multinational Corporation, *Journal of International Business Studies*, 34, 2003, pp. 356-373.
Martinez, J. I./Jarillo, J. C., The Evolution of Research on Coordination Mechanisms in Multinational Corporations, *Journal of International Business Studies*, 20, 3, 1989, pp. 489-514.
Meso, P./Smith, R., A Resource-based View of Organizational Knowledge Management Systems, *Journal of Knowledge Management*, 4, 3, 2000, pp. 224-234.
Nohria, N./Ghoshal, S., *The Differentiated Network: Organizing Multinational Corporations for Value Creation*, San Francisco, CA: Jossey-Bass 1997.
Nonaka, I., Managing Globalization as a Self-renewing Process: Experiences of Japanese MNCs, in Bartlett, C. A./Doz, Y./Hedlund, G. (eds.), *Managing the Global Firm*, London: Routledge 1990, pp. 69-94.
Nonaka, I./Takeuchi, H., *The Knowledge-creating Company: How Japanese Companies Create the Dynamics of Innovation*, Oxford: Oxford University Press 1995.
Penrose, E., *The Theory of the Growth of the Firm*, London: Basil Blackwell 1959.
Pedersen, T./Petersen, B./Sharma, D., Knowledge Transfer Performance of Multinational Companies, *Management International Review*, 43, Special Issue 3/2003, pp. 69-90.
Polanyi, M., *The Tacit Dimension*, London: Routledge & Kegan Paul 1966.
Porter, M. E., Competition in Global Industries: A Conceptual Framework, in Porter, M. E. (ed.), *Competition in Global Industries*, Boston, MA: Harvard Business School Press 1986, pp. 15-60.
Prahalad, C. K./Doz, Y. L., *The Multinational Mission*. New York: Free Press 1987.
Simonin, B. L., Ambiguity and the Process of Knowledge Transfer in Strategic Alliances, *Strategic Management Journal*, 20, 1999. pp. 595-623.
Sölvell, Ö./Birkinshaw, J., Multinational Enterprises and the Knowledge Economy: Leveraging Global Practice, in Dunning, J. H. (ed.), *Regions, Globalization, and the Knowledge Economy*, Oxford: Oxford University Press 2000, pp. 82-105.
Subramaniam, M./Venkatraman, N., Determinants of Transnational New Product Capability: Testing the Influence of Transferring and Deploying Tacit Overseas Knowledge, *Strategic Management Journal*, 22, 2001, pp. 359-378.
von Krogh, G., Develop Knowledge Activists!, *European Management Journal*, 15, 5, 1997, pp. 475-483.
von Krogh, G./Ichijo, K./Nonaka, I., *Enabling Knowledge Creation: How to Unlock the Mystery of Tacit Knowledge and Release the Power of Innovation*, Oxford: Oxford University Press 2000.
Welge, M. K./Holtbrügge, D., Motive für die Auslandstätigkeit, in Gerhard und Lore Kienbaum Stiftung/Gutmann, J./Kabst, R. (eds.), *Internationalisierung im Mittelstand. Chancen-Risiken-Erfolgsfaktoren*, Wiesbaden: Gabler 2000, pp. 315-325.
Welge, M. K./Holtbrügge, D., *Internationales Management*, third edition, Stuttgart: Schäffer-Poeschel 2003.
Zahra, S. A./George, G., Absorpotive Capacity: A Review, Reconceptualization, and Extension, *Academy of Management Review*, 27, 2, 2002, pp. 185-203.
Zander, U./Kogut, B., Knowledge and the Speed of the Transfer and Imitation of Organizational Capabilities, *Organization Science*, 6, 1995, pp. 76-92.

Management International Review

Neuerscheinungen

Doris Lindner
**Einflussfaktoren
des erfolgreichen
Auslandseinsatzes**
Konzeptionelle Grundlagen –
Bestimmungsgrößen – Ansatzpunkte
zur Verbesserung
2002
XX, 341 S. mit 38 Abb., 21 Tab.,
(mir-Edition),
Br. € 59,–
ISBN 3-409-11952-3

Tobias Specker
**Postmerger-Management in den
ost- und mitteleuropäischen
Transformationsstaaten**
2002
XX, 431 S. mit 60 Abb., 28 Tab.,
(mir-Edition),
Br. € 64,–
ISBN 3-409-12010-6

Jörg Frehse
**Internationale
Dienstleistungskompetenzen**
Erfolgsstrategien für die europäische
Hotellerie
2002
XXVI, 353 S. mit 48 Abb.,
(mir-Edition),
Br. € 59,–
ISBN 3-409-12349-0

Anja Schulte
**Das Phänomen
der Rückverlagerung**
Internationale Standortent-
scheidungen kleiner und mittlerer
Unternehmen
2002
XXII, 315 S. mit 17 Abb., 2 Tab.,
(mir-Edition),
Br. € 59,–
ISBN 3-409-12375-X

Andreas Wald
**Netzwerkstrukturen und
-effekte in Organisationen**
Eine Netzwerkanalyse
in internationalen Unternehmen
2003
XVIII, 238 S. mit 19 Abb., 61 Tab.,
(mir-Edition),
Br. € 49,90
ISBN 3-409-12395-4

Nicola Berg
Public Affairs Management
Ergebnisse einer empirischen
Untersuchung in Multinationalen
Unternehmungen
2003
XXXIV, 471 S. mit 20 Abb., 67 Tab.
(mir-Edition),
Br. € 64,–
ISBN 3-409-12387-3

Betriebswirtschaftlicher Verlag Dr. Th. Gabler, Abraham-Lincoln-Str. 46, 65189 Wiesbaden

Management
International Review
© Gabler Verlag 2004

Jan Hendrik Fisch

Allocating Innovative Activities in International R&D with Fuzzy Logic

Abstract

- This paper develops a model to predict the appearance of specific R&D units in international locations. Grounding on information processing theory, the model evaluates the local supply of technological information and demand for R&D information processing using fuzzy logic in order to determine the appropriate type of R&D unit.

- The model is tested with data from German and Swiss MNCs. After further refinement and validation, R&D managers may use the model to analyze and optimize their international R&D organizations.

Key Results

- The model correctly predicts the configuration of four out of six international R&D networks by locational factors.

Author

Dr. Jan Hendrik Fisch, Senior Lecturer and Research Fellow at the Chair of Business Policy, Organization and Human Resource Management, University of Hohenheim, Stuttgart, Germany.

Jan Hendrik Fisch

Introduction

After the scholarly interest in the internationalization of research and development (R&D) in multinational corporations (MNCs) reached several peaks since the end 1970ies, the turn of the millennium brought a new wave of publications on this topic. *Research Policy* devoted its issue 2/3 of volume 28 (1999) exclusively to the internationalization of R&D; *Management International Review* presented a special issue on this subject in volume 40 (2000). Novel trends are identified to enable new insights (Gerybadze/Reger 1999). Also, novel methods may be introduced to enable new solutions.

There is a great variety of approaches in literature that differentiate types of R&D units in international locations. Not only contributions from the 1980ies (Behrman/Fischer 1980, Freudenberg 1988) but also more recent typologies (Pearce/Singh 1992, Brockhoff/Schmaul 1996, Nobel/Birkinshaw 1998) find new terms to describe the different innovative activities of internationally spread R&D units but basically express the same thing as Ronstadt's early typology of 1978 (Ronstadt 1978). *Transfer Technology Units* receive existing technologies from other R&D units and modify them for local products. *Indigenous Technology Units* cannot rely on technological support from other parts of the MNC and thus have to develop new products especially for the local markets. *Global Technology Units* also conduct original R&D but have the mandate to transfer their technologies to the whole MNC. *Corporate Technology Units* have an MNC-wide mandate, too, but focus on research rather than on development.

Håkanson investigated the emergence of different types of R&D units (Håkanson 1992). Corporate Technology Units are frequently founded on green field. If foreign companies are acquired by an MNC the related R&D units tend to become Transfer Technology Units or Indigenous Technology Units. Nearly all types of R&D units can appear in an evolution from a Transfer Technology Unit to a Global Technology Unit. Hewitt searched for the preconditions for an R&D unit to reach a new stage of evolution (Hewitt 1980). Both the location conditions within and outside a subsidiary may change over time and suggest having an appropriate type of R&D unit. Beckmann found in his empirical study that the potential quality and the interaction quality of a location have a major influence on the decision to establish a certain kind of R&D unit (Beckmann 1997).

For the time being, there is solid knowledge about what types of R&D units MNCs set up in international R&D networks and why they appear at the presence of distinct location conditions. There is no shortage of explanatory factors but there might be a deficit of grounding in terms of organizational theory. Moreover, practitioners have received little payback from empirical studies providing them with support for R&D location decisions.

This paper tries to enrich the theoretical base of R&D location decisions by information processing theory. On this basis, the predominant line of thought, which strives for explanations, is turned upside down in order to gain a model that is able to predict efficient choices in international R&D location decisions. Because common calculations in crisp logic are very sensitive to minor errors in classification, I use fuzzy logic to cope with the difficulties in predicting the efficient decisions. The model is tested with a sample of MNCs from the German-speaking countries. After a more embracing validation it may serve as a decision support tool for R&D managers.

R&D as Information Processing

In general, the quality and frequency of communication appear to increase the performance of organizations (Snyder/Morris 1984). There is also empirical evidence for the fact that particularly the success of innovations depends on R&D-related communication (Allen/Tushman/Lee 1979, Ebadi/Utterback 1984, Souder 1987). The dominance of communication aspects in R&D suggests to focus on information processing and therefore to refer to the information processing approach by Galbraith (Galbraith 1977).

Information processing theory views organizations as open systems that process information in order to reduce uncertainty. Uncertainty is the difference between the amount of information an organization needs in order to fulfill a task and the amount of information it already owns for this purpose. The amount of information an organization has to process depends primarily on the task itself. Diverging goals and division of labor involve specialization of sub-groups and raise the amount of information to process. The desired level of performance also increases the amount of information that has to be processed. In international R&D, the amount of information is very high because an MNC's product and process technologies have to keep pace with the world's top competitors.

Galbraith considers organizations efficient if their ability to process information (information processing capacity) fits the amount of information they have to process in order to reduce uncertainty. There are two basic ways towards an improvement of the information processing capacity. One is to establish vertical information systems that increase the throughput of hierarchical communication channels. Because information flows in R&D are less hierarchical, the second way bears more importance: enabling lateral communication. Lateral communication in international R&D is facilitated when participants of innovation processes, namely R&D units, other corporate functions such as marketing/sales and manufacturing, and external information sources such as public research institutions or competitors' R&D units face little obstacles to interaction. Such obstacles increase with geographical distance (Allen 1991).

According to Daft and Lengel, reducing uncertainty is only one aspect of information processing (Daft/Lengel 1986). When there is even uncertainty about what information is necessary to reduce uncertainty, processing a defined amount of information lacks a direction. Daft and Lengel call this sort of uncertainty "ambiguity". In order to reduce ambiguity, successful information processing depends on the richness of information rather than on its sheer amount. Richness is the ability of a piece of information to change the understanding of a problem in a given span of time. There are several media to transmit information at specific degrees of richness. Richness decreases from direct personal contact to video conferencing and telephone calls down to written communication such as letters and e-mail or even anonymous databases.

Daft and Lengel hold that uncertainty and ambiguity originate from three sources: the task, the relationships between organizational units, and the environment. Tasks are very different and poorly analyzable in R&D when true technological innovations are at stake. Innovation processes create various interdependencies with many different organizational units. The environment has a strong meaning for technological activities but is difficult to analyze when holders of technological knowledge try to keep it as a secret. Consequently, international R&D activities do not only require a large amount of uncertainty reduction but also a great deal of ambiguity reduction. Ambiguity reduction is facilitated when participants of innovation processes are able to use media of high richness, preferably direct personal contact. Direct personal contact is more available for communicating partners whose workplaces are situated close to one another.

Tushman and Nadler (1980) as well as Moenaert and Souder (1990) summarized the arguments of information processing theory in their models of R&D units. These models highlight the importance of the collaboration between R&D units and other communicating partners. They characterize R&D units as information processing systems that absorb information from the environment, combine it with existing knowledge and transfer the newly generated information to their environment. The transfer of information into and from an R&D unit may sometimes be bi-directional but has a general order from the technological environment, which serves as a supply of information, to the R&D unit, and finally to the production and sales units, which represent the demand for R&D information processing induced by the market. Because much of the relevant information is difficult to codify and hardly fits pre-defined communication structures, Tushman and Nadler interpret R&D units as members of informal and mainly verbal communication networks.

Both the high amount and the high richness of information needed for international R&D information processing suggest to place appropriate R&D units in proximity to their international communicating partners. Geographical

(Hough 1972) and cultural distances (Hofstede 1980) hinder international communication. A network of internationally spread R&D units faces internal problems in the communication over large distances but also has to yield communication issues at external interfaces, which can be even more sensitive than internal interfaces. The choice of the type of local R&D units will therefore depend on the conditions of the local supply of technological information and the local demand for R&D information processing.

A Fuzzy Location Model of International R&D

Supply of Information and Demand for Information Processing

Information processing theory is able to integrate several of the known factors of R&D internationalization. For example, the supply of technological information embraces tapping into foreign sources of knowledge (Dunning/Wymbs 1999) and employing highly qualified foreign personnel (Håkanson 1992). Factors such as better reacting to country-specific customer needs (Kuemmerle 1999) and supporting foreign production units (Caluori 1993) are reflected by the local demand for R&D information processing. *Figure 1* shows what types of R&D units hypothetically match the information processing characteristics of distinct location conditions. The matrix builds a model to predict the efficient choice of R&D units for foreign locations. Since this efficient choice is derived from a perspective of information flows, it will be called *communication-efficient*. It is more adequate to consider communication efficiency than cost efficiency in innovation processes. Their primary goal is generating new ideas at a given cost rather than saving money in having ideas; ideas are not "given" but emerge under suitable circumstances. In order to gain a prognostic sentence of R&D location choice, the common logic of explanation needs to be inverted as follows.

If an MNC can apply or adapt existing technologies to new local products, the *demand* for local R&D information processing is *low*. If the technological environment of a potential location offers little stimuli, the *supply* of information for local R&D is *low* as well. At a low demand for information processing and a low supply of information, the model expects a *Transfer Technology Unit* to be communication-efficient in this location.

If the local market requires creating products whose underlying technology is not available from other parts of an MNC, the *demand* for local R&D information processing is *high*. Still the technological environment in the respective country may be poorly developed. The informational resources for R&D are scarce; the *supply* of information is *low*. At a high demand for local information processing and a low supply of information, the MNC will run an *Indigenous Technology Unit*, which develops products exclusively for the local market.

Jan Hendrik Fisch

Figure 1. Types of R&D Units Depending on the Local Supply of Information and the Local Demand for Information Processing

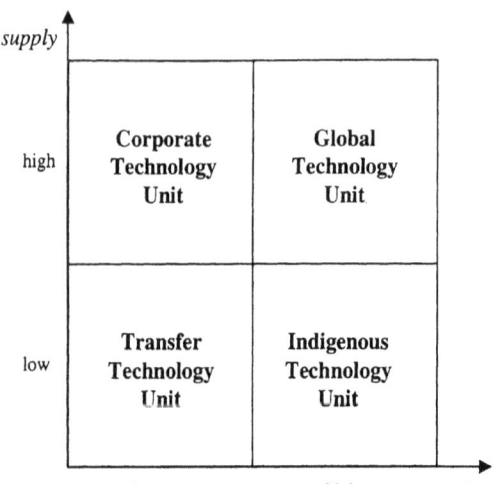

If, once again, the local market requires developing completely new products whose technological base is missing in an MNC, the *demand* for local R&D information processing is *high*. If, furthermore, the technological environment in this country offers a variety of co-operating partners in private or public research institutions, the *supply* of information for R&D information processing is *high*. Under these circumstances, it will be efficient to establish a *Global Technology Unit* that takes over an MNC-wide mandate for the new technology and transfers its results to other R&D units in order to exploit them elsewhere as well.

Finally, the local subsidiary may have little interest in specific R&D services. The local *demand* for R&D information processing is *low*. By contrast, the prerequisites for research in the related country may be excellent because the local *supply* of R&D-related information is *high*. In this constellation, the location is ideal for a *Corporate Technology Unit* that is able to operate rather independently of the local subsidiary's necessities and thereby concentrate on tasks of (applied) research for the whole MNC. Now recall the concept of communication-efficient choices. The international R&D network of an MNC may consist of all of the four different R&D unit types according to the respective communicational conditions. It represents a set of efficient location decisions:

Hypothesis 1. MNCs build their international R&D networks from communication-efficient R&D units.

The model in *Figure 1* looks like a common conceptual model. Such models are very popular in management science in order to structure and clarify a field of analysis. The model at hand shall moreover serve as a tool of prognosis. On the base of the explaining factors of R&D internationalization, it tries to *predict* the international *allocation* of innovative activities in MNCs as a dependent variable from the independent variables *supply* of technological information and *demand* for local R&D information processing. There is, however, a hidden challenge: The prognosis is expected to hit its goal although the independent variables are poorly defined. The matrix dimensions suggest that *high* and *low* represent distinct sections of a defined scale. In fact they do not. What exactly means *"high"*, and what is actually *"low"*? Introducing an artificial, clear-cut borderline between *high* and *low* works on the language level but may result in grave random and systematic errors when predicting these types by calculation.

Figure 2 presents a modified, less determined view of differentiating R&D types by the local supply and demand of information. In the fuzzy R&D location model, there are gray zones between *high* and *low*, i.e.; supply and demand within the intermediate ranges can be a bit high and a bit low at the same time.

Figure 2. Fuzzy Types of International R&D Units

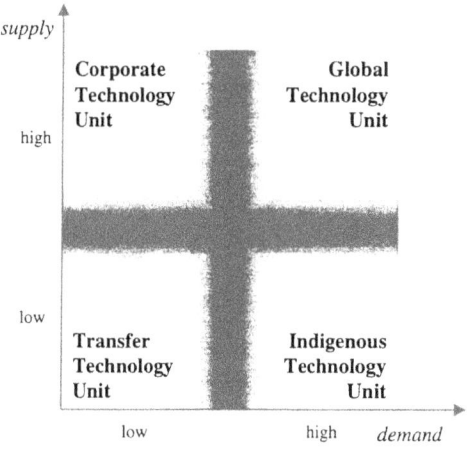

Jan Hendrik Fisch

Fuzzy Logic in R&D Location Decisions

Intuition and experience enable human decision makers to act efficiently even in poorly defined decision problems (Zeleny 1994). Fuzzy logic tries to project experiential decision rules to fuzzy variables in order to automate human decision behaviour by means of a fuzzy controller.

In classical crisp logic, x is an element of a set X, or it is not. Fuzzy logic allows for a less exclusive assignment of elements to sets. The membership function

$$\mu_F(x) : X \to [0, 1]$$

expresses that the element x is part of the set X to a certain extent between 0 and 1. The border cases of 0 and 1 correspond to an assignment in common crisp logic while the intermediate range mirrors the fuzziness of the relation (Kartalopoulos 1996). Membership functions may have different kinds of shape. Mostly it is sufficient to use a piecewise linear function. As long as a precise distinction between two terms is impossible it makes little sense to assume highly complicate membership functions for the range between them. In intermediate zones, membership functions overlap and add up to 1.

Accordingly, the fuzzy R&D location model embraces three ranges for both scales of *supply* and *demand*. In the outer ranges the memberships of *high* and *low* are 1, respectively. In the intermediate range the *supply* (or *demand*) is considered both *high* and *low* depending on the membership functions $\mu_{supplyH}$ (*supply*) and $\mu_{supplyL}$ (*supply*). It is difficult to determine the "right" value of *supply* (or *demand*) from which on the membership functions shall overlap. The model assumes that these points are at the 20% and 80% quantiles q^{20}_{supply} and q^{80}_{supply}, see *Figure 3*. These quantiles are bound to the context of each individual MNC. This requires

Figure 3. Fuzzification of the Supply of Information from the Technological Environment

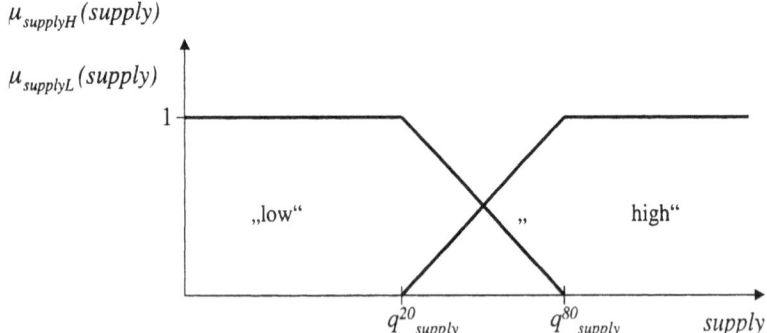

testing the model on the level of the international R&D network of a single MNC rather than through all R&D locations of an entire sample of MNCs.

The supply of information from the technological environment may be in the range of *high supply* $\mu_{supplyH}$ *(supply)*. As *Figure 3* shows, the membership function *supply of information is high* is 0 up to q^{20}_{supply}, has a constant slope in the interval $[q^{20}_{supply}, q^{80}_{supply}]$ and is finally 1 above q^{80}_{supply}:

$$\mu_{supplyH}(supply) = \begin{cases} 0; & supply < q^{supply}_{20} \\ \dfrac{supply - q^{supply}_{20}}{q^{supply}_{80} - q^{supply}_{20}}; & q^{supply}_{20} \leq supply < q^{supply}_{80} \\ 1; & supply \geq q^{supply}_{80} \end{cases}$$

The supply of information can be in the range of *low supply* $\mu_{supplyL}$ *(supply)* as well. The related membership function *supply of information is low* has the inverse shape

$$\mu_{supplyL}(supply) = \begin{cases} 1; & supply < q^{supply}_{20} \\ -\dfrac{supply - q^{supply}_{80}}{q^{supply}_{80} - q^{supply}_{20}}; & q^{supply}_{20} \leq supply < q^{supply}_{80} \\ 0; & supply \geq q^{supply}_{80} \end{cases}$$

and adds up to 1 with $\mu_{supplyH}$ *(supply)* for all possible values of *supply*. The local demand for R&D information processing is fuzzified in the same manner.

Many rules used by human decision makers have an *if-then* structure. In the *if* part, fuzzy sets may be integrated by Boolean operators such as *and* or *or*. The *then* part of a rule formulates the logic consequence of the inference. The fuzzy R&D location model embraces four decision rules predicting the type of R&D from the supply and demand of information:

1. **If** *demand* low **and** *supply* low **then** Transfer Technology Unit.
2. **If** *demand* high **and** *supply* low **then** Indigenous Technology Unit.
3. **If** *demand* high **and** *supply* high **then** Global Technology Unit.
4. **If** *demand* low **and** *supply* high **then** Corporate Technology Unit.

In fuzzy logic, Boolean operators can be implemented in various ways. The simplest way is to use the minimum (*and*, ∩) or the maximum (*or*, ∪) of both membership functions that are to be integrated. The logic integration of two fuzzy sets is again a fuzzy set. The fuzzy R&D location model requires *and* operators only. The membership functions resulting from the inference are

$\mu_{demandL \cap supplyL}(demand, supply) = \min[\mu_{demandL}(demand), \mu_{supplyL}(supply)],$

$\mu_{demandH \cap supplyL}(demand, supply) = \min[\mu_{demandH}(demand), \mu_{supplyL}(supply)],$

$\mu_{demandH \cap supplyH}(demand, supply) = \min[\mu_{demandH}(demand), \mu_{supplyH}(supply)],$

$\mu_{demandL \cap supplyH}(demand, supply) = \min[\mu_{demandL}(demand), \mu_{supplyH}(supply)].$

In order to derive a crisp decision from the fuzzy inference, the result reflected by the integrated memberships needs to be defuzzified. One method to defuzzify a result from multiple memberships is to calculate the centre of gravity (average) of the different consequences on a continuous scale, see *Figure 4*. The four membership functions are integrated via *and* gates and point to distinct spots on a scale that indicates the degree of innovation (*doi*) of the predicted R&D unit's type. The fuzzy R&D location model assumes Transfer Technology Units to be least innovative and therefore rates them at a *doi* of 1. Indigenous Technology Units develop products that are new to the local market but have little meaning for the MNC as a whole. Their *doi* shall be 2. Global Technology Units receive a *doi* value of 3 since their innovatory work is relevant to the entire MNC. Corporate Technology Units are characterized by a *doi* of 4 because their research results may be even new to the world of science.

Let e_1 be a concrete value of *demand* and e_2 a concrete value of *supply*. The centre of gravity in the case of e_1 and e_2 is calculated from

$$doi(e_1, e_2) = 1^* \mu_{demandL \cap supplyL}(e_1, e_2) + 2^* \mu_{demandH \cap supplyL}(e_1, e_2)$$
$$+ 3^* \mu_{demandH \cap supplyH}(e_1, e_2) + 4^* \mu_{demandL \cap supplyH}(e_1, e_2).$$

Figure 4. Inference and Defuzzification of R&D Unit Types

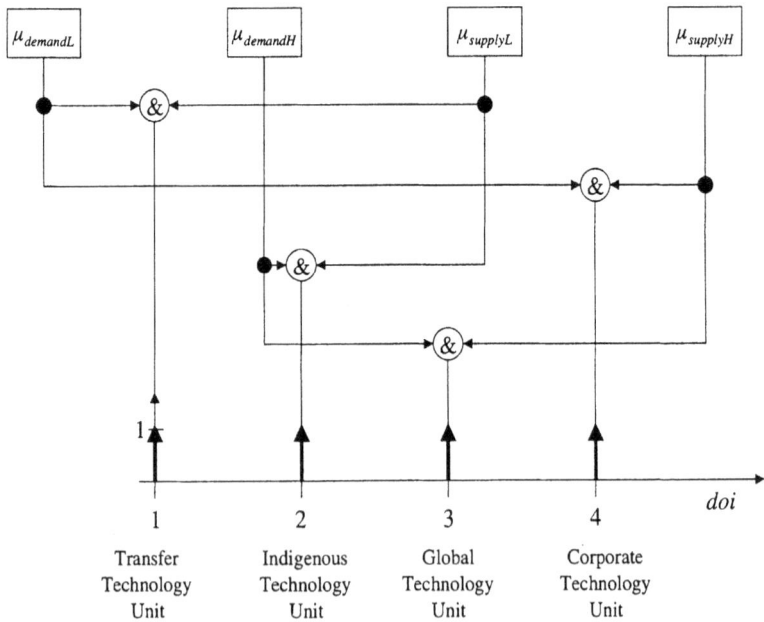

To sum up, the fuzzy R&D location model consists of three steps. In the first step, the supply of technological information from the environment and the demand for R&D information processing are translated into certain degrees of membership to the terms *high* and *low* (fuzzification). The second step applies the decision rules in the matrix of *Figure 2* to the membership functions and derives a fuzzy decision (inference). At last the fuzzy result is re-converted into crisp logic in order to determine the appropriate type of R&D unit at a location (defuzzification). In crisp logic, tiny inaccuracies in the *high* vs. *low* classification would lead to harsh misinterpretations of the location conditions. The fuzzy controller, by contrast, reacts fairly robust to vague inputs.

Method

Sample

The empirical test of the hypothesis formulated above requires data from MNCs that own several R&D units in foreign locations. The chemical, pharmaceutical, and electronics industries are highly internationalized (Taggart 1991, Kenney/Florida 1994, Kuemmerle 1998). I gathered data from the largest MNCs in these industries whose revenues exceeded € 2.56 billion (DM 5 billion) in 1997 and whose share of foreign revenues was at least 50 percent. In the German-speaking countries, there are 15 such MNCs: 12 in Germany, three in Switzerland, and none in Austria. I contacted their financial officers by questionnaires. Seven MNCs completely denied supplying information, two were only ready to give out data on a regional level. The remaining six MNCs delivered complete data sets. The sample embraces a total of 70 R&D locations.

As *Table 1* shows, the shares of revenue abroad do not differ significantly in the sample and the total. The R&D intensities, defined as the ratio of R&D expenses and revenue, are nearly the same. Neither do the affiliations to the different industries in the sample deviate too much from the total. The sample appears sufficiently representative of the total. Some MNCs insisted to treat their answers confidentially, so the presentation of data in this paper shall not enable the reader to assign them to the MNCs under consideration.

Table 1. Characterization of the MNCs in the Sample and the Total

	Foreign Revenues	R&D Intensity	Pharmaceutical	Chemical	Electronics
Sample	80%	7%	33%	50%	17%
Total	81%	8%	40%	40%	20%

Jan Hendrik Fisch

Measures

The *information supply* from the national technological environments is not directly related to the individual MNCs. I obtained country-specific data on the relative importance of the individual technological environments from international patent application statistics for the pharmaceutical, chemical, and electronics industries from the *ifo Institut fuer Wirtschaftsforschung*, Munich/Germany. The advantage of these data over common patent statistics is that only applications in at least two countries are taken into account. This eliminates most of the bias from different national patent laws. Patent data of each country in the world were condensed by calculating sliding averages over the years 1987 until 1996. The resulting value contains information about the whole period and puts higher weights on recent patent applications.

The *demand for R&D information processing* is the second independent variable of the model. The demand originates from corporate functions other than R&D, in particular the local management, marketing, sales, and production departments. I measure the demand for R&D information processing by the 1997 revenues of the MNCs' subsidiaries in the related countries. The revenue is a more suitable measure than the value added by country because it also carries information on the meaning of the markets that the subsidiaries serve.

Information on the *degree of innovation* (*doi*) as the dependent variable of the model was gained from respondents' estimation. The questionnaire characterized the four types of international R&D units and presented a list of the countries with potential R&D locations of the respective MNC. The country name was followed by a scale on which the respondents were asked to mark the predominant type of R&D activities. Indications between types were allowed. The replies were transformed to a *doi* between 1 and 4. A χ^2 test is able to judge whether the predictions of the model fit reality.

Fuzzy Controller

The fuzzy controller was implemented in the programming language Matlab; see *Figure 5* for a flow chart. Matlab is an interpreted language that offers a variety of built-in numerical functions and is especially designed for matrix operations, which is very useful for the fuzzy location model.

The fuzzy controller program reads the independent variables from a .txt file. This file contains a table of the supply of technological information and the demand for R&D information processing for all countries in the international R&D network of the MNC at hand. In a loop, *supply* and *demand* are fuzzified for each country. The program integrates the membership functions and derives a fuzzy decision. The result is defuzzified and stored in another .txt file.

Figure 5. Flow Chart of the Fuzzy Controller

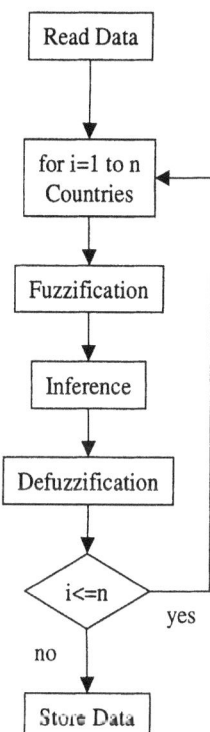

Results

For each MNC, the fuzzy controller predicted a communication-efficient allocation of R&D activities. *Figure 6* shows the expected *doi* in the hatched bars and the actual *doi* in the solid bars. The MNCs are sorted by decreasing number of R&D locations, the countries are sorted by rising actual *doi*.

Table 2 presents the results of the χ^2 tests with $\alpha = 0.01$ for all MNCs I to VI. The international R&D network of MNC I deviates from the communication-efficient solution to a considerable extent. The fuzzy location model predicts much more innovative R&D units in Japan, France, and the UK and does not expect such units in Norway and Poland. These differences can be partly explained by the strong focus on certain local markets but contradict the common ratio of establishing international R&D sites. *Hypothesis 1* must be rejected for MNC I.

Figure 6. Expected and Real Degree of Innovation at International R&D Locations

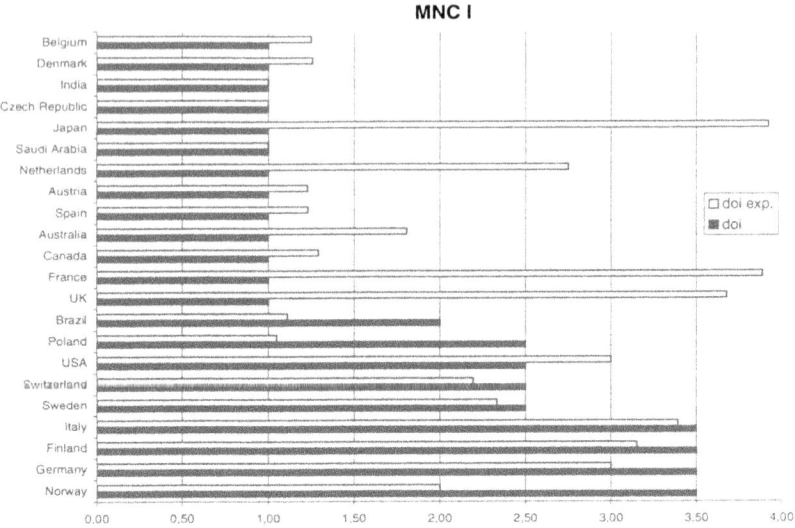

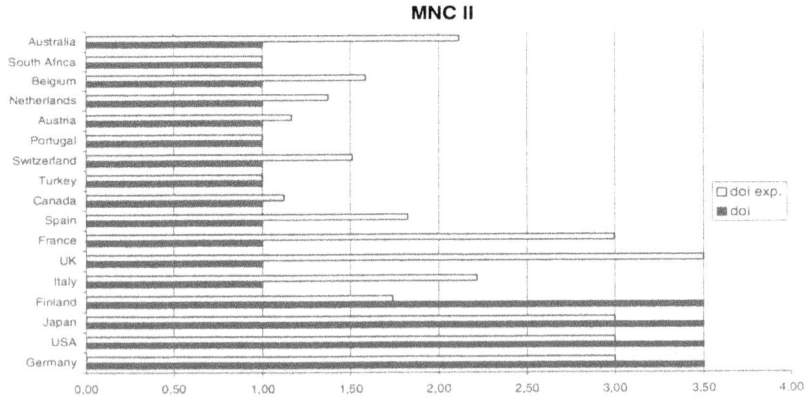

Figure 6. (continued)

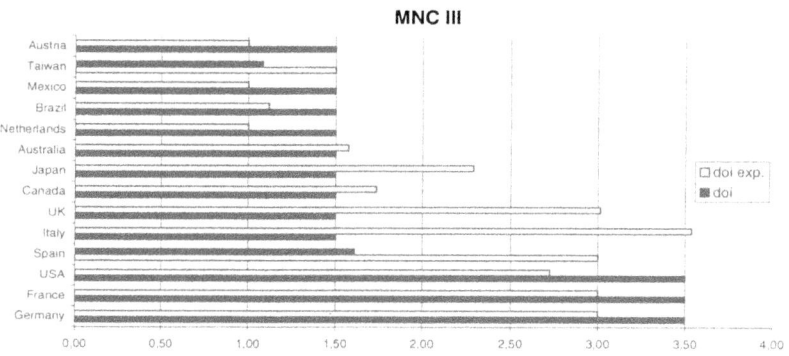

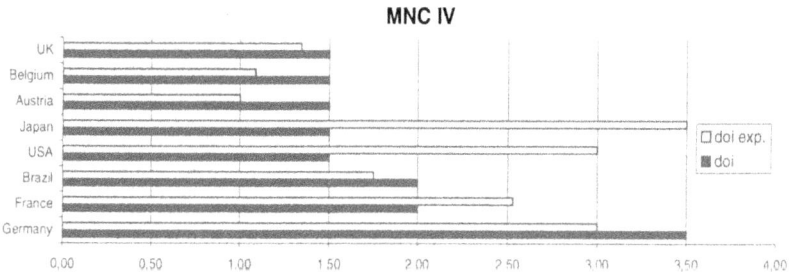

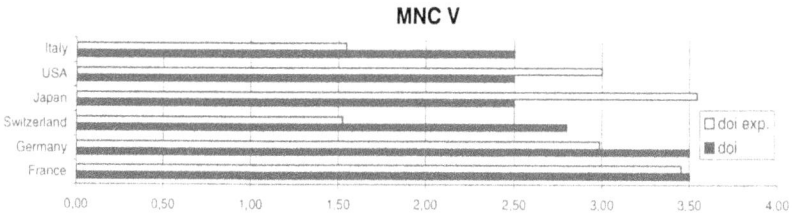

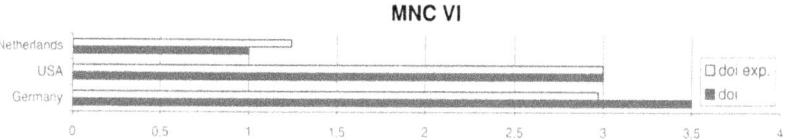

Table 2. χ^2 Test of the Fuzzy R&D Location Model

MNC	test value	critical range	Hypothesis 1
I	$\chi^2 = 151.10$	$\chi^2 \leq 38.93$	reject
II	$\chi^2 = 77.63$	$\chi^2 \leq 32.00$	reject
III	$\chi^2 = 21.40$	$\chi^2 \leq 27.69$	do not reject
IV	$\chi^2 = 15.69$	$\chi^2 \leq 18.48$	do not reject
V	$\chi^2 = 3.11$	$\chi^2 \leq 15.09$	do not reject
VI	$\chi^2 = 0.69$	$\chi^2 \leq 9.21$	do not reject

MNC II's R&D network reveals unexpected priorities in its international locations as well. France, the UK, and Italy are, in principle, attractive locations for innovative activities in the related industry but remain widely neglected by MNC II. MNC II clearly distinguishes between a limited number of research units in Finland, Japan, the US, and Germany on the one hand and typical Transfer Technology Units in many countries on the other. This division of labour has mainly historical reasons. Again, *Hypothesis 1* must be rejected for MNC II.

MNC III has built its international R&D network in a way that is more comprehensible by an analysis of the location conditions. Differences are visible in the UK, Spain, and Italy while the R&D units in the remaining countries reveal an expected *doi*. The location choices of MNC III are communication-efficient within the bounds of α. *Hypothesis 1* cannot be rejected.

The international R&D network of MNC IV mainly behaves accordingly to the fuzzy location model's expectations but foregoes much of the innovative potential of locations in Japan and the US. The respondent from MNC IV explained this by the European R&D units' strong effort to keep the research activities centralized in the traditional R&D sites. Still the χ^2 test considers the R&D network of MNC IV communication-efficient. Communication efficiency will increase even further when the R&D site in the USA has its planned size and meaning.

MNC V focuses on a small number of countries for its R&D activities. Within this circle of countries, MNC V puts an unexpected weight on Italy and Switzerland while it gives Japan a minor R&D mandate. The differences, however, are comparably little so the predicted R&D network passes the χ^2 test. *Hypothesis 1* cannot be rejected.

The range of countries covered by MNC VI's international R&D network is limited to three. The model predicts the assignment of innovative activities quite accurately. *Hypothesis 1* cannot be rejected. Altogether, *Hypothesis 1* had to be rejected for two and could not be rejected for four R&D networks.

Discussion

Implications for R&D Management

The fuzzy location model predicts the establishment of Transfer, Indigenous, Global, and Corporate Technology Units correctly in four out of six international R&D networks of MNCs from the German-speaking countries. On the one hand, this suggests that the model is realistic and delivers results that are similar to the outcome of precedent decision-making in practice. One the other hand, the differences between the predicted and the actual establishment of R&D units could indicate potentials of improvement in these R&D networks. While explanatory models give practitioners a hint on what information could be relevant for their decisions, this predictive model provides them with a theoretical reference or recommendation. R&D managers may want to check their past decisions against this benchmark or even direct their future decisions along with it.

The fuzzy location model evaluates the suitability of a potential R&D location for an individual MNC rather than the general location quality of a country. The success of its prognoses gives support to the findings of precedent explanatory studies, which sought for the influencing factors of R&D internationalization. Its prognostic orientation, however, makes it a decision support tool for R&D managers. On an overall level, we observe from the differences displayed in *Figure 6* that the location conditions in some countries appear underestimated by several MNCs in the survey. Japanese laboratories, e.g., could play a much more important role according to their communication properties than they obviously do in the cases of MNC I, III, IV, V, and also VI, which completely neglects this option. Some MNCs hesitate to set up R&D sites even in adjacent European countries. R&D units in France and particularly in the UK could make considerable contributions to the innovatory performance but their mandates are frequently restricted to adapting existing ideas for the local markets. Some MNCs even omit qualified R&D activities in the US. This is not only striking with respect to the objective location conditions but also to the fact that their local R&D staff could benefit from knowledge in the proprietary marketing or production units, which are already in the country.

If R&D managers wish to redesign their international R&D organizations in order to facilitate inter-organizational and inter-functional communication, they could let the fuzzy location model go through all potential R&D locations and suggest appropriate types of R&D units for these countries. With relatively little input data, which should be easily accessible internally, they obtain a proposition for a communication-efficient R&D organization. MNC III, for instance, would be encouraged to upgrade its innovative activities in Japan to at least an Indigenous Technology Unit. Italy and the UK ought to host Global Technology Units, which develop new technologies rather than implement minor changes to the known product design. This theoretical proposition and other suggestions given by the fuzzy location model cannot replace human decision-making but add to its rationality. Note, however, that the model is not sufficiently validated yet.

Limitations and Future Work

The model relies on two independent variables, the supply of technological information and the demand for R&D information processing. The supply is measured by the share of patent applications in the related country. Even though using international patent applications mainly eliminates the bias from different patent laws, this operationalization is rather an indicator than a direct measure of technological information supply. Similarly, the shares of revenue in the related countries are merely a proxy of the local demand for R&D information processing. More detailed data on the international conditions of R&D information processing will probably allow for a more accurate prediction in a future study.

Prior research as well as the results of this study suggest that there are additional variables influencing international R&D location decisions besides the local conditions of communication. Host governments frequently control the local content of economic activities. Differences in the cost of labour could have an impact as well. Productivity of labour, though, compensates for a reasonable part of these differences. Furthermore, information transfer between different R&D sites as well as between R&D units and corporate units in other countries are neglected by the present version of the fuzzy location model although the related communication barriers could also have a strong effect on the efficiency of international R&D networks (Fisch 2003). Problems of intercultural communication might be able to explain why Japan hosts comparably few Corporate and Global Technology Units of mid-European MNCs.

The fuzzy controller strictly implements the argumentation of the model in *Figure 2*. Its decisions cannot be "better" than human decisions as long as the underlying ratio is the same. However, the automated decisions require less time-consuming handwork and are more objective than human intuition: The fuzzy controller's decisions in the gray zones are fully reproducible. Traditional calculation methods, which may serve as an alternative to the fuzzy controller, do not work with gray zones. The fuzzy controller is therefore largely immune against methodological concerns. However, the present model uses only part of the potential of fuzzy logic. When the model is enhanced by additional variables, one may implement new and much more complicate decision rules. The fuzzy controller could check existing R&D sites at the local and neighboring locations and decide whether it will be efficient to establish a supplementary R&D unit of a different type. It could also use information about possible synergies between technological fields or consider subsidies from host governments.

The small sample size and its conceptual simplifications notwithstanding, this study is a first attempt to turn the known location factors of R&D internationalization into a predictive model. Predicting phenomena is considerably more difficult than explaining them because a causal prognosis has to specify the influence of independent variables whereas an explanation merely has to identify the relevant influencing factors. In this respect, the fuzzy R&D location model advances the analysis of R&D internationalization.

Conclusions

Information processing theory was used to integrate influencing factors of R&D internationalization in a perspective of communication efficiency. The local supply of technological information from the environment and the corporate demand for R&D information processing suggest establishing R&D units of a specific degree of innovation at different international locations. The resulting matrix of Transfer Technology Units, Indigenous Technology Units, Global Technology Units, and Corporate Technology Units was transformed into a fuzzy location model. Fuzzy logic operates with values in the "gray zones" between types and thereby requires less reliable informational input. While such a technique could be used in general to turn conceptual work into quantitative models, this study concentrates on predicting the appearance of certain R&D units in international R&D networks of MNCs. The prognoses of the model held true in four out of six cases. Although future work is necessary to enhance and further validate the model, R&D managers might consider using it as a decision support tool and improve their international R&D organizations towards more efficient information flows and innovative performance.

References

Allen, T. J., *Managing the Flow of Technology – Technology Transfer and the Dissemination of Technological Information within the R&D Organization*, 5th edition, Cambridge, MA: MIT Press 1991.

Allen, T. J./Tushman, M. L./Lee, D. M. S., Technology Transfer as a Function of Position in the Spectrum from Research through Development to Technical Services, *Academy of Management Journal*, 22, 1979, pp. 694–708.

Beckmann, C., *Internationalisierung von Forschung und Entwicklung in multinationalen Unternehmen – Explorative Analyse der Einflußfaktoren auf die Gestaltung internationaler F&E-Netzwerke am Beispiel der deutschen chemischen und pharmazeutischen Industrie*, Aachen: Shaker 1997.

Behrman, J. N./Fischer, W. A., *Overseas R&D Activities of Transnational Companies*, Cambridge, MA: Oelgeschlager, Gunn & Hain 1980.
Brockhoff, K./Schmaul, B., Organization, Autonomy, and Success of Internationally Dispersed R&D Facilities, *IEEE Transactions on Engineering Management*, 43, 1996, pp. 33–40.
Caluori, M., *Internationalisierung der Forschungs- und Entwicklungsaktivitäten*, Hallstadt: Rosch-Buch 1993.
Daft, R. L./Lengel, R. H., Organizational Information Requirements, Media Richness and Structural Design, *Management Science*, 32, 1986, pp. 554–571.
Dunning, J. H./Wymbs, C., The Geographical Sourcing of Technology-based Assets by Multinational Enterprises, in Archibugi, D./Howells, J./Michie, J. (eds.), *Innovation Policy in a Global Economy*, Cambridge: Cambridge University Press 1999, pp. 184–224.
Ebadi, Y. M./Utterback, J. M., The Effects of Communication on Technological Innovation, *Management Science*, 3, 1984, pp. 572–585.
Fisch, J. H., Optimal Dispersion of R&D Activities in Multinational Corporations with a Genetic Algorithm, *Research Policy*, 32, 2003, pp. 1381–1396.
Freudenberg, T., *Aufbau und Management internationaler Forschungs- und Entwicklungssysteme*, Zuerich: ADAG 1988.
Galbraith, J. R., *Organization Design*, Reading, MA et al.: Addison-Wesley 1977.
Gerybadze, A./Reger, G., Globalization of R&D – Recent Changes in the Management of Innovation in Transnational Corporations, *Research Policy*, 28, 1999, pp. 251–274.
Håkanson, L., Locational Determinants of Foreign R&D in Swedish Multinationals, in Granstrand, O./Håkanson, L./Sjölander, S. (eds.), *Technology Management and International Business*, Chichester et al.: Wiley 1992, pp. 97–115.
Hewitt, G., Research and Development performed Abroad by US Manufacturing Multinationals, *Kyklos*, 33, 1980, pp. 308–327.
Hofstede, G., *Culture's Consequences – International Differences in Work-related Values*, Newbury Park, CA et al.: Sage 1980.
Hough, E. A., Communication of Technical Information between Overseas Markets and Head Office Laboratories, *R&D Management*, 3, 1972, pp. 1–5.
Kartalopoulos, S. V., *Understanding Neural Networks and Fuzzy Logic – Basic Concepts and Applications*, New York: IEEE Press 1996.
Kenney, M./Florida, R., The Organization and Geography of Japanese R&D – Results from a Survey of Japanese Electronics and Biotechnology Firms, *Research Policy*, 23, 1994, pp. 305–323.
Kuemmerle, W., Optimal Scale for Research and Development in Foreign Environments – An Investigation into Size and Performance of Research and Development Laboratories Abroad, *Research Policy*, 27, 1998, pp. 111–126.
Kuemmerle, W., The Drivers of Foreign Direct Investment into Research and Development – An Empirical Investigation, *Journal of International Business Studies*, 30, 1999, pp. 1–24.
Moenaert, R. K./Souder, W. E., An Information Transfer Model for Integrating Marketing and R&D Personnel in New Product Development Projects, *Journal of Product Innovation Management*, 7, 1990, pp. 91–107.
Nobel, R./Birkinshaw, J., Innovation in Multinational Corporations – Control and Communication Patterns in International R&D Operations, *Strategic Management Journal*, 19, 1998, pp. 479–496.
Pearce, R. D./Singh, S., *Globalizing Research and Development*, Basingstoke, London: Macmillan 1992.
Ronstadt, R. C., International R&D – The Establishment and Evolution of R&D Abroad by Seven US Multinationals, *Journal of International Business Studies*, 9, 1978, pp. 7–24.
Snyder, R. A./Morris, J. H., Organizational Communication and Performance, *Journal of Applied Psychology*, 69, 1984, pp. 461–465.
Souder, W. E., *Managing New Product Innovations*, Lexington, MA, Toronto: Lexington Books 1987.
Taggart, J. H., Determinants of the Foreign R&D Locational Decision in the Pharmaceutical Industry, *R&D Management*, 21, 1991, pp. 229–240.
Tushman, M. L./Nadler, D. A., Communication and Technical Roles in R&D Laboratories – An Information Processing Approach, *TIMS Studies in the Management Sciences*, 15, 1980, pp. 91–112.
Zeleny, M., Fuzziness, Knowledge and Optimization – New optimality Concepts, in Delgado, M. et al. (eds.), *Fuzzy Optimization – Recent Advances*, Heidelberg et al.: Springer 1994, pp. 3–20.

mir *Edition*

Stefan Eckert

Aktionärsorientierung der Unternehmenspolitik?

Shareholder Value – Globalisierung – Internationalität

2004, XXXII, 518 pages, pb., € 64,00 (approx. US $ 64,00)
ISBN 3-409-12569-8

During the 1990s "shareholder value" has become a popular catchphrase for German companies. In his book the author examines whether this tendency is accompanied by a fundamental change in corporate attitudes towards shareholders. The argumentation is based on an in-depth case study, which stretches across a period of nearly 30 years. The author uncovers the ambiguity of the changes in corporate policy taking place and comes to the conclusion that the turn to shareholder value cannot just be seen as the consequence of competitive changes in a company's markets, but has to be interpreted as a cultural phenomenon.

This book is essential reading for students, lecturers, and researchers who are interested in topics such as International Management, Corparate Policy, and Corporate Governance. It should also be of special interest to corporate managers as well as decision makers working in investment funds or in shareholder associations.

Betriebswirtschaftlicher Verlag Dr. Th. Gabler GmbH, Abraham-Lincoln-Str. 46, 65189 Wiesbaden

mir *Edition*

GABLER

Heiko Hamann

Informationsversorgung in Transnationalen Unternehmungen

Konzeptionelle Grundlagen – Anforderungen – Technologien

2003, XXXIV, 404 pages, pb., € 64,00 (approx. US $ 64,–)
ISBN 3-409-12464-0

Corporations that operate globally have special requirements with respect to their information supply. The author has constructed a model from which he derives suitable criteria for those requirements. The theoretical study is supplemented by an empirical case study conducted at Siemens AG. Current information technologies are described and analysed.

This book is addressed to researchers and students of Strategic Management, especially of International Management, Controlling and Economical Informatics. It ist equally interesting for management consultants and managers in international corporations and IT-departments.

Betriebswirtschaftlicher Verlag Dr. Th. Gabler GmbH, Abraham-Lincoln-Str. 46, 65189 Wiesbaden

Management
International Review
© Gabler Verlag 2004

EDITORIAL OBJECTIVES

MANAGEMENT INTERNATIONAL REVIEW presents insights and analyses which reflect basic and topical advances in the key areas of International Management. Its target audience includes scholars and executives in business and administration.

EDITORIAL POLICY

MANAGEMENT INTERNATIONAL REVIEW is a refereed journal which aims at the advancement and dissemination of international applied research in the fields of Management and Business. The scope of the journal comprises International Business, Transnational Corporations, Intercultural Management, Strategic Management, and Business Policy.

MANAGEMENT INTERNATIONAL REVIEW stresses the interaction between theory and practice of management by way of publishing articles, research notes, reports and comments which concentrate on the application of existing and potential research for business and other organizations. Papers are invited and given priority which are based on rigorous methodology, suggest models capable to solve practical problems. Also papers are welcome which advise as to whether and to what extent models can be translated and applied by the practising manager. Work which has passed the practical test of successful application is of special interest to MIR. It is hoped that besides its academic objectives the journal will serve some useful purpose for the practical world, and also help bridging the gap between academic and business management.

PUBLISHING · SUBSCRIPTION · ADVERTISEMENTS

Published quarterly, fixed annual subscription rate for foreign countries: Individual subscription 114 Euro (approx. US $ 129.–), institutional subscription 228 Euro (approx. US $ 258.–), single copy 62 Euro – (approx. US $ 64.–). Fixed annual subscription rate for Germany: Individual subscription 104 Euro –, institutional subscription 218 Euro. Payment on receipt of invoice. Subscriptions are entered on a calendar basis only (Jan.–Dec.). Cancellations must be filed by referring to the subscription number six weeks before closing date (subscription invoice); there will be no confirmation. There may be 1 to 4 supplementary issues per year. Each supplementary issue will be sent to subscribers with a separate invoice allowing 25% deduction on the regular price. Subscribers have the right to return the issue within one month to the distribution company. – Subscription office: VVA, post-box 7777, D-33310 Gütersloh, Germany, Tel. 0049/(0)5241-8019 68/802891, Fax 80 96 20. Distribution: Kristiane Alesch, Tel. 0049/(0)611/7878-359. Advertising office: Thomas Werner, Tel. 0049/(0)611/7878-138. Editorial Department: Susanne Kramer, Tel. 0049/(0)611/7878-234, e-mail: Susanne.Kramer@gabler.de. Annelie Meisenheimer, Tel. 0049/(0)611/7878-232. Production: Frieder Kumm, Tel. 0049/(0)611/7878-175, Fax 7878-400. Internet: Publisher http://www.gabler.de; Editor http://www.uni-hohenheim.de./~mir; Managing Director Dr. Hans-Dieter Haenel; Publishing Director Dr. Heinz Weinheimer; Senior Publishing Editor Claudia Splittgerber; Sales Manager Gabriel Göttlinger; Production Manager Reinhard van den Hövel. Produced by Druckhaus „Thomas Müntzer" GmbH, Bad Langensalza – Contributions published in this journal are protected by copyright.

ISBN 978-3-409-12719-6   ISBN 978-3-322-91001-1 (eBook)
DOI 10.1007/978-3-322-91001-1

© Springer Fachmedien Wiesbaden 2004
Originally published by Betriebswirtschaftlicher Verlag Dr. Th. Gabler/GWV Fachverlage GmbH, Wiesbaden in 2004

No part of this publication may be reproduced, stored in a retrieval system or transmitted in any form or by any means: electronic, magnetic tape, mechanical, photocopying, recording or otherwise, without permission in writing from the publisher. There is no liability for manuscripts and review literature which were submitted without invitation.

ISSN 0938-8249

Have you already visited our **mir** homepage?

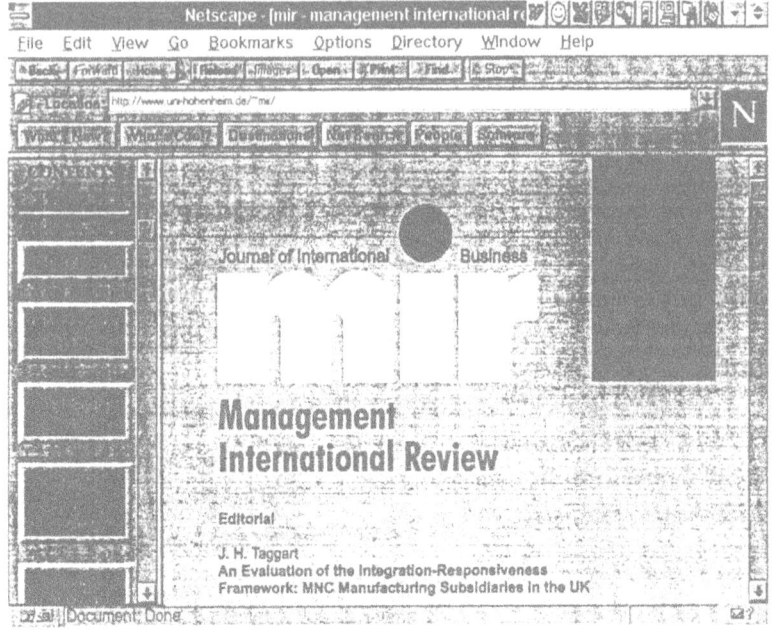

If not, then it is high time you did!

http://www.uni-hohenheim.de/~mir

ISBN 3-409-12719-4
VVA 126/02719

GPSR Compliance
The European Union's (EU) General Product Safety Regulation (GPSR) is a set of rules that requires consumer products to be safe and our obligations to ensure this.

If you have any concerns about our products, you can contact us on

ProductSafety@springernature.com

In case Publisher is established outside the EU, the EU authorized representative is:

Springer Nature Customer Service Center GmbH
Europaplatz 3
69115 Heidelberg, Germany

www.ingramcontent.com/pod-product-compliance
Lightning Source LLC
LaVergne TN
LVHW011941070526
838202LV00054B/4745